The Rise and Fall of Arab Presidents for Life

The Rise and Fall of Arab Presidents for Life

With a New Afterword

Roger Owen

Harvard University Press
Cambridge, Massachusetts
London, England

First Harvard University Press paperback edition, 2014

Library of Congress Cataloging-in-Publication Data
Owen, Roger, 1935–
The rise and fall of Arab presidents for life / Roger Owen.
p. cm.
Includes bibliographical references and index.
ISBN 978-0-674-06583-3 (cloth : alk. paper)
ISBN 978-0-674-73537-8 (pbk.)
1. Arab countries—Politics and government—1945–
2. Middle East—Politics and government—1945–
3. Presidents—Arab countries—History.   4. Presidents—Middle East—History.
5. Arab countries—Kings and rulers.   6. Middle East—Kings and rulers.
7. Monarchy—Arab countries.   8. Monarchy—Middle East.
9. Authoritarianism—Arab countries.   10. Authoritarianism—Middle East.
I. Title.
DS39.O84   2012
352.230917'4927—dc23   2011045764

To the members and Teaching Fellows of the Harvard History 1891 classes of 2009/2010 and 2010/2011

Contents

Contents

Preface

I became interested in the particular subject of Arab republican presidents for life in the spring of 2009 when I learned that President Abdelaziz Bouteflika of Algeria had engineered a constitutional amendment allowing him to remain in office for a third term and so, in effect, for as long as his wished. In so doing he joined an exclusive band of Arab rulers, five in North Africa and two in the Arab east, who governed more or less as kings with every intention of creating dynasties for themselves, just as Hafiz al-Asad had managed to do in Syria. The decision to write a book on the subject followed almost immediately, and the project was virtually completed by the end of December 2010, just as the first rumblings of opposition to President Zein El Abidine Ben Ali of Tunisia suggested that these systems of quasi-monarchical government were much more vulnerable to popular pressure than almost anyone had previously imagined.

This unexpected situation created an obvious dilemma. Should I publish the manuscript as it was before any of the presidents had been actually pushed from office, or should I seek to incorporate the beginnings of that extraordinary story by which insistent demands for the removal of dictatorial presidents and for personal freedom suddenly appeared almost everywhere in the Arab world? In the end I decided on what was necessarily an only partially satisfactory compromise: I would adapt my manuscript to take account of the fall of two presidents, Ben Ali of Tunisia and Hosni Mubarak of Egypt; the tremendous pressure faced by three more, Bashar al-Asad of Syria, Ali Abdullah Saleh of Yemen, and Muammar Qaddafi of Libya; and the announcement by Omar al-Bashir of Sudan that he would not seek another term as president when his present term expired in 2015. This meant, in effect, the end of the system that my book seeks to explicate as a particular form of modern Arab political practice.

Presidents were also very much in the spotlight when my own interest in Middle East politics began in the 1960s. Like other academic observers I believed that the strong presidential regimes of that time were an inevitable outcome of the drive toward complete independence, easily justified by the attention that was paid to remedying the enforced backwardness of the colonial period with programs of land reform, industrialization, and educational development. Only in the 1970s did I begin to realize that they also involved the creation of structures of centralized personal rule, soon to be identified as authoritarian, while showing few signs of transforming themselves into plural systems of power based on contested elections and the more open, more competitive economic structures to be seen in parts of postcolonial Asia, sub-Saharan Africa, and Latin America.

Disillusion came in two stages. First, there was the widespread recognition that Arab authoritarianism was much more durable than had originally been supposed. Next there was the realization that more and more presidents were becoming, in effect, presidents for life, with every intention of passing on their office to one of their family, a process first observed in Syria, where President Hafiz al-Asad began grooming his sons to succeed him in the early 1990s. Soon some of the republics were beginning to look more like monarchies, a condition wonderfully captured by Egyptian sociologist Saad Eddine Ibrahim's newly minted word *"gumlukiya"*—meaning a state that was half republic and half monarchy—which, though coined while he was reporting on Hafiz al-Asad's funeral in Damascus, was rightly taken to apply to President Hosni Mubarak's plans for Egypt as well. That Ibrahim was arrested as soon as he got back to Cairo seemed only to confirm the truth of what he was saying. Republican presidents were now behaving more like kings, just as the kings of Jordan, Morocco, and, later, Bahrain were adopting many techniques of government borrowed from their presidential neighbors.

My attempt at a comprehensive answer to the many questions about the development of Arab presidencies for life builds on the research of numerous political historians and political scientists of the Middle East working along much the same lines, whose ideas, I hope, it fully acknowledges. Nevertheless, as far as I know, there is no other book devoted solely to the subject, nor one that examines its historical etiology all across the Arab world from Morocco to the Persian Gulf, as well as analyzing its many unusual features in terms of rulers determined not only to defy the passage of time but also to find ways of defeating the whole logic of what is supposed to be a republican form of government.

One last preliminary note: while the subject of rule by presidents for life was an intrinsically depressing one while it lasted, I would like to end this brief preface by testifying to the excitement and entertainment I have experienced from talking with knowledgeable colleagues, teaching the enthusiastic Harvard students of History 1891, and persuading many friends to act as my eyes and ears in places in the Arab world that I have been unable to visit myself.

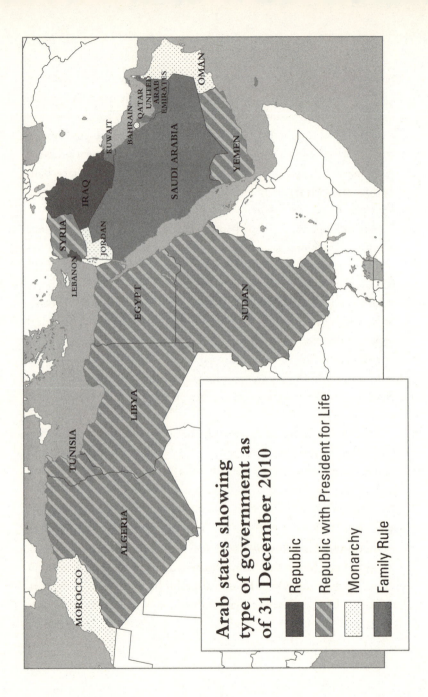

Arab states showing type of government as of 31 December 2010

- Republic
- Republic with President for Life
- Monarchy
- Family Rule

MOROCCO, ALGERIA, TUNISIA, LIBYA, EGYPT, SUDAN, LEBANON, SYRIA, JORDAN, IRAQ, KUWAIT, BAHRAIN, QATAR, UNITED ARAB EMIRATES, SAUDI ARABIA, YEMEN, OMAN

Introduction

The systems of Arab presidents for life were many decades in the making, having their origins with the (mostly military) leaders who came to power from the late 1960s onward and soon learned how to construct the coup-proof regimes that would allow them to remain in office for as long as they lived. From then on, only one Arab republican president, Abdul Rahman al-Iryani of North Yemen, left office more or less of his own free will when his term expired in 1974. Other unusual exceptions were Ahmad Hassan al-Bakr of Iraq and Habib Bourguiba of Tunisia, who got pushed aside by ambitious subordinates, while two more, Gafar Nimeiri of Sudan and Chadli Bendjedid of Algeria, were removed by fellow military officers in 1985 and 1992, respectively.

As of 31 December 2010, the list of longtime presidential survivors included Muammar Qaddafi, who got rid of the Libyan monarchy in 1969; Ali Abdullah Saleh of North Yemen (1978–) and a United Yemen (1991–); Hosni Mubarak of Egypt (1981–); Zein El Abidine Ben Ali of Tunisia (1987–); and Omar Hassan al-Bashir of Sudan (1993–). By then, just one—Hafiz al-Asad of Syria (1970–2000)—had managed to pass on power to his son, Bashar. But there was every reason to suppose that others, like Mubarak, Saleh, and Qaddafi, fully intended to try. Meanwhile, at least two of the Middle East's remaining monarchies, Morocco and Jordan, had become significantly more presidential in their exercise of royal authoritarian power.

Perhaps this should come as no surprise to those who have read the long history of political republics, beginning with the emergence of powerful figures such as the Caesars of ancient Rome. Then, too, there are the cases of the two powerful leaders of the revived form of republicanism represented by the American and French revolutions, with George Washington fighting off the various influences suggesting that he become another type of monarch and Napoleon Bonaparte agreeing to become emperor in the interest of ensuring that the revolution could be continued on a permanent basis.

Nevertheless, it took some little time to understand how, in a roughly similar republican context, roughly similar pressures encouraged the leaders of the world's newly independent states to take their first step in the process toward permanency by allowing themselves to serve on and on without thought of retirement. It remains true that, in the Arab world at least, the general rationale of such systems, their structures, their politics, and the ways in which they sought to legitimize themselves remain little researched and poorly understood. All this in spite of the work of a small group of academic researchers, mostly political scientists, who have begun either to explore the present political dynamics of individual Arab presidential security states such as Algeria, Egypt, Syria, and Tunisia or to look comparatively at certain aspects of these same dynamics either across the Middle East or, in a few cases, across all or most of the former colonial world.[1]

It is known, for example, that almost every Arab republic contained an interlocking, and relatively small, elite composed of senior army officers, bureaucrats, and cronies who had a vested interest in protecting both the regime and themselves by limiting and controlling the impact of Western-inspired political and economic reform. It is also becoming known that, in such systems, members of the presidential family were deeply involved in business themselves; that elections were managed in such a way as to secure a reasonable turnout and so to give the impression that they were exercises in pluralist competition; that opposition was co-opted or repressed; and that information about the major mechanisms of privatization and the award of state contracts was virtually unobtainable, leaving rumor as the only source of political information. Finally, some pathbreaking work is being done on the expansion of the role of many Arab armies in the direction of becoming monopolistic economic actors in their own right.[2]

What, so far, has been lacking is any attempt to examine all these elements on a systematic basis as an example of a new form of rule, practiced intermittently across the non-European regions of the globe, but seen in its most concentrated form in the Arab world, where incumbent presidents all benefited from the same general context—oil revenues, Western support as bulwarks against Islamic extremism, and largely apathetic populations—and, to an increasing extent, from the type of demonstration effect in which ruling families and their advisers readily learned techniques of management from their Arab neighbors.

Looked at from this comparative perspective, the main features of the system, of its contradictions and laws of motion, become more clear. On the one hand, there were centralized structures of power based on a presidency supported by the army and the security services. On the other, a set of practices designed to legitimize the system, most notably the importance attached to the constitution and to managed elections, touted by the presidents themselves, in spite of all proof to the contrary, as providing authentic evidence of the people's will.

My approach will build on the one I employed in *State, Power and Politics in the Making of the Modern Middle East*, which, though providing much of the necessary background, stopped short (in its edition in 2004) of indicating the common nature of the then-evolving systems of permanent presidential government. This current book is based, as before, on synthesizing the recent primary research of others with my own long experience of working in and on the Middle East, as well as on data provided by my extensive networks of Middle Eastern colleagues and friends, in order to develop a series of middle-level theories analyzing local structures of economic and political power.

There are two great advantages of such an approach. One is that it helps to overcome some of the problems stemming from the fact that Middle Eastern regimes were, and largely remain, unusually secretive about the way they exercise power. Indeed, they had a great deal to be secretive about when it came to the practice of patronage, the awarding of state contracts, the budgets of both the military and the security services, the harassment of the opposition, the sources of presidential-family wealth, and so on. Furthermore, none of them that I am aware of encouraged the storage of government records in a national archive, let alone opening them up to the public in accordance with something like a thirty- or fifty-year rule. True, important though scrappy pieces of information about past presidential practice and presidential corruption have appeared since the popular revolts against their authority began in late 2010, both from witnesses and, coincidentally, from the WikiLeaks project as it related to U.S. State Department dispatches from the Arab world. I use items from both sources selectively in what follows. But it also has to be stressed that it is in no way to be regarded as a proper substitute for the absence of official records, which, though known to exist, remained totally inaccessible to public scrutiny so long as the regime itself was in power.

Here is where the notion of structures and processes comes in. If properly identified, they can provide an idea not only of what is more or less likely to be true, but also of why hard evidence is so hard to find, of what types of activity are being hidden, and of how the public is being willfully deceived. In these circumstances, looking at politics through the lens of a collection of set practices associated with presidential succession everywhere in the non-European world is a particularly useful way to give structure and meaning to what might otherwise appear to be a string of random, and usually mysterious, political announcements and events.

Furthermore, obtaining a notion of the way in which power is organized, of regime priorities, and of the incoherence and even contradictions on which regime maintenance and survival depends is a necessary precondition for understanding not only the strengths and weaknesses of each regime, but also the ways in which such regimes undermined their own stability over time. As I argue later, two of the central priorities of the monarchical presidential regimes—the smooth succession of power after the death of each president for life and its legitimation by the use of managed plebiscites and elections, manipulated constitutions, and economic success—involved considerable problems of political organization that, in the event, proved large and explosive enough to derail the whole process more or less by themselves.

The existence of structures containing contradictory features that cannot be held together for long or, at least, not without considerable political cost is another vital clue to anticipating future trajectories. One obvious before 31 December 2010 was the possibility that either a disputed succession or a total collapse of public confidence would bring new political forces to the fore—perhaps the army, perhaps a partnership between a section of the army and some organized civilian group, perhaps a popular movement with an ill-defined but revolutionary agenda. Equally helpful is Steffen Hertog's useful notion of "hub and spoke" when applied to systems of governance in which each part is connected to the center but not directly to the other parts.[3] Lacking internal coherence, such systems experience the greatest difficulty in coordinating many of the ordinary tasks of government, such as the implementation of nationwide plans designed to raise more taxes or to address serious problems such as price inflation or food shortages.

The significance of trying to reconstruct some of the general structures created by the various presidents for life to cement their family rule is the more valuable because, so far as successful successions are concerned, there had been only one Arab example thus far: the transfer of power from Hafiz al-Asad to his son, Bashar, in 2000. Even here, much about the difficulties involved—including the possibility that the transfer was opposed by certain important sections of the Syrian elite—remains little known even inside the country itself. Yet the way in which the politics of succession played itself out in Egypt, and may still play itself out in Algeria, Libya, Sudan, and Yemen, will certainly have a profound influence on future practices and policies in some of the surrounding Arab states.

Nevertheless, I am also aware that a systematic analysis of the structures of political and economic power can take one only so far. Far more than once supposed, modern Arab politics became a matter of personality, of personal character, and of family relationships in which questions of temperament, age, physical and mental health, and individual political skills stood, and sometimes still stand, at the center of political life. Of course, there is a sense in which this was always the case. However, in the days of President Nasser, or the first two decades of Hafiz al-Asad, the personal idiosyncrasies of the leader, and the nature of his relations with his close relatives, were sufficiently well hidden behind a wall of national institutions and, to some extent, constitutional constraints to play only a small observable role in the making of public policy. It was only once the government of the Arab republics had become distinctly more monarchical that intrafamily rivalries and a concern with the production of heirs entered forcefully into the public domain. Presidents with sons of their own appeared to have the advantage. Yet, even then, as in Libya and Yemen, the possibility of strife between the president's own offspring suggested serious problems ahead.

How can we find the jealously guarded personal information needed to understand how such a highly personalized system of family rule really worked? Apart from the single exception of Iraq, where the government and Ba'th Party documents seized in 1991 and again in 2003 provide wonderful insights into Saddam Hussein's methods of day-to-day management and control, the would-be observer of similar practices elsewhere is reduced to obtaining tiny scraps of information from anyone who has some experience of what goes on behind the palace walls.

For the rest, the best strategy that I have been able to devise is to concentrate on trying to work out the significance of a few central issues as they relate to the logic of a system based on maintaining, and then passing on, a machinery of power "well-tailored," as Holger Albrecht puts it, "to suit the person in office."[4] First and foremost, there was the question of the age and life expectancy of the president himself. By the end of the year 2010, all the Arab presidents for life were in their late sixties or older, with the single exception of Bashar al-Asad, who was born in 1965. From this single fact derived a very obvious concern with the health of the president, as well as, from his point of view, a desire to appear as youthful and energetic as possible, dying his hair, using old pictures of himself, disseminating stories of his continued vigor.

Second, there was the question of whether a president had direct heirs and, if so, how many and how old. As of 2010, three presidents (Qaddafi, Mubarak, and Saleh) had sons old enough to succeed them, while one (Ben Ali) had a son still some years from maturity, a fact that engendered much speculation about a family regency should the father die before his offspring became an adult.

Third, there was the question of each president's number of years in office and, as this extended to thirty years in the case of Mubarak and even forty years in the case of Qaddafi, of either their willingness or their ability to put in as hard a day's work as they once did.[5] Such systems of centralized power that involve all the major, and many of the minor, decisions being made by one man must be enormously time consuming to run, and so must become more and more arduous as the years go by. Hence there may well have been a desire to engage in some form of delegation to members of the family or to trusted lieutenants. Political gossip from Egypt and Libya certainly suggested that this might well be the case.

Fourth, and finally, there was the recognition of something like a presidential management style. As a senior official told a member of the International Crisis Group in Damascus in May 2008 about the difference between Hafiz and Bashar al-Asad: "The father used to say little and his decisions were final. Today, the president may settle on a proposal which his advisers later discourage him from following through."[6]

Styles may also change several times during a particular president's long rule. Libya is one notable example, especially after Muammar Qaddafi allowed his eldest son, Saif, to take the lead in many aspects of policy making in the 1990s, only to allow Saif's efforts at reform to be defeated by men close to him in 2009/2010. Other aspects of style included a personal preference for a particular number of close advisers, including senior cronies; the willingness to delegate; and the ability to tolerate personal criticism.

These and many other questions form the subject matter of the book. All the chapters, though linked, address discrete aspects of the rise and fall of Arab republican presidents for life. Chapter 1 introduces the various structures of power that emerged at the end of the colonial period. At this time, a concern both to legitimize and to protect the new and often fragile form of sovereignty almost always led to some type of authoritarianism in which whatever types of pluralism had previously existed were replaced by a centralized, usually one-party state ruling over a set of corporate structures, trade unions, the universities, and the media, all of which were molded or remolded to serve the purposes of the regime itself.

Chapter 2 examines various attempts to understand the origins of the monarcho-republican system as, one after the other, incumbent presidents developed systems of personal power based in large measure on the myth of their own unique governing skills and so on their own indispensable role as guardians and promoters of their country's security and national progress. The chapter goes on to address how, after many of the first generation of revolutionary leaders passed away, their equally single-minded successors adapted the way presidential power was organized, most notably to accommodate the global waves of economic and political liberalizations beginning in the 1970s in ways that, paradoxically, provided them and their associated elites with both the incentive and the resources to keep economic power monopolized in a small number of hands.

Chapter 3 discusses the essential components of these new structures of presidential power, typified by the notion of the "security state" in terms of the role of its key institutions: the presidency and its associated elite of aides and cronies, the army and security services, and the policies used to legitimate them. Chapters 4 and 5 then look in detail at the trajectories of seven such systems, first those where the central government was relatively strong, as in Tunisia, Syria, Egypt, and Algeria; then where its weakness required a much more elaborate practice of accommodations, negotiations, and compromise, as in Sudan, Libya, and Yemen. Here a major argument is that, though most such systems contained many of the same features, the ways in which these component parts related to each other, as well as how these relationships changed over time, were particular to each. All were the result of different historical trajectories, combined with a number of different variables such as the size of the country and its economy, the presence of revenues from domestic oil and gas, the historical role of its armed forces, and the process by which public assets were sold off in the cause of so-called liberalization to create a class of regime cronies that usually included members of the ruling family itself.

Chapter 6 deals with the systems of rule in the Arab republics with, at present, weak presidencies—Lebanon and Iraq—while Chapter 7 considers the various forms of monarchical structures to be found in Jordan, Morocco, Bahrain, and Oman, which share many of the administrative and security features of their republican neighbors but where problems of regime legitimation and succession are much more easily solved. Chapter 8 looks specifically at the politics of succession from two points of view. One concerns the specific measures taken in a number of states to prepare a member of the presidential family to succeed his father, beginning with Syria in the 1990s. The second is the impact of such preparations on the wider political process in general.

Finally, Chapter 9 returns to the pan-Arab arena seen in its global context. One important theme is the existence of a type of demonstration effect by which Arab presidents learned certain techniques of management and survival from each other. This was certainly argued by observers in the case of Bouteflika's decision to seek a third term in office in Algeria in 2009. It can also be seen in the similarities among many of the individual states' laws, practices, and procedures. A second theme that leads on naturally from the first is the question of Arab exceptionalism—that is, the extent to which the emergence of the presidential security states with their presidents for life is a particularly Arab, rather than a more general Third World, phenomenon.

The book concludes with Chapter 10 and a discussion of the strengths and weaknesses of the various presidential systems looked at from a position of hindsight in terms of the huge popular opposition they engendered and the revolutionary process of political change that then ensued. It also comments on some of the main features of the process that led to the overthrow of some presidents and to a serious challenge to the position of others in the first half of 2011.

Looked at in its entirety, this is an attempt to address some of the principal questions that the development of monarchical presidencies for life suggests. How did this sorry state of affairs come about? What were its laws of motion and likely consequences? And why did the situation in the Arab world, where the system became nearly universal, differ from that of Africa and other parts of the former colonial world where it proved much more difficult to establish?

Shakespeare is present in the human and family drama of it all: think of the Macbeths' ambitious drive for power, and of Lear's vanity and lack of imagination, making elaborate arrangements for the future rule of his kingdom only to disrupt them in his petulant old age. So too is Machiavelli with his advice that a ruler's counselors should tell him only what they think he wants to hear.

Viewed from this perspective, it is politics and power that become, as they did for many historians before the present era, the main motive force of history. Nevertheless, given my own concerns with another old tradition—that of political economy—I do not wish to suggest either that powerful men can do exactly what they like or that socioeconomic and cultural forces have little or nothing to do with the case. Rather, I would like to suggest that the formula "Mubarak's Egypt" only makes sense if it is accompanied by the equally powerful notion of "Egypt's Mubarak," the one imperfectly understood without the other, with both existing in the larger context of the Middle East and a globalizing world.

1 The Search for Sovereignty
in an Insecure World

The Arab state system that now exists across the Middle East and North Africa, and the origins of its particular style of presidential rule, are the result of a combination of colonialism, Arabism, and the new world order of sovereign states that was introduced after 1945 under the aegis of the United Nations.

Although Europe established very few formal colonies in this region, the boundaries of three sets of Arab states—those in North Africa, in the Fertile Crescent, and in the Arabian Peninsula—and their international acceptance were largely the work of British and French governments anxious to establish spheres of influence on the far side of the Mediterranean Sea and along the land and sea routes running east to India. This process began in Arab North Africa, starting with the French invasion and occupation of Algeria in 1830. It continued with the establishment of a protectorate in Tunisia in 1881, followed by the British occupation of Egypt in 1882 and of Sudan in 1898, and then the Italian invasion of Libya in 1911. Finally, it was rounded out by the French declaration of a protectorate of Morocco a year later.

European military and political expansion east of Suez, though not the establishment of spheres of cultural and commercial influence, was checked by the existence of the Ottoman Empire, which was closely allied to Britain in an effort to prevent Russian influence from spreading outward toward the Mediterranean and the Persian Gulf. However, once the Ottomans decided to enter World War I on the German side, plans were put in place for an European carve-up of the Arab provinces of the empire. The result was that the British established themselves in what was to become Iraq, Palestine, and—after 1922—Transjordan (later Jordan). Meanwhile, the French created new states in Syria and Lebanon.

All these structures were technically termed "mandates," a form of international trusteeship devised by the powers controlling the new League of Nations to conform to what was seen as "the spirit of the age," a reference to Woodrow Wilson's call for national self-determination in Europe. Nevertheless, they were run more like colonies than nations-to-be, notwithstanding a certain amount of international oversight and Britain's obligation to adhere to the Balfour Declaration of November 1917 promising to encourage the development of a Jewish national home in Palestine. As is well known, the disputes engendered by this promise were to lead, by 1947, to Palestine's violent partition into what emerged as the new state of Israel in May 1948 and two Palestinian entities, the West Bank and Gaza, under, respectively, Jordanian and Egyptian rule.

In the Arabian Peninsula, power before World War I was divided among several entities: the Ottoman Empire, Britain, and a few family administrations that had managed to maintain an uneasy form of local independence, notably the successive states created by the house of House of Saud based in Riyadh, the imams who controlled the mountainous interior of western Yemen, and the sultans of Oman in the east. This system continued largely intact into the oil era, which began in the 1930s with the ruling families cementing their hold on power with the use of their new wealth, distributed along familiar lines of patronage to their relatives and tribal and merchant supporters.

The Colonial Legacy

The impact of the colonial period was vital not just for the creation of the new Arab state structures but also in terms of its continuing influence on the process by which they became independent and on many of the policies they then pursued. On the one hand, the British and the French created internationally recognized statelike entities with central administrations, legal systems, geographical boundaries, and the ability to sign treaties and concession agreements. Such agreements and treaties could be entered into not just with the departing colonial powers themselves but also with private companies anxious to exploit their mineral resources in the form of metals and oil. On the other hand, the way in which these new entities were put together out of a mélange of different ethnic and religious groups involved a difficult balancing act that was, in some cases, to pose enormous problems for nation building.

These problems were especially evident in the new states carved out of the Ottoman Empire, which included not just Palestine (where the British attempt to create a single political community was sabotaged almost from the start by rival Arab Palestinian and Jewish Zionist agendas) but also Iraq (where a Sunni elite ruled uncomfortably over a majority of Shi'is and Kurds), and Lebanon (where institutionalized neglect of the interests of the growing Shiite community was one of the primary factors leading to the long civil war in that country, from 1975 to 1989). Colonial encouragement of foreign settlement also played a major role in the history of Algeria, where some two million French and other European residents conducted a fierce fight after World War II to prevent Algeria's independence as a separate Arab nation.

There were other important types of legacy from colonial influence as well. In some cases, notably across most of North Africa including Egypt and Sudan, the anticolonial struggle produced a coherent nationalist movement that provided not only the first leaders at independence but also their programs for establishing control over their national assets, while reversing what were identified as the worst features of colonial policy, such as the neglect of education and of local industry. East of Suez, nationalism itself was a more problematic issue, partly because of competition between rival ethnic and religious groups, and partly because of the widespread significance of an Arabism that claimed a higher loyalty than that of the individual states.

The Importance Attached to Sovereignty and Strength

The majority of Arab states obtained their independence after World War II. They were ruled by regimes whose legitimacy was immediately very much weakened, first by defeat in the 1948 war with Israel, and then by the fact that their elites were all too easily accused by their people of being allied too closely with the former colonial powers. Members of the various successor regimes were also aware of the possibility that, if they ran afoul of European or American interests, they might be attacked and reoccupied, as the British and French attempted to do in Egypt in 1956, menaced by Israel or subjected to some form of foreign-influenced political change. The result, in Mohammed Ayoob's words, was an "acute sense of internal and external insecurity" that they shared with much of the former colonial world and that derived from a similarly "inadequate stateness" that prevented them from imposing a legitimate political order at home, while making them "uniquely vulnerable to external pressures—political, military, economic or technological—from other and usually more developed states."[1]

The establishment and protection of sovereignty—what President Nasser described in 1954 as the "aspiration" of the Egyptian people to "be the masters of their fate" and to live in an Egypt "now free and strong"—was all.[2] Domestically, the response of the newly independent regimes was to try to augment their hold over their own populations using institutions and techniques, notably an increasing emphasis on policing, security, and the management of elections, borrowed directly from the practices of their former colonial masters. There was also a tendency, reinforced by their defeats at the hands of the new Israeli army in 1948/1949, to increase, and then to reequip, their own small armies. Most importantly, this process necessitated a considerable increase in the number of middle- and lower-middle-class officers produced by their own military academies, most of them imbued with an intense patriotism that was to have significant consequences once they began to influence or, in some cases, remove civilian politicians.

Meanwhile, the new regimes did everything they could to strengthen their international sovereignty while, in some cases, using the outbreak of the Cold War to obtain military and diplomatic support from either Britain and America or the Soviet Union. Other important policy initiatives included reinforcing inter-Arab ties via the creation of the League of Arab States (1945), as well as, more spectacularly, President Gamal Abdel Nasser's participation in the Afro-Asian Solidarity Conference at Bandung in 1955. This had the immediate effect of encouraging Egypt's president to call for greater solidarity between the newly independent, nonaligned countries of Africa and Asia in the interests of making a final attack on the last remaining outposts of colonialism.

Nevertheless, the Arab Middle East remained a dangerous place for sitting postindependence governments, as outside interference continued. Examples include rival British/American and Soviet plots to exert influence in Syria in 1957, as well as more radical domestic political movements—often allied with the military—that pushed for changes in the existing distribution of wealth and power. There were major Middle East wars in 1956 and 1967. There were also many years of fierce fighting between the French and the Algerian nationalists, as well as the more intermittent French military interference in Tunisia and Morocco. And, starting with Syria in 1949, there were numerous attempts at military coups: fifty-five of them between September 1961 and September 1969 alone, of which twenty-seven were successful.[3] Only the states of the Gulf, secure under British protection until the early 1970s, remained largely exempt such turmoil. But even there, individual rulers like those in Abu Dhabi and Oman who were thought to stand in the way of such modernizing measures as the building of schools and hospitals and roads were removed in family coups masterminded from London.

The Second-Generation Arab Regimes

In much of the Arab world, the postindependence governments were sooner or later replaced by more radical regimes that, usually in name of "revolution," made a concerted effort to remove all traces of colonial influence. These attempts included disbanding the remaining foreign military bases, encouraging the exit of most of what remained of the non-Muslim and foreign populations in countries such as Algeria, Egypt, Libya, and Syria, and nationalizing much of what had been a flourishing globally connected private sector in the interests of a protectionist and state-led economic and social development. Meanwhile, the notion of electoral democracy was delegitimized and disvalued by its association with what was seen by most of the elite as a shameful era of domestic division and national defeat. So, too, was the existence of any alternative to a uniform secular nationalism, for example, one based on particular interpretation of the major principles of Islam.

The primary exemplar of this new system was the Nasser-led military coup in Egypt in 1952, spearheaded by the Revolutionary Command Council, and the establishment the next year of a set of revolutionary courts. The aim of these courts was not only to vilify members of the old monarchical establishment but also to supply a revolutionary legitimacy for the new regime based upon a single authoritative narrative concerning Egypt's long struggle for independence. This was followed by roughly similar coups in Iraq and Sudan in 1958, Algeria in 1965, and Syria in the late 1960s. Paler imitations of the same process took place in Yemen from 1962 onward and Libya in 1969.

Note too that in Egypt, Iraq, Libya, and Yemen, the installation of revolutionary regimes involved the removal of kings or other hereditary heads of state. This was also true in Tunisia, where the modernizing regime of Habib Bourguiba came to power directly after independence in 1956. Meanwhile, the monarchs of Jordan, Morocco, and Saudi Arabia only just managed to survive a series of attempted military coups or assassinations, events that pushed them to assume the mantle of centralizing modernizers in roughly the same way as their republican neighbors.

The preferred political structure of most of the second wave of postindependent Arab regimes was the authoritarian one-party state with its monopoly of political power and control over the process of planned, "scientific" development and the measures taken to improve social welfare via a large-scale redistribution of wealth. This structure was seen as serving the essential tasks of nation building and of providing regime legitimacy, often through some vague notion of Arab socialism, while allowing a tight control over people, borders, and the official brand of Islam.

Similar postindependence regimes were being constructed all over the former colonial world for more or less the same reasons. Where the Arab world differed from other postcolonial entities was in the degree to which its regimes were able to obtain significant resources, directly or indirectly, from oil and from Cold War aid, a form of rent that accrued to them as a result of the region's geographical importance augmented by the internationalization of the Arab-Israeli dispute. The sense of Arabism shared by these regimes was also important, promoting a process of sharing, as techniques of rule were passed from one to another, sometimes voluntarily, sometimes as the result of the short-lived drive for Arab unity led by Egypt in the late 1950s and early 1960s.

Bankruptcy and Ideological Defeat after 1967

The comprehensive defeat of the Egyptian, Syrian, Iraqi, and Jordanian armies, combined with the Israeli occupation of the whole of pre-1948 Palestine, sent shockwaves throughout the Arab world, where this was seen not just as a military disgrace but also as a demonstration of the bankruptcy of the secular, Arab socialist, postindependence, self-styled revolutionary regimes themselves. Algeria, with its proud tradition of resistance to the French still intact, was the sole notable exception. In the short run, the military disaster led to further coups in Iraq (1968) and Syria (1970), as well as to the rise of the Palestine Liberation Organization (PLO) under Yasser Arafat. It also created something of an ideological vacuum, allowing the reemergence of religious ideologies backed, in some instances, by the activities of small *jihadi* groups such as those that took over the Grand Mosque in Mecca in 1979 and those that assassinated President Anwar Sadat of Egypt in 1981.

Yet, over time, the shock of defeat encouraged several significant new trends in political thinking. One was the need, if not for peace, at least for an accommodation with Israel, exemplified by Sadat's highly controversial visit to Jerusalem in 1977. A second trend was a reconsideration of the implications of an aggressive unitary Arab nationalism, with the result that all Arab regimes now sought ways to avoid further acts of union like the short-lived Egypto-Syrian one of 1958–1961, as well as preventing themselves from being drawn into yet another damaging war with Israel in pursuit of such central Arab causes as the plight of the dispossessed Palestinians.

Dangers of this type had never been a great problem for the regimes in North Africa, whose countries were sufficiently removed geographically from the Israeli-Palestinian dispute that they did not feel the need to take part in such pan-Arab causes. But as far as the leaders of the new Ba'th Party regimes in Iraq and Syria were concerned, and with the single exception of their participation in the short October war of 1973, they managed to perfect a way of talking tough about the need to assist the PLO without actually doing anything that might force them into a military confrontation with their obviously more powerful Israeli enemy.

Four other significant developments began to make an impact in the late 1960s and early 1970s. The first was the start of the process best described as the "reprofessionalization" of the Arab armies. This can be seen most clearly in the case of Egypt, where part of the poor performance of its army in the 1967 war can be attributed to the way in which promotions under Field Marshal Abdel-Hakim Amer, Nasser's confidant, had been based more on personal favors than on merit. With Amer removed after the defeat, it was then possible to address the pressing need to retrain the army in order to be able to dislodge the Israelis from their positions just across the Suez Canal. President Nasser, and then, after his death in 1970, President Anwar Sadat, managed both to reestablish control over the military and then to turn it into a proper fighting force whose goal was not self-aggrandizement but national defense. Something of the same process took place in Syria and Iraq as well, where a series of military presidents had previously failed to maintain control over a highly politicized officer corps anxious to use the army for its own factional purposes.

Second, the 1967 war coincided with the moment when several Arab countries began to experience difficulty financing their expensive programs of investment and social welfare, due to a combination of scarce foreign currency and of limited domestic resources. This in turn encouraged the idea of trying to obtain money from outside the country through what in Egypt came to be known as *infitah*, a form of liberalization that involved a selective opening up of the economy to make it more attractive to foreign investors. The new spirit of liberalization also made it possible for several million Egyptians to migrate to the oil-rich states of Saudi Arabia and the Gulf, making their remittances a major source of local funds.

As time went on, the process expanded to include other features as well: the creation of a more pluralistic political system with a revived government party taking part in managed elections against a controlled opposition and, in the 1990s, the sale of selected state assets to private-sector entrepreneurs with close ties to the regime. Much the same process took place in many other Arab republics as well, hastened by the collapse of oil prices in the mid-1980s, as well as by pressures to open up to global political and economic forces emanating from the United States, Europe, and international financial institutions following the end of the Soviet empire in 1989.

A third development, though little noticed at the time, was the steep decline of the successful military coup. In the years after the major Libyan and Sudanese coups of 1969, only two Arab presidents' former generals—Gafar Nimeiri of Sudan and Chadli Bendjedid of Algeria—were ousted by the army, and then only by palace coups, not full-scale armed takeovers. According to the Israeli analyst Eliezer Be'eri, this was due in part to the disgrace of the Arab officer corps in the 1967 war and in part to the measures taken to bring the reprofessionalized armies back more securely under presidential control.[4] Other factors included the increase in the size of the army, which made it more difficult for any one part of it to consider making a joint coup; the creation of alternative armed units such as Iraq's Republican Guard; and the wider use of both the intelligence services and, in Iraq and Syria, members of the ruling party to keep an eye out for barracks-room discontent.

Fourth, with the waning of the revolutionary legitimacy of the first generation of leaders, several of their successors began to look for alternative ways to legitimize their regimes. These were usually based on some notion of economic liberalization supported by what Kristina Kauch styles "engineered electoral processes."[5] The result, however, was a new set of problems, many of which are discussed in subsequent chapters, leading presidents to base their rule even more heavily on the creation of a large security apparatus and so to produce that "sense of inevitability" designed to make it futile to think that they could ever be easily removed.[6]

BY THE 1970S, IT SEEMS safe to say, apart from the states in the Persian Gulf, the direct influence of Arabism and the colonial legacy had been transformed into autonomous indigenous political structures, each with its own logic, its own dynamic, and its own modes of operation. True, some of the old problems of nation building in religiously and ethnically divided communities such as Iraq, Lebanon, and Sudan remained. True, too, many of the problems created in Palestine and Kurdistan as a result of the post–World War I settlement continued, including the very obvious lack of a separate Palestinian state. And in Arabia and the Gulf at least, a considerable dependence on the umbrella of great-power protection and support remained firmly in place.

Nevertheless, as has often been observed, the new world order that began to emerge in the 1980s did not require states of the non-European world to subordinate themselves slavishly to the interests of the United States, Europe, or any other centers of world power in exchange for aid and support. Nor were there any boundary issues of pressing concern either among the Arab states or between them and their non-Arab neighbors, the one exception, soon rectified, being that of Iraq's desire to eliminate Kuwait in 1990. Furthermore, the Arab states all recognized each other's legitimacy via the Arab League, while also finding their own place in the international order through membership in the United Nations. It was the secure form of sovereignty thus established that, combined with the much-increased security of tenure for incumbent heads of state, paved the way for the next major development: the appearance of an increasing number of republican presidents for life.

2 The Origins of the Presidential Security State

As Sami Zubaida has observed, the most popular political formula for newly independent states was provided by what he calls the "Jacobin model," based on the notion that sovereignty derives from the people and on the central importance of institutions of popular representation (usually a single national assembly), of constitutions, and of the legal systems dependent upon them. And although many new republican regimes soon took to amending their constitutions and manipulating their electoral and legal systems in the interests of removing checks on presidential power, Zubaida correctly notes that the complex of ideas associated with the model "continued to exercise great influence upon . . . political actors, ideologies and practices."[1] This is more true, it would seem, in states once ruled by France, where republican constitutions are held in a kind of veneration less often found in the British colonial world.

Nevertheless, though true, such observations do not tell us much about the supposed advantages of a republican as opposed to other possible forms of government. My own argument is that, while it had the initial merit of distancing new regimes from their monarchical and colonial pasts, it would seem likely that, over time, what really mattered was the enormous license that manipulation of the notion of the sovereignty of the people appeared to give to presidents when it came to legitimizing their own personal rule. To take just one example among many, here is President Gamal Abdel Nasser describing the sources of the 1952 revolution on the occasion of its eleventh anniversary in July 1963:

> Feudalism and capitalism had usurped power in order to en-slave the majority, for the benefit of the minority. The people rebelled against this, led by the revolutionary vanguard of the Armed Forces in order to destroy this usurpation and return power to its rightful owners, the people.[2]

Appeals to the existence of constitutional propriety and to the sup-posed rule of law based upon it had many of the same advantages, not least in the way that such an appeal provided a tiny, if not always con-vincing, fig leaf behind which to conceal some of the harsh realities of arbitrary and despotic actions from the eyes of would-be supporters in Europe and the United States. It is also possible that, over time, the rulers themselves came to believe—perhaps even to have to believe—in their own sovereign popularity and to be puzzled at even the slightest evidence of opposition. This was certainly true of Iraq's Saddam Hus-sein as well as many of the rulers faced with popular opposition dur-ing the beginnings of the Arab uprisings of 2011.

All this is not to say, however, that there were no occasions when powerful Arab presidents, from Habib Bourguiba to Saddam Hussein, debated the pros and cons of returning to some type of monarchical system. One such moment occurred very early on when Bourguiba, hav-ing disposed of the hereditary Dey of Tunisia in 1957, was soon chal-lenged by colleagues who wished to place limits on his own presidential powers. In reply, he noted that, although he could have reconstituted the Deyship in royal fashion for his own benefit, "He preferred a republic."[3]

Equally, there were also moments when the behavior of a monarchical president such as Bourguiba was compared unfavorably in certain vital respects to that of a real king. The editors of the radical journal *Afrique-Action* made just such a vital point in 1961:

> In the twentieth century we see not the abolition of monarchy but its transformation into a power that differs from it in only two respects: it is not inherited, it is seized (and consequently must be guarded); it cannot be bequeathed and thus creates the permanent problem of its inheritor. This is personal power, wielded by men who are presidents of republics and, in reality, untitled monarchs....
>
> Because personal power is in an individual's hands, it is a most fragile and precarious thing. Because it nurtures pride and scorn in its holder, submissiveness and servility in others, it is inherently dangerous to the well-being of the nation. Because it does not stimulate the search for factual truth or thoughtful appraisal and discussion, it can easily be disoriented in the real sense of the word. Finally, and most important, because it leaves no heir ... it dooms the nation, its faithful companion, to chaos.[4]

The reply of Bourguiba's supporters in the journal *Al-Amal* is just as telling: "The responsibility of power was entrusted to the President under the control of the Assembly and the people—who elect him directly."[5] Nevertheless, a great deal of both political and conceptual uncertainty remained, and must probably always do so. Here is General Mohamed Touati, President Bouteflika's adviser on security affairs, trying either to sum up the situation or, just as possible, to muddy the political waters after Bouteflika's second electoral victory in 2004: "The regime is neither dictatorial, nor democratic, not presidential, not parliamentarian.... We are certainly not living in a monarchy but are we really a republic?"[6]

As for the republican presidents for life themselves, there must also have been quite an element of bad faith involved in their increasingly monarchical practices. Even the most uneducated people generally understand what it is that distinguishes republics from monarchies and why, in theory at least, a president should live in a "White House" rather than a palace. Nevertheless, Arab rulers from at least the time of Anwar Sadat in the 1970s onward began to assume some of the trappings of monarchy, adopting a more regal style, accumulating residences, surrounding themselves with huge entourages, and, in general, living lives undreamed of by the majority of their people.

Much the same thinking existed for those presidents who also began to show signs of trying to make the very unrepublican move of creating dynasties for their own families. This is certainly one of the reasons why first President Hafiz al-Asad and then President Hosni Mubarak took such great care to hide their initial intentions concerning their sons, worried about what other parts of the elite might think, as well as, just possibly, being not quite sure as to what they thought about it themselves. No wonder that the result was a kind of fudge in which only some of the people, perhaps even a distinct minority, were persuaded that their own personal interest in stability and predictability could best be secured by the succession of a son, and then only if it was done with some nod toward popular acclamation by members of the parliament and party, however hand-picked, however tame.

Building the Presidential Security State

From 1952 onward, Arab republics began to be ruled by strongmen of a certain type who used their growing powers to entrench themselves firmly in office, including Gamal Abdel Nasser and Habib Bourguiba in the 1950s, Houari Boumedienne (Algeria) and Muammar Qaddafi (Libya) in the 1960s, and Hafiz al-Asad (Syria) and Ali Abdullah Saleh (North Yemen) in the 1970s. Such men saw themselves as national unifiers, had little time for political pluralism, and saw their main task as lifting their (largely peasant) populations out of their alleged back-wardness through expanded programs of education and welfare, a task that they saw as taking many, many decades to accomplish. Typically, they had a low view of the capacities of the less educated of their own people: "we will lift them up in spite of themselves," as Egypt's deputy prime minister observed in 1954. And if they talked of "democracy," it was as a practice that did not require representative government.[7] Most of all they believed in themselves as powerful agents of history, and that "time was on their side."[8]

Men of this type turned out to be secretive, suspicious, and inclined to see enemies everywhere. They were also ruthless, as they had to be to survive, cutting down rivals and imprisoning, torturing, and often exe-cuting members of organizations they regarded as dangerous, such as the communists everywhere and the Muslim Brothers in Egypt and Syria. Then, as they established themselves more firmly in power, their belief in themselves—in their political and managerial skills and, of-ten, in their own indispensability—continued to expand and expand. One can see this in Bourguiba almost as soon as he was proclaimed (and may even have proclaimed himself)—the "sole leader," *"l'homme providentiel."* There is also little doubt that Nasser regarded himself not only as the protector of the Egyptian revolution but also as its main guide and sole interpreter.

Even so, there is no reason to suppose that the life of a president was anything but an extremely difficult and often dangerous one in the early years of most of the Arab republics, just as it was in sub-Saharan Africa and other parts of the newly independent world where the turn-over rate at the top, due to assassination, imprisonment, and enforced exile, was initially very high. As Jean-François Bayart notes of the Af-rican case, colonialism often left behind not only huge economic and social problems but also plural sources of power and a whole host of ambitious and power-hungry politicians with links to the army, to the tribes, and, in some cases, to influential foreign embassies.[9] Books

27

written about the Middle East in the 1970s generally focused on what were seen as the reasons for its particular instability and violence. "The Arab world is hard to govern," as Michael Hudson summed up in his analysis of the question in his *Arab Politics*, which came out in 1977. And he backed this up with an appendix, "Political Events," suggesting a remarkably high incidence of what he and his colleagues characterized as "riots, armed attacks and political deaths."[10]

In these difficult circumstances, presidents and their entourages desirous of staying permanently in power had to find ways of accumulating enough authority to secure themselves against actual or potential rivals, both military and civilian. There was no obvious template except that derived from aspects of the colonial experience itself or from the institutions to be found in the Soviet Union and its satellites—large and intrusive security services, ministries of national guidance, and so on—making for a great deal of trial and error. Crucial to the whole process was the centralization and personalization of political power by presidents who surrounded themselves by men they felt they could trust to manage an enlarged bureaucracy and a set of interlocking intelligence services, as well as, in most cases, a single government party designed both to mobilize popular enthusiasm and to act as the eyes and ears of the regime throughout society. Put simply, in such cases the people were subordinated to the state, the state to the party, and the party itself to the single ruler who was himself either responsible for its creation or who had become its master.

The most basic imperative of all was control over the army so as to ensure that neither its commanding generals nor those majors and colonels who had direct access to the troops in barracks were in a position to make political trouble. James T. Quinlivan sets out some of the vital ingredients:

- the use of officers with a loyalty to the president based on friendship, family, or ethnoreligious loyalties in key positions;

- the creation of parallel armed forces, not necessarily larger than the regular army but big and loyal enough to defeat any disloyal force; and
- the development of multiple security agencies to monitor loyalty— including, in Iraq and Syria, those associated with the party.[11]

Another important tactic, as Philippe Droz-Vincent notes, was to bind the officer corps into the regime hierarchy via the creation of a sense of shared interest.[12]

The success that attended such measures first began to be noticed here and there in the early 1970s. For example, the new vice president of Iraq, Saddam Hussein, told a British journalist in 1971, "With our party methods, there is no chance for anyone who disagrees with us to jump on a couple of tanks and overthrow the government."[13] This was, of course, more or less what he and his fellow Ba'thists had done in 1968, giving them a compelling reason to make sure that such an event would never happen again.

The Personification of Personal Power

It has long been the case in world history that heads of state who are able to rule unchecked sooner rather than later begin to think of themselves as omniscient and indispensable. Power holders in the Arab world were and are no different. But, given the secrecy that surrounded the lives of the presidents and the way they exercised their power, it is difficult to assess what weight to give to their personalities, their style of management and personal predilections, and the influence of members of their close family, let alone to determine how these features may have changed over time. What outsiders see is only what they are allowed to see and very little more.

Nevertheless, attempts to make some sense of this conundrum go back at least as far as Jean Lacouture's *The Demigods: Charismatic Leadership in the Third World,* published in French in 1969. As its English title suggests, Lacouture made use of Max Weber's notion of charisma, defined as a "charm" that elevates the individual above ordinary men, confers "exceptional powers" on him, and confirms him as a leader.[14] He then employs the notion to analyze the role of Gamal Abdel Nasser in Egypt and Habib Bourguiba in Tunisia, as well as Cambodia's Norodom Sihanouk and Ghana's Kwame Nkrumah. It is easy to see its attraction for anyone trying to understand the politics of the postcolonial period. Strong leaders with a powerful personal rapport with their people appeared in many parts of the non-European world to steer their country through that uneasy period when the old colonial order had not yet been replaced by something new. Many also seemed to try to follow the Weberian logic by which their charisma had to be what he called "routinized" within a newly created institutional structure, even though only a few were actually able to accomplish such a difficult task.

As far as Nasser is concerned, Lacouture identifies a two-stage process: first the "concentration" of power, complete by 1954/1955; and then its "personification," involving the establishment of a two-way relationship between Nasser and the Egyptian people, beginning with his triumphant return from the Bandung Non-Aligned Conference in April 1955. From then on, by a further process that Lacouture terms "identification," he *was* Egypt and "spoke in the name of Egypt."[15] Key speeches—such as the one he gave informing the country of his arms deal with the Soviet Union (known as the "Czech Arms Deal") in September 1955, and the one announcing the nationalization of the Suez Canal Company in July 1956—were now greeted with "wild acclamation." They also began to be given in a new style that, in Lacouture's words, "caught the accents of everyday life, of country brawls, of suburban banter." And he goes on to assert that by this stage Nasser himself "had become part of the crowd: speaking its language, he was its spokesman."[16]

Lacouture also charts another process of personal change in the leader himself, in which Nasser moved from a position of stressing the importance of being "humble" in service of country (1953) to one involving the organization of mass adulation to be seen, he writes, "everywhere" by the mid-1950s: at electoral meetings, visits to factories, inaugural ceremonies, and the stage-managed visits of foreign leaders.[17] Arriving at each and any of these events, the president's appearance was much the same:

> Pumping his arm like a seasoned champion, he smiles and steps forward in his slightly bent, deliberate manner. He is the "great," the "generous," the "victor" and the "just." He is the father of the revolution, the "nation's liberator."[18]

There is every reason to view this as part of a calculated effect in which Nasser himself, as Lacouture describes, had taken a personal role, closely supervising what was said in the government-controlled press and exhibiting great interest in the content of the new television service opened in 1962.[19] Perhaps instinctively he seemed to understand that "charisma needs constant rejuvenation."[20]

As elsewhere in the newly independent world, this cult of personality appeared with what seems like remarkable rapidity, as Nasser distanced himself from his former military colleagues and was distanced by them. Already by 1955, a member of the original Revolutionary Command Council, Major Salah Salem, was telling a radio audience: "He [Nasser] is moving away from us, in our very midst, through his own humility, as the Saviour did from his disciples. But among us there is no Judas."[21] A remarkable statement indeed.

It is true that Nasser made some attempt to mitigate the impact of the growing adulation by living simply in his old house in the Cairo suburb of Heliopolis, by rarely dining out, and by spending many domestic evenings in study and discussions with experts. It is also true that he rarely spoke in the first person, preferring what Lacouture calls the "we of co-responsibility," but one that involved a "mixture of joint deception and sincerity," at times using it to share responsibility with the people, at others to upbraid them as in his 1956 exhortation: "We fought a revolution against injustice. What have you done? The enemy is not simply imperialism, it is within you."[22]

All this is not to say that the revolution under Nasser's leadership did not implement a formidable program of economic and social reforms, from a restructuring of rural relations to an enormous transfer of wealth from the old landed and business class to the poorer classes of the Egyptian population. Nor that he did not make some attempt to create a substantive new structure of government based on a charter, a single party—the Arab Socialist Union—and an elected popular assembly. But it all came at great cost: opposition was silenced and Egypt's wonderfully vibrant interwar intellectual life was brought to an end. Meanwhile its people were subject to what the writer Tawfiq al-Hakim identified as a paralysis of the mind, surrendering their own powers of action and decision to a powerful ruler on whom they relied to solve all their problems for them.[23]

Then, as often happens, the big man, the "boss," began to make big mistakes. Beginning in the late 1950s, Nasser presided over a period of incoherent economic planning, which led to the creation of a bloated and inefficient public sector, followed by the huge miscalculation involved in his decision to go to war with Israel in June 1967. It is greatly to his credit that he offered to resign as a response to this last disaster. He also sacrificed what was left of his failing health by trying to help put both Egypt and the Arab world back on their feet in the remaining three years before he died in 1970. Nevertheless, Lacouture's final quote from one of his knowledgeable Egyptian sources provides a damning indictment of Nasserite rule: "because he (Nasser) did not recognize or could not resolve Egypt's problems, he incarnated them."[24]

As Lacouture tells it, Habib Bourguiba's assertion of personal power was much more dramatic. Here was someone whose leadership of the anticolonial movement had already been marked by an extraordinary egotism and sense of personal destiny even before the country's independence in 1955. Witness a statement from a letter written when he was a prisoner of the French in 1952: "if my life were taken, the people would suffer an irreparable loss in losing not so much their leader and moral counselor as the fruit of all their past sacrifices."[25]

Not surprisingly, such an attitude led to a continuous expansion of presidential power after he assumed office, adopting the title of "supreme commander" and becoming the virtually unique subject of daily press, radio, and TV newscasts, with his portrait everywhere and with the "entire population marshaled to meet him" in towns and villages on domestic tours.[26] There was, as Lacouture points out, a "sense of [his] being everywhere, [that] everything flows from him, that everything speaks of him."[27] In this "endless ceremony of collective identification," critics—and there were a number of powerful ones in his first decade in office—were "faithless dissenters," to be quickly isolated, imprisoned, or exiled.[28] Yet though true as a general account of Bourguiba's early years in power, by not paying particular attention to context or chronology, Lacouture makes it seem all too inevitable, too uncalculated, and too easy.

A second major contribution to the study of personalized power is provided by Lisa Wedeen. She eschews the concept of charisma for one that draws on the notions of power and spectacle to be found in the works of Michel Foucault and Clifford Geertz, using them to explain the presence of a cult that, beginning almost as soon as Hafiz al-Asad assumed sole power in November 1970, combined huge amounts of rhetorical excess with an enthusiasm that, she observes, did not go very deep. This she identifies as a strategy of domination based on "compliance rather than legitimacy," in which citizens act, not wholeheartedly, but only "as if" they revere their leader.[29] As a result, though it served many of the functions of leadership cults in other Arab countries—acting, for instance, to personify the state and to set it above society—it was also nicely tailored to Asad's obvious lack of physical charisma.

Unlike his neighbor, Saddam Hussein, who found ways of exuding a vital sense of energetic masculinity after he assumed sole power in Iraq in 1979, the Syrian president exhibited a quiet, deliberative persona, almost always wearing a suit and tie, slow of speech, his body stooped and his movements sluggish.[30]

Wedeen's second significant observation is that, in its Syrian context, the cult of personality did not simply intensify over time but waxed and waned according to political circumstances. It was particularly prominent—for example, in its demand for "outlandish declarations of loyalty"—at times of crisis, such as the period of growing domestic opposition in the late 1970s and again during Asad's health crisis of 1983/1984, when he faced another internal challenge from his brother, Rifaat.[31] Used in this way, she argues, the cult allowed considerable flexibility, permitting it to "change direction, to return to prior points of emphasis in response to any new crisis that challenged the regime's idealized representation of events, conditions, people."[32]

Flexibility of this type also provided a partial answer to the perennial problem of what to do when the cult of personality has reached the limits of rhetorical excess, as in Wedeen's argument that Syria did in 1985. Just as you cannot get more than 100 percent support in a referendum, it is difficult to cap such early epithets as "omniscient," "immortal," or "leader forever." In Iraq, the same problem was, fortuitously, overcome by the regime's turn to religion in the late 1980s, which opened up a whole new vocabulary of praise for Saddam Hussein as second only to God. In Syria, more prosaic themes could be introduced to vary the mix, the most notable of which was the emphasis on the Asads as a kind of "holy" family in the late 1980s and early 1990s.[33]

It follows that such cults not only legitimize the notion of a president for life but also encourage the belief that he should be succeeded by a member of the same revered family. In Syria, this began in the late 1980s with the refashioning of Hafiz al-Asad's son, Basil, from a playboy to a "potential incorrupt leader," followed in 1991 by an orchestrated effusion of banners and posters referring to the president as "Abu Basil" (father of Basil).[34] Some of this, suitably amended to suit the difference in personalities, was then transferred to Asad's second son, Bashar, after Basil's death in a car crash in 1994.

A STUDY OF THE ESTABLISHMENT of the three presidential systems just considered—those of Egypt, Tunisia, and Syria—suggests the existence of a number of powerful factors that promoted the arrival of Arab presidents for life. At their roots, they included the creation of a security state devoted to the task of a long-term program of planned economic and social development and managed by a single leader whose skills, complemented by a cult of personality that placed him—and, in the case of Asad, his whole family—above society, party, and the elite, allowed him to rule more or less unchecked for as long as he chose. And so, invariably, for life. To begin with, this process involved some attention to republican forms marked, for example, by the absence of palaces to act as what Wedeen calls the "physical center of sacred power." There was also no hint of a ruling family.[35] But, over time, the presidents became more monarchical in character, demanding greater and greater adulation from their people while setting themselves apart as essentially different human beings, more wise, more far-sighted, more courageous than those they ruled.

Even so, there are no signs that these first powerful presidents thought very much about who should succeed them. Never, for a single moment, did they imagine that it might be one of their sons. Both Nasser and Bourguiba seem to have been content with creating a constitutional mechanism for choosing a new president. In Nasser's case, this was by a nomination by a two-thirds majority in parliament ratified by a national referendum. Then, having paid little further thought to the matter, Nasser died at the young age of fifty-three. Bourguiba, too, seems to have paid little attention to his own succession before he was deposed by the ambitious Ben Ali after thirty years in power. It was only in Syria, and then as a result of a combination of the president's ill health, the challenge from his brother, and, no doubt, the urging of highly privileged members of his own minority community, the Alawis, that Hafiz al-Asad began to think seriously about preparing one of his sons to take over after his death.

In the Arab republics of Algeria, Libya, Sudan, and Yemen, presidencies for life either emerged in different ways or took different forms, sometimes with less emphasis on the cult of personality, sometimes with little or no reference to the other members of the president's nuclear family.

3   Basic Components of the Regimes

The "Arab security state" had its origins in the authoritarian presidential regimes established soon after independence. These regimes then passed through a statist phase before being restructured to accommodate selected private economic interests as well as some form of managed democracy. But at all times, their main function was to maintain a president in power for life. Given their many decades of existence and the networks of security officials they still contain, it is likely that parts of their structures will outlast the era of the strong personal presidencies that engendered them in the first place.

Security states were, and are, highly personalized and individualized affairs, generally built up over time by rulers who, whatever the concessions they might have employed to win people over during their first years in power, presided over structures that tended to harden over time. The effect on the lives and liberties of their subjects became increasingly unequal, allowing great freedom to a few and imposing considerable constraints on the life chances and expectations of all the rest. Arab kings, most notably those of Jordan and Morocco, built up more or less the same types of security-based structures with many of the same effects.

The security state is also a "fierce" state, with considerable powers of repression, in part, as Nazih Ayubi wisely notes, to make up for the fact that it lacks the reach and coherence required either to tax efficiently or to provide a wide range of public goods to its citizens.[1] For one thing, its high degree of centralization, with all power concentrated in a very few hands, means that civilian ministers are allowed little personal initiative. At the same time, the links between the component parts of the government necessary for concerted effort remain weak and underdeveloped. Furthermore, a general lack of resources, as well as a desire to build up personal support, encouraged such presidential regimes to farm out what would normally be considered central government activities either to their crony followers or to self-interested organizations such as the army, none of whom can be said to have the concerns of the civilian population very much at heart. It also goes without saying that state regulatory powers and judicial oversight were, and remain, correspondingly weak.

At the apex of such systems stands the presidential office, the presidential family, and a small group of advisers drawn from the military, the security services, and the business elite. Next in order of importance come the senior members of the army, the intelligence agencies, and the police, together with a small group of crony capitalists who obtain access and influence in exchange for a role in providing additional resources for the regime in terms of money and, sometimes, organizational skills. Under them are the main agencies of civilian administration, the ministries, and the provincial governors, as well as the most important centers of ideological legitimation and control: the educational apparatus, the official media, the tame judiciary, and the equally tame religious establishment.

To this should be added the role of well-organized government parties where they existed. Examples are the National Democratic Party with its three million members and nationwide network of offices in Mubarak's Egypt and the Constitutional Democratic Rally in Tunisia, which had an even more overwhelming national presence with huge propaganda functions as well as ancillary police duties involving surveillance and information gathering.

At their inception, most Arab presidential regimes made use of some version of Arab socialism, either in its Nasserite or its Syrian or Iraqi Ba'thist form. Over time, however, this was modified to include a greater emphasis on economic liberalization with, at times, just a hint of political liberalization as well. Then, as rulers went to greater and greater lengths to rid themselves of anything that might constrain their own flexibility and freedom of action, regime ideologies became so watered down as to become little more than endless variations on the twin themes of nationalism and development. In most cases, the old nostrums were simply allowed to wither away. Less typical but more honest was Saddam Hussein's famous statement in the late 1980s that Ba'thism had become whatever he himself said it was and, "The law is anything I write on a scrap of paper."[2]

Consideration also needs to be given to what might be called the central imperatives that began to drive such presidential security regimes. One of these involved issues related directly to the security of the regime itself. Most important here was the need to find the resources required to sustain the army and the police both in terms of the morale and well-being of their higher echelons, and as employers of a significant proportion of what might otherwise be unemployed and so disaffected youth.

A second imperative concerned what are generally lumped together as the mechanisms for regime legitimation. These involved the government party, the constitution, the practice of holding regular elections and referendums, and the presence of official and semiofficial human rights organizations that, in most countries, still have to be registered with, and supervised by, the Ministry of Social Affairs. Just how valuable these mechanisms for legitimation were for regime survival, given the huge amounts of actual force at their disposal, remains an open question. But the more significant point is that they were treated by the regime itself as of major importance, not just in terms of engineering popular acquiescence but also as a way of ensuring foreign financial support. This is particularly the case for those forms of economic assistance that depended on some type of conditionality in terms of reciprocal improvements in transparency, the rule of law, and the promotion of democracy. Fortunately for these presidential regimes, most donors and donor countries have been, historically, willing to work with only the most limited definition of what constitutes a democracy: the conduct of contested elections even when there is not the slightest possibility that the incumbent party will be defeated, let alone leave office if it is.

The third imperative was the implementation of the economic policies needed to combine regular growth and reasonably low inflation with the ability to provide welfare services for the poor and public services such as electricity, water, and transport for those who could afford them.

The Presidency

In most cases, the inner workings of presidential security regimes, both past and present, remain largely hidden, with only few occasions when it has been possible to observe presidents at work or to learn how decisions are or were actually made. The fundamental task for any powerful Arab republican president has been to build, and then to maintain, a system that preserves him in office while concentrating most of the decision-making process in his own hands. Typically this was a doubly personal matter, for not only did the presidents for life perfect their own systems of management and control, but also they did it in ways congruent with their own individual styles of leadership. By the same token, it was this that made concerns about the succession so pressing for members of their families and close associates. How could they be confident that whoever came next—most likely a much younger man—would have the abilities necessary to replicate such a highly personalized method of presidential rule?

Basic to each system was a species of balancing act in which the leaders of institutions, as well as powerful members of the elite, were dealt with individually in such a way as to prevent them from forming coalitions that might inhibit the president's freedom to act or allow them to accumulate enough knowledge of how the whole system worked to make concerted opposition possible. Some simply owed the ruler their obedience. Others were provided with substantial benefits of one kind or another. All knew that whatever privileges they enjoyed could be easily removed. All understood that no one of them could be considered indispensable.

How this was actually managed in practice was, of course, up to the individual ruler. Something of importance can be learned about their exercise of quasi-royal authority by their choice of residence, which tended to become grander and more monarchical over time. In the case of Tunisia, for example, President Ben Ali and his immediate family lived in a huge complex of buildings in Carthage (a suburb of the capital, Tunis), which contained not only the residence itself but a complete set of shadow ministries that acted as the real agents of government. Other rulers, such as Egypt's President Mubarak, and his predecessor Anwar Sadat before him, preferred to move around from one palatial residence to another. Others again, such as Yemen's Ali Abdullah Saleh, continued to live in what were, in effect, military encampments, well protected from assassination or attack. There is also room for modesty, Libya's Qaddafi being described in one of the WikiLeaks American cables as keeping a low profile in Tripoli with his Bab al-Azizia complex "not lavish in any way" compared with the ostentatious palaces of the Gulf's ruling families.[3]

Being centers of enormous power, the comings and goings at the palace also provide a fair indication of the role of those visitors who possessed that most valuable of all political commodities: access, such access often being measured out with what Patrick Seale, writing of Hafiz al-Asad's Syria, described as "minute care."[4] Having access, of course, not only meant having the opportunity to influence policy or to make a case but also conferred other significant benefits, such as the ability to present the case of friends and colleagues or the possibility of inclusion in lucrative business deals. Access to close members of the presidential family had many of the same advantages.

Each president developed his own way of commanding respect, organizing his time, choosing his advisers, and anticipating possible threats. Some, such as Nasser, Hafiz al-Asad, and Ben Ali of Tunisia, spent long hours at their desks, in Asad's case working a fourteen-hour day, which often included dealing with relatively trivial matters passed up to him by subordinates fearful of making decisions on their own.[5] Others, such as Hosni Mubarak, may have put in such a heavy working day when they were younger but, as they got older, preferred to delegate most of the business of government to others, rarely if ever reading the newspapers and keeping only the very important decisions to themselves. Meanwhile, any rival who might consider using either his position or his personal charisma to build up a rival center of power had better beware. As a rule, charisma in others proved anathema to noncharismatic leaders.[6]

Rulers also varied a great deal in how many advisers they were comfortable seeing on a regular basis, in some cases—Mubarak, Hafiz al-Asad, and Ben Ali for example—drastically limiting that number as they got older. Meanwhile, meetings with the general public were usually confined to a few formal public occasions or were organized in the form of carefully managed personal encounters at regular assemblies or *diwan*s such as those in Sudan or Yemen.

Then there is the question of style. While the majority of Arab presidents seem to have wanted to present themselves as grave and sober custodians of the country's interests, a few, such as Anwar Sadat and

Muammar Qaddafi, took or take obvious pleasure in presenting a more exuberant personality, dressing in extravagant costumes of their own design and turning their every public appearance into a form of theater.

The role of the ruler's family also varied considerably. Some, like Ali Abdullah Saleh of Yemen, used nearly thirty members of his extended family to control important parts of the army and the security apparatus. Others again, such as Sadat, Bourguiba, and Bashar al-Asad, encouraged their wives to assume the role of something like a cross between a queen and an American first lady, pleased to see them obtain academic degrees and to engage in charitable activities, particularly those politically neutral ones that gave the impression of the existence of a vibrant civil society with a special concern for the rights of women. But not all: Hafiz al-Asad, Muammar Qaddafi, Omar al-Bashir, and Ali Abdullah Saleh kept, or keep, their wives very much out of sight. And, in just one case—that of Zein El Abidine Ben Ali—his wife emerged as the country's leading businesswoman, owning and managing some of the largest enterprises in the Tunisian economy. Here, as in a number of other instances, the monarchical president seems to have had much more license in the allocation of family roles than did the traditional king, sometimes summarily summoning a son back from abroad to assist him, at others actively defining the part he expected his wife to perform.

Sons and sons-in-law also had important roles to play, whether as potential successors (Egypt, Libya, Tunisia, Yemen), as political managers (Egypt, Tunisia), or as loyal commanders of key units of the army and security services (Libya, Yemen). To do so they generally had to pass through a period of testing in which, for example, some, like Mubarak's elder son, Ala'a, might choose not to serve as a potential successor, or, like Uday Hussein in Iraq, might be found wanting as far as his military skills were concerned. Others, like Mubarak's second son and presumed heir, Gamal, played a secondary role as a principle source of the very large sums of money he obtained from the enforced partnerships he imposed on foreign companies wishing to invest in Egypt.

It follows that sons and other relatives must all be considered as part of a single team dedicated to the promotion of a mutual family interest. But it has also been possible to imagine some sons as also potential rivals, both to each other, as in Libya and Yemen, or, in certain circumstances, to their father himself. This at least was the view of Saddam Hussein in Iraq when asked by one of his American interrogators whether he had ever considered a family succession, to which he replied, only half-seriously no doubt, that he had but that he was also aware of what had happened in Oman in 1970 where the sultan (with British help) had deposed his own father.[7] Sometimes daughters had a role to play as well, notably where the leader's wife chose not to appear much in public. This is the case in Libya, for example, where Aisha Qaddafi had her own charity and was also involved in promoting social welfare for women and children.

The Army and Security Services

The army is almost always the ultimate source of domestic protection for an Arab president, although, in a few cases, it is overshadowed by various security services, including the paramilitary police. Whether the army is also large enough or well equipped enough to go to war with a neighbor is another matter. For those states that have borders with Israel, this remains a consideration, although an increasingly distant one. Others have more or less given up the pursuit of a military-backed foreign policy.

For historic reasons, the largest armies, fed by a universal or near-universal conscription, still belong to Egypt, Syria, and monarchical Jordan and Morocco, as well as (at various times) Iraq. This has allowed the armies to serve the extra function of employing a sizable proportion of otherwise unemployed youth, as well as keeping them in the military loop after they retire (usually in their late thirties or forties) though various veterans' clubs and associations. Soon, however, the cost of imposing such a burden on each country's resources forced their regimes to become pioneers in encouraging their militaries to defray at least some part of their expenses—most notably salaries, wages, and pensions—by engaging in various forms of profitable enterprise. These included military and domestic industry and certain forms of agricultural activities in some cases, as well as more Arab or international cross-border services such as construction or training or security in others. In addition, in Algeria, Egypt, Libya, Syria, and Yemen, individual members of the officer corps are known to have been provided with lucrative opportunities, either to participate in private business while in the army or to move on to such businesses after they retired, thus incorporating them firmly as members of each country's crony elite.

Republics with smaller armies, such as Tunisia and Lebanon, have been able to follow a different path, paying their retired officers pensions large enough for them not to have to find extra employment opportunities if they do not wish to do so.

Keeping the officer corps "sweet" is, of course, only one of the ways of ensuring that the army remains loyal to the president. More direct methods involve dividing the armed forces up into several distinct clusters, rotating their commanders, creating a separate presidential guard, and subjecting the military to constant surveillance by one or more special intelligence organizations. An even more extreme form of micromanagement was practiced by Hafiz al-Asad, who is said to have read every officer's file before committing its personal details to memory. Anxious too to preserve Alawi control over what he regarded as not just the national army but also the main agent protecting the interests of his community, he also made sure that every combat unit was commanded by an Alawi and that none of its equipment could be moved without his permission.[8]

Nevertheless, military docility can never be quite taken for granted. The army has its own special interests to protect in terms of its budget, its control over its own system of promotion, and, in some cases, its particular concerns with security policy and the management of the national economy in which its own military businesses are embedded. Typically these interests are protected by appointing a senior general as the minister of defense. But there have also been times, such as during the process of a presidential succession, when the generals seem to have wanted guarantees in advance before supporting the new man. And even when divided up into separate components, the army typically retains sufficient coherence to make it far and away the most powerful force within the country and so an institution to be handled carefully by the president, with due deference to the wishes of its senior figures. Hence the desire to identify both the president and his sons—where they existed—directly with the military establishment. Hence too, the need to assure the senior commanders that their institutional interests would remain securely protected.

In most Arab republics, the number of persons employed by the various police and security forces was, and remains, many times larger than the number of those serving in the army. Furthermore, and unlike the armed forces, their size and the proportion of the budget needed to sustain them tended to grow, sometimes as a result of purposefully exaggerated fears of a growing internal opposition, sometimes as a way of giving jobs to more of the unemployed youth. Of equal or perhaps even more importance was the special internal logic that absolved the police and internal intelligence services from official constraints on expenditure in the name of meeting newly identified threats to national security, for example, the need to monitor and, if possible, control the use of the Internet and cyberspace. As of only a decade ago, many persons in the Arab security services—particularly those in senior positions—were computer illiterate. It took an extensive program of recruitment from the universities to catch up with the ability of young people to use the new electronic technology for organizing sudden strikes and demonstrations against the various regimes. Even then, regime attempts to keep track of what was going on did not always work, as was well demonstrated by the failure to control the use of the social media in the huge popular protests that ended the rule of Ben Ali and Hosni Mubarak.

Given the obvious problems in obtaining information, facts about the security services are hard to come by. Perhaps because Egypt is, and has been, slightly more open than other Arab countries in terms of its press and its sources of information, sources suggest that it increased its spending on its security intelligence services—notably State Security Intelligence and General Intelligence, akin to the FBI and the CIA respectively—from 3.5 percent of its official budget in 1987 to 4.8 percent in 1997, with a consequent expansion of police personnel from 9 to 21 percent of total government employment during the same ten years.[9] They also suggest that by 2006 its total security budget had reached U.S. $1.5 billion, a sum that, as Robert Springborg points out, was substantially more than that spent on health care.[10] Another source asserts that, by 2002, the Egyptian Ministry of Interior controlled a force of one million police, security, and intelligence personnel, up from some 150,000 in 1974.[11] And a more recent estimate put the number "employed" in Egyptian security at three million, although this figure is surely too large unless one includes an extra army of plainclothes thugs, agents-provocateurs, informers, and others that make up what Springborg describes as a large "undercover community able to control and affect most important civilian institutions" such as the universities, the media, and the official trade unions.[12] Nonuniformed persons of this kind also have come to play an increasing role in breaking up peaceful antigovernment demonstrations, sit-ins, and rallies, particularly those monitored by the foreign press, where photographs of policemen attacking women would incur greater international opprobrium.

In Egypt, police and security activity under Mubarak was legitimated by a battery of laws, including the existence of a state of emergency that, until its abolition in 2011, permitted the government to ban strikes, demonstrations, and public meetings, censor or close down newspapers, and arrest or detain individuals without charge, a set of practices that, as the leaders of the small legal opposition frequently pointed out, was used primarily to "stifle political dissent."[13] In ordinary times, and even without some of these powers, there is much evidence to suggest that the security services remained able to act outside the law, torturing arrested persons and threatening them with re-arrest, or the arrest of their relatives, if they tried to lodge a complaint.[14]

As with the army, the security forces also looked after their own, for example, by getting them jobs after retirement in companies run by former colleagues.[15] But, unlike former army officers, many of these persons had the extra advantage of having accumulated a great deal of sensitive political and economic information during the course of their security work, which made them particularly in demand after they retired.[16]

Even if the names of the different security services in the other Arab states are generally known, their size, the relationship between their sometimes rival parts, the exact details of their role, and how they carried out their functions are not. In Libya, for example, the Intelligence Bureau of the Leader was created in the early 1970s, soon after Qaddafi's military coup, with the assistance of the East German Ministry of State Security. This bureau controlled all the other intelligence services, including the Military Secret Service that, according to Dirk Vandewalle, was responsible for the leader's own personal security.[17] In Yemen, by contrast, there are said to be two main agencies—the National Security Bureau and the Political Security Organization—which compete with each other, are in league with different foreign intelligence services, and do not share information.[18] And in Syria under Hafiz al-Asad, there were four different intelligence and security bodies under the control of the National Security Bureau.[19]

Cronies and Other Rent Seekers

Arab republican presidents in states with little or no oil were almost always closely associated with only a small number of individuals or groups of men and women. These included, on occasion, members of their own close or extended families who used their privileged access to obtain favorable business terms in exchange for various political and economic services. This also remains true in general of the large oil states such as Algeria or Libya. But in these latter states it involved, and still involves, both an inner circle of regime cronies and a larger one of peripheral persons and institutions who benefit at one remove from the major oil revenues that are the main source of regime patronage. In the case of Libya, for instance, a leaked U.S. Embassy dispatch of May 2006 notes that "all of the Qaddafi children and favorites are supposed to have income streams from the national oil company and oil service subsidies."[20]

With few exceptions, the vast majority of the cronies came from a different stratum than the one that existed in preindependence or prerevolutionary days under the old capitalist regime, which had been either forced to leave or were dispossessed by the nationalization of their property in the 1950s and 1960s. Hence, unlike the members of the former elite, these new cronies were entirely dependent on the state and its policies for their own enrichment. Opportunity came mainly from the regime's initial need for local contractors to build roads, bridges, and airports for military purposes and then, from the 1970s onward, from the process of controlled liberalization when state assets were sold or otherwise given to men close to the regime along with new opportunities to create joint ventures—usually monopolies—with foreign enterprises.

One central feature of this whole process was the use of state banks to provide capital for the new ventures, often in the shape of nonperforming loans. Another was the way in which a privileged few were

allowed to convert public monopolies into private ones while still using state power to prevent potential competitors from cutting into their
market. Yet another variation is the situation in Libya after its own
"opening up" from 2006 onward, which saw the creation of a small
number of huge parastatal organizations such as the Economic and
Social Development Fund, which uses oil money to invest in upstream
enterprises, sometimes in partnership with foreign companies that are
forced to become its local partner if they want to do business there.
Although little or nothing is known about the people who run these
gigantic enterprises, it is generally assumed that they include some of
Qaddafi's seven sons, as well as members of military families connected
with the 1969 coup. Cronyism, as elsewhere in the world, obviously
flourished on the continued existence of monopolies, of privileged access to state resources, and of rules and regulations that only insiders
are allowed to break.

The role played by the presidents themselves, and the role of the
regimes they commanded in the construction of a crony elite, obviously
differed from state to state. In some, like Egypt, strenuous efforts were
made by members of the fledgling business community to corrupt
members of the ruler's family. In others, such as Syria, the president,
Hafiz al-Asad, felt called upon to nurture a new capitalist class, but
with great reluctance due to his dislike of capitalist enterprises and so
without really knowing how do it. Others may have felt more comfortable dealing with the devil they knew, in the shape of relatives and
friends, than the one they did not know, formed from social groups
they distrusted or despised.

Nevertheless, it is possible to make some general comments about
the conditions under which the first important cronies appeared as well
as the working relationships that were then established to the mutual
benefit of all insider parties. To begin with, capitalists were in demand
as a result of crises in which the authoritarian regimes simply ran out of
money, particularly the foreign exchange they needed to finance their

attempts to create heavy industry, to engage in major public projects, and to create better health, education, and welfare systems for their people. This crisis was acknowledged as early as the 1970s in Egypt and Syria, followed by Tunisia, Sudan, and Libya in the 1980s. In all cases the acknowledgment was accompanied by arguments about the need to encourage private foreign investment in selected parts of the domestic private sector as well, sometimes, as in Egypt, beginning with tourism, and sometimes with activities designed to improve productivity in the agricultural sector.

The whole process was then given a further fillip by the changes in the world economy, signaled by the advent of greater global openness and interconnectedness promoted by Western governments and international financial institutions under the general rubric of the so-called Washington Consensus by which financial assistance was provided to indebted countries in exchange for promises to shrink the public sector, encourage the private sector, establish stock exchanges, and so on. People identified as capitalists were now at a premium, both to provide the entrepreneurial input and resources now in much demand and to act as window dressing as far as possible donors and investors were concerned. In this spirit, many secret deals were completed in which a select few were permitted to buy up state resources, create chambers of commerce, and encourage foreign private investment, all at great profit to themselves. The crony capitalists could also be used, on occasions, to provide employment, finance ventures that the state could not easily afford, top up state salaries, establish pro-government newspapers, and assist the government party by putting money into referendums and elections.

It goes without saying that the cost to state finances from these uncompetitive fire sales was very high, in spite of some attempt in countries such as Egypt to monitor the price at which the more public of the privatizations were carried out. So too was the cost in terms of what might have been left of public integrity, as new ways of raping state resources were constantly being found, from closed contracts to the purchase of cheap state land along the coast or around the major cities.

The result: huge fortunes were made by a few while the cost of bribes and middlemen's commissions rose exponentially. Then, as criticism of the exploitative behavior of the wealthy few began to bite, allegations of secrecy and deception had themselves to be met by threats, greater government censorship, and, in the case of groups like the Muslim Brothers that gave the notion of corruption a powerful religious connotation, imprisonment or exile. True, a few of the new "fat cats," as they were called in Egypt, were fined or imprisoned as a public example. Nevertheless, the majority continued to prosper so long as they maintained presidential favor and did nothing to cause so much public outrage that the authorities felt they had no alternative but to act against them.

As for the exact numbers of major cronies in each case, some have detected a logic depending on the management style of the president himself—Hafiz al-Asad, for example, being comfortable with having contact with less than a dozen—combined with the size of the market to be divided between the major crony conglomerates.[21] Other variables involve the presence of a voracious business member of the president's close family—a cousin in the case of Bashar al-Asad, the wife of Ben Ali, and almost all the males closely related to Ali Abdullah Saleh in Yemen—who were, and sometimes still are, in a position either to limit competition or, in some instances, to engage in forced buyouts of other profitable concerns. Bashar al-Asad's cousin, Rami Makhlouf, provides a particularly egregious example. By the beginning of 2011 he was said to control as much as 60 percent of the country's economy through a complex web of holding companies involved in telecommunications, oil and gas, banking, air transport, and retailing, a concentration of power that, according to many observers, made it "almost impossible" for outsiders to consider conducting business in Syria without his consent.[22]

The role of those who held top positions in the army and security was also important because, not being entrepreneurs themselves, they were anxious to find business partners with whom they could make money from their official connections. In this way, as Bassam Haddad has argued, the cronies and their partners have come, over the last two decades or so, to form part of the same elite. They were united by money, the exchange of favors, generally a common interest in particular economic policies, and, most important of all, a president who was willing to see to the preservation of their interests even after he died.[23]

One last aspect of the role of cronies in the system is worthy of special note. Given the way in which state assets began to be sold off or distributed by particular presidents at a particular time, many of the cronies were more or less of the same age as the president himself. Hence they were just as anxious as he to pass on their family business empires to a chosen successor, not always an easy task given the general absence of laws governing the orderly process of such transfers. In consequence, they became ever more bound to the president's solution to his own succession problem in spite of the fact that this could well be deleterious to their own immediate economic interests, as would-be investors, both domestic and foreign, began to hold off important decisions while they waited to see how the whole process would turn out.

Legitimacy and Constitutions

Apart from the overriding concern with keeping themselves in power and cultivating elite support, presidential security regimes paid a great deal of time and attention to two other essential priorities. One was to find ways to demobilize their populations politically while still persuading them to vote in the elections and referenda they used to support the appearance of constitutional legitimacy and of their recognition of the notion of the popular will. The other was the promotion of economic well-being through economic growth, consumption, and welfare. Whereas the former was something the incumbent presidents wanted to manage themselves, the latter was usually left to economists and other "experts" who could easily be disposed of and replaced if things did not work out as planned.

Historically, constitutions have been part and parcel of the republican model, their majestic presence seen as central to the process of using the law to limit the behavior of an arbitrary and capricious monarch. This was as true of the Arab Middle East as elsewhere, and the idea continued to maintain some vitality while being stripped, for the most part, of any of its old meaning. As Daniel Brumberg has pointed out, "in the Arab world, constitutions are written to ensure that the president or king has ultimate power."[24] The same was also true, with even greater force, of the electoral process. Even after decades of manipulation and misuse, elections still retained some capacity to get people to the polls, even in circumstances when they well knew that would have little or no political effect. Hence for most presidential security regimes the question was not whether to have a constitution, laws, and elections in the first place, but how to use them to maximum advantage to "dignify," if not actually legitimize, their rule internally and before their American and European allies.[25]

The problem, as observant political scientists such as Lisa Blaydes and others have begun to note, is that both exercises—the one of attending to constitutional niceties and the other of organizing regular elections—soon became extremely time consuming because both involved considerable political risk, a risk made worse by the constant chopping and changing of the rules that became an essential part of the process itself.[26] In Tunisia, for instance, Ben Ali felt it necessary to begin by ingratiating himself with the Tunisian elite by introducing a three-term limit to the presidency, in contradistinction to Bourguiba's presidency for life, before spending the next eight years creating a mechanism that would allow him to introduce a plebiscite for an amendment that would, in turn, allow him to stand more for more than three terms after all. In Egypt, a more recent problem was how to deal with what from the regime's point of view were flaws in the 2005 election process. The result was a complex series of amendments that, at one and the same time, gave the appearance of addressing the popular demands for reform while making it easier to manage the 2010 People's Assembly elections and the projected 2011 presidential elections as well. In both cases, although there was no doubt at all that such goals could easily be achieved in practice, the way each was handled was enough to give the impression of sufficient chicanery and manipulation as to provide a ready focus for those willing to draw attention to the harsh realities of presidential power that they enshrined.

As for the actual electoral process in those countries where the regime took them seriously, such as Egypt and Yemen and, to a lesser extent, Tunisia, this involved even more presidential time as the members of his inner council debated the best way to achieve certain defined aims—such as obtaining the two-thirds majority that under most constitutions was required to elect a president—without running the risk that elections would be the occasion for either major disturbances or major allegations of manipulation, both of which would be difficult to hide safely away from foreign and domestic eyes. Plebiscites and referendums proved the easiest to manage, as they required little more than getting out a large enough "yes" vote. But presidential elections presented more of a problem, particularly those that involved providing the appearance of competition as an alternative to the patently manufactured 98 or 99 percent vote. Antiseptic though the actual event might seem to be, the regimes that tried such elections—notably those in Algeria, Egypt, and Tunisia—still ran into difficulties drawing up rules specifying who could and could not run against the incumbent president. These were then compounded when having to deal with the challenges presented by well-known persons who, without tame party support, were excluded from the new system, such as Mohamed ElBaradei in Egypt in 2010.

But it was the conduct of parliamentary elections that proved to be the most time consuming and, often, the most worrying problem of all. The fact that it was usually taken as a matter of course that each election should be held under different rules—indeed, this was an essential part of the aim of keeping potential opposition off guard—only made it all the more taxing because each new proposal had to be carefully weighed for all possible consequences. Even when left to the president's most loyal and clever advisers, this proved a tricky business indeed. A mismanaged election such as that of Egypt in 2005, when supporters of the Muslim Brothers obtained many more seats than intended, proved to have serious consequences for all concerned. Worse was to come in Egypt in 2010, when an overmanaged election was subjected to intense public scrutiny after video cameras poked through the barred windows of polling stations showed supporters of the government party filling in blank ballot papers that were then taken away to be stuffed into waiting boxes while uniformed policemen looked on.[27]

Basic to the management of elections was the identification of just which parties were to be allowed to stand against the regime's own political apparatus. In most republics, this usually followed some version of Egypt's 1977 parties law with its particular list of exclusions—no parties that are based on religion, class, regional loyalties, or foreign associations—designed specifically to produce a tame "national" opposition with no access to a coherent set of easy-to-mobilize constituencies. Next in importance came questions regarding the mechanics of the election itself: proportional representation or winner takes all; the question of thresholds and of the numbers of representatives per constituency. Ancillary issues involved decisions regarding the time allowed to prepare for elections, the use of election monitors (for example, domestic or foreign), methods of voter registration, and the involvement of local human rights organizations, both government and nongovernmental organizations. It is easy to see how such a variety of choices offers a huge repertoire of opportunity, offset, to some extent, by the tricky problems involved in achieving a balance among the different, and perhaps incompatible, goals of securing a respectable turnout while also being able to produce predictable outcomes.

Given both the possible risks and the effort necessary to counter them, observers have often had difficulty in working out just why such regimes think elections are worth all the worry involved. Some, of course, such as the Syrian regime, do not feel the need to make too much of an effort in the first place. Others, such as the Libyan one, get around the problem by a system in which local people are allowed to elect the members of the people's congresses and revolutionary committees that, themselves, have very little power to make serious decisions of major national importance. But where the conduct of what are often called "elections without choices" is, or has been, taken seriously, as in Egypt and Tunisia, it is assumed to be based on the elections' utility as a system of allocating resources, managing the members and would-be members of the ruling party, testing public opinion, and allowing some small scope for individual competition and initiative among its supporters.[28]

A last form of controlled elections was those for the *shura* and similar councils based on the Egyptian model as a second chamber designed to provide a further set of constraints on the actions of a parliament. In Egypt itself, where 174 members of the 264-person council were directly elected, the vast majority were members of the government party, while great care was taken to prevent anyone who represented a significant social constituency from being elected. In other North African states with similar councils, such as Algeria, Tunisia, and Sudan, roughly the same proportion of members obtained or continue to obtain their seats via different types of managed constituencies such as trade unions and regional and municipal councils. The remainder were, or are, appointed by the presidents themselves, who used this power to nominate persons from minority groups and women, in a rather transparent attempt to give the country an image of greater pluralism than it actually possessed.

Producing Economic Growth

Postcolonial regimes first relied on the state to initiate a process of growth and development, supported where possible by foreign aid and occasional transfers from their oil-rich neighbors. Then, in the general process of economic restructuring that took place from the 1970s onward, greater reliance began to be placed on the private sector, on workers' remittances from the oil-rich states, and on attracting foreign private capital. In this way, most presidential regimes were able to generate a reasonable level of consumption for a growing middle class, even if the poor and unemployed remained dependent on subsidies and other safety nets. In Egypt, for instance, it is calculated that 87 percent of homes now have a refrigerator, 97 percent have access to piped water, and 99 percent have electricity; and the numbers of cars have doubled since 2000.[29] In Tunisia 99.5 percent of homes had electricity by 2009, 98 percent had access to piped water, and automobiles were owned by a quarter of all households, versus 15 percent a decade earlier.[30]

In all circumstances, successful management of the economy became a particularly important matter. It was usually placed in the hands of some reliable and technologically competent prime minister, and often subject to fierce battles within the elite itself over what policies were and are best pursued. Most of the republican presidential regimes have seen such internal conflicts pitting those who believe in a system of state-controlled management via tariffs and monopolies against those who believe that the future lies in greater openness through closer contact with the global economy. This has been as true of the large oil states—such as Algeria and Libya, where sharp falls in the price of oil triggered heated discussions about diversification and loosening of controls—as it has of those that depend more on a combination of taxation and external rents from aid, tourism, remittances, and so on.

Be that as it may, economic performance generally remained something of an Achilles' heel, a constant source of worry to the presidents themselves and a potentially divisive political issue. This division seemed particularly apparent when one of their sons became strongly involved in support of a policy that threatened the interests of members of the economic old guard, as seems to have been the case with Saif al-Islam Qaddafi in Libya in recent years and, to some extent, with Gamal Mubarak in Egypt before his father's fall, who advocated reduced tariffs and a shift to a more export-oriented economic strategy. Other major sources of presidential concern involved the potential impact of world economic depressions, inflation, natural disasters, and fears about future supplies of cheap food and water.

THERE CAN BE NO DOUBT that, as a result of what Eva Bellin has called the "robustness of [their] coercive apparatus," the Arab republican presidents for life were able to sustain themselves in power before 2010/2011 with only the occasional serious difficulty.[31] They were also helped in the first decade of the twenty-first century by a favorable international context in which almost all of them became openly or covertly allies of the United States in its international war on terror.

Nevertheless, even before their downfall such regimes can be seen to have contained weaknesses that either might have forced them to adapt to new circumstances or, in the event, might have led to their sudden demise. In terms of the analysis of their component parts just mentioned, there were dangers at every level, from their complete dependence on the health, the character, and the judgment of one man, his sometimes venal family, and his untested successor, through their reliance on the army and the deeply unpopular security services to keep them in power, to the problems that stemmed from their need to legitimize their rule by regular elections and by economic success sufficient to keep the majority of their populations content.

Other problems that could be identified even before their fall stemmed from their lack of ability to deal in a coordinated way with the sudden hikes in the price of basic necessities like food and fuel and the distortions in the economy produced by crony activity, for example, the unwillingness of ordinary Tunisian entrepreneurs to make large investment in businesses which might then suddenly be wrested from them by the president's wife and her grasping associates.

Just when one or all of these essential features of such regimes would become sufficiently damaging to produce a real crisis, no one could predict. Writing before the outbreak of the popular uprisings of 2011, what seemed a reasonable assumption was that, barring unforeseen circumstances, they would be likely to be at their weakest at the moment of presidential transition, as then appeared to be the case in Egypt. But this only goes to show how difficult it was for either the regimes themselves or outside observers to understand the interlocking natures of their problems, the enormous sense of popular alienation and, as it proved, the ease with which youthful demonstrators in Tunisia and Egypt were able to bring them to their knees.

4   Centralized State Systems in Egypt, Tunisia, Syria, and Algeria

Egypt, Tunisia, and Syria exhibited roughly similar patterns in their movement toward monarchical-style presidential systems in the years after independence. All three built strong centralized presidencies based in part on institutions, such as Tunisia's ruling party, created before independence, in part as a result of either a political revolution or a series of revolutionary events aimed at removing what were seen as the last obstacles in the way of establishing full national sovereignty. In each country, too, the preservation of the regime became paramount. This resulted in the creation of multiple security services and, after a certain amount of trial and error, the creation of a depoliticized army. Meanwhile, regime legitimacy was based on programs of modernization and development, supplemented by various forms of constitutional and electoral arrangements designed to give the appearance of a new republican legal order based on popular will.

Systems of economic management were, to begin with, heavily statist and left little room for cooperation with what was regarded as a socially irresponsible and foreign-oriented capitalist bourgeoisie. But then, when the state sector proved unable to generate sufficient resources to pay for itself, the regimes sought to encourage foreign (often

Arab) private investment in association with a small number of favored local entrepreneurs who were given increasing access to state contracts and, from the 1980s onward, to sales of state economic enterprises. The result was the emergence of a small group of cronies whose wealth served to finance a new elite composed of certain members of the ruling family, top military officers and security officials, and senior bureaucrats and ruling party apparatchiks, united in their defense of the regime, their own privileges, and the existing status quo.

Algeria was something of an outlier in that it was born directly out of a long and bloody struggle for independence against France, a circumstance that directly informed its postindependence trajectory under a long set of military governments in which power was held by a relatively small number of senior generals. Furthermore, its particular divide-and-rule method of government was made possible only by the existence of much larger oil resources than Egypt, Tunisia, or Syria possessed. Nevertheless, Algeria's development of a strongly centralized state system, its tentative moves toward managed elections and a mixed economy, and its eventual domination by yet another president for life give it sufficient elements in common with Egypt, Syria, and Tunisia to include it in this chapter rather than leave it to stand on its own as a unique case.

In Egypt, a series of presidential transitions—from Nasser to Sadat in 1970 and from Sadat to Mubarak in 1981—encouraged a number of experiments involving the president and his deputy before culminating in the prolonged process of deciding who should succeed President Hosni Mubarak after his retirement or death. Tunisia's president, Habib Bourguiba, became the first self-proclaimed Arab president for life (1975), and Syria represented the first case of family succession (Hafiz al-Asad to his son Bashar in 2000). In Algeria, decades of military rule came to an uneasy end with Abdelaziz Bouteflika's accession to the presidency in 1999.

Egypt

Egypt became a republic in 1953 after its monarchy had been effectively overthrown in a military coup in July 1952. Its first president was General Muhammad Naguib, the titular head of the Free Officers Movement that instigated the change. Given little real power, however, he was shunted aside in January 1955 by the other officers of the Revolutionary Command Council and replaced by the coup's real leader, Colonel Gamal Abdel Nasser.

As Kirk Beattie describes it, the Free Officers themselves were both well aware of Nasser's "increasingly obvious drive to concentrate power in his own hands" and sharply divided between those who approved of the process, like Anwar Sadat, and those who resisted.[1] In the event, Nasser's primacy, well established by the summer of 1955, did answer one of the major problems the officers faced in institutionalizing their revolution: deciding whether to retain power as a group or hand it over to their leader to safeguard it for them.[2] This same primacy soon found expression in the new 1956 constitution, written secretly in the presidential office and then approved, together with Nasser's own presidency, in a national referendum.[3]

The result of such personal moves was the establishment of an authoritarian system of government in which, as in most parts of the post-colonial world, the size of the state apparatus and its command over national resources was greatly increased, while independent institutions were either dissolved or co-opted by the new regime. And also as elsewhere, the preferred development strategy was one involving planning, a program of import substitution, and the nationalization of most of the private sector. In Egypt's case, as later in Syria, this process was taken much further than anywhere else in the world except the communist bloc, and led to the almost complete elimination of the old entrepreneurial class.

Bolstered by his own charisma, as well as by his emergence as a statesman of global importance, Nasser developed a system of leadership and decision making that combined consultation with those of his military colleagues who had followed him into civilian administration with a devolution of responsibilities that gave command of the army to his close friend, Abdel Hakim Amer, and an extensive "pyramid" of "complementary and competitive" security services, staffed largely by active or retired military officers, to another colleague, Zakaria Mohieddin.[4] A third, increasingly powerful figure, Ali Sabri, was given the management of the Arab Socialist Union, created in 1962/1963, as the regime's main ideological and popular tool for mobilization.

Nasser himself had some idea of the dangers this process of devolution posed. He made strenuous efforts to bring the army under presidential control in late 1962, only to be beaten back by Amer, whose insistence on his own independence can be blamed for a train of unhappy events: the politicization of the top ranks of the officer crops, a lackluster approach to military efficiency, and a desire to compensate for the army's poor performance in Yemen. As a result, Egypt's top military commander, together with Nasser himself, bore considerable responsibility for Egypt's humiliating defeat by Israel in June 1967.

Nasser too was greatly damaged by his own headstrong lack of judgment and the poor advice of his economic experts. One result was that the country experienced a huge balance-of-payments crisis in the middle of the implementation of the first five-year plan (1960–1965), bringing a central part of the state-led developmental process more or less to a halt. In the light of these disasters, it is difficult to avoid making a direct connection between the impact of some of the president's better qualities—his wide reading, his interest in economic and political theory, his loyalty to his colleagues—and some of his less good ones, like his growing sense of his own omniscience.

In a rare show of humility, Nasser accepted responsibility for the 1967 defeat by offering to resign, only to be compelled back into office by the shouts—"Gamal, Gamal, don't desert us, we need you"—from a huge Cairo crowd. He also moved quickly to reassert control over the military by securing the "suicide" of Amer and the trial of some of his leading generals.[5] Other acts had more unexpected results. For example, his naming of Zakaria Mohieddin as his successor was so much disliked by the same Cairo crowd that Mohieddin resigned from office and disappeared into private life the next year. This left Ali Sabri and, after 1969, Nasser's vice president, Anwar Sadat, as the two leading contenders for the succession.

What role Nasser's advanced diabetes, the painful arteriosclerosis in his legs, and his periodic attacks of angina played during the last hectic years when he tried to cope with the aftereffects of the 1967 disaster cannot be known with certainty. According to sources quoted by Kirk Beattie, Soviet doctors told him after his heart attack in September 1969 that he had only a year to live.[6] If Anwar Sadat is to be believed, this understanding forced him to pay some small attention to his own possibly imminent mortality by leaving Sadat himself in charge while he made a last trip to Morocco in December 1969, mentioning the possibility of assassination and saying that he did not want to "leave a vacuum."[7] Even so, not one of the high-level sources interviewed by Beattie believed for a moment that Nasser was actually thinking of Sadat as his successor.[8] Perhaps, as Beattie himself suggests, he remained wary of giving anyone else too much power.[9] Or perhaps, like other presidents for life, he remained so firmly convinced of his basic indispensability that he simply could not envisage his own end.

Becoming president after Nasser's death in September 1970, Anwar Sadat faced opposition from a powerful group of ministers who had coalesced around Ali Sabri, one of Nasser's vice presidents. But, after assuring himself of the loyalty of the army, he had Sabri and his colleagues jailed in May 1971, denouncing them for having constituted a rival "power center" and proclaiming the start of his own "corrective revolution," only six months after Syria's Hafiz al-Asad had used more or less the same words in describing his own coup against his colleague, Salah Jadid, in Damascus. Sadat increased his authority further by ousting Egypt's Soviet military advisers, and then using a reprofessionalized army to secure a limited, but highly acclaimed, victory against the Israeli forces occupying the eastern side of the Suez Canal in October 1973.

Military success was followed by an "October" Working Paper of April 1974 in which Sadat outlined his plans for the liberalization of both the economy and the political process that was to prove one of the defining features of his regime. The paper included the introduction of a new system of government based on a managed electoral and parliamentary competition between a reorganized Arab Socialist Union (later retitled the National Democratic Party, NDP) and a number of smaller opposition parties, carefully defined by the Parties Law of May 1977 to exclude organizations formed on a "class, sectarian or geographic basis, nor upon sex or race"—in other words, excluding any political grouping based on a preexisting, cohesive, social constituency.[10] Another innovation was the introduction in 1980 of a second chamber, the *shura* council, with a third of its members nominated by the president himself and which was clearly designed to act as an alternative source of legislation while providing a useful check on the activities of what might in certain circumstances have become a less controllable lower house.

As for the presidency itself, Sadat transformed Nasser's activist, charismatic use of the office to one that an American report of 1990 described as a kind of "presidential monarchy," consisting of a "royal family of influential relatives" connected to a "strong client network of politicians allowed to enrich themselves by often illicit manipulations of the economic opening his policies afforded" and hence, having a "strong stake in his success."[11] Almost all major decisions, including the significant one to visit Jerusalem in November 1977 as part of a successful effort to sign a peace treaty with Israel, were now taken by Sadat himself.

In May 1980, Sadat took the first steps toward becoming a president for life, amending Article 77 of the constitution of 1971 to allow a sitting president to be elected for more than one six-year term. Aged only sixty-two at the time, it is unlikely that he had given serious thought to who should succeed him. He had a son, Gamal, who was kept very much in the background; he also had a politically lightweight military vice president, Hosni Mubarak, appointed in 1975. Neither of these men would appear to have been considered serious contenders before Sadat's assassination at an Army Day Parade in October 1981.

Mubarak's long presidency can be divided up into three main segments. The first, lasting until Egypt's participation in the American-led coalition that ended the Iraqi occupation of Kuwait in early 1991, was a period of consolidation in which he continued most of his predecessor's economic policies while encouraging a lively political life involving reasonably free elections in 1984 and 1987. Where he differed from Sadat was in his effort to secure the loyalty of the army by an increase in military spending, which had been cut back dramatically after the Camp David peace agreement with Israel in 1978.[12] This had two important consequences. One was the pressure put on the domestic budget leading to an increased level of international borrowing that was brought under control only when Egypt was offered a significant amount of debt forgiveness as a reward for its participation in the military liberation of Kuwait from Iraqi occupation in 1990–1991.

The second was the growth of the army as both a military and an economic center of power under its influential chief, Defense Minister Field Marshal Abd-Halim Abu Ghazala. This development was part of a trend seen in a number of other Arab countries in the 1980s as a way of allowing the army to offset some of its own costs. Sensing that he was losing control of the military to such a powerful rival, and no doubt mindful of the uneasy relationship between President Nasser and Abdel Hakim Amer, Mubarak sacked Abu Ghazala in 1989.

The next phase of Mubarak's rule began in 1991, with a debt settlement with Egypt's creditors that involved a great deal of conditionality in terms of promises to balance the budget, open up the economy, and reduce the size of the public sector in exchange for further credit. One result was the beginning of the sale of state assets to a new group of businessmen who were soon to become the regime's major political allies. Given the secrecy surrounding the process, it is neither possible to chart this process in any detail nor to assess whether, at least at the start, there was any master plan behind it. But in its great haste it certainly bears close resemblance to the similar sell-off that took place in Yeltsin's Russia in the early 1990s. There too, state monopolies were rapidly transferred into the hands of private supporters of the regime whose wealth was then available for certain political purposes, including the funding of the regime's political party and the topping up of the salaries of senior bureaucrats and security officials.

A second feature of Mubarak's second decade was the economic warfare practiced against the regime by a new breed of Islamic militants who were based largely in a region south of Cairo. It took some years before their activities were savagely put down by the police. Perhaps fortuitously, these and other challenges provided an excuse for not going ahead with further political liberalization, for managing elections more tightly in the 1990s than the 1980s, and for exercising censorship of the press and other sources of criticism with a much heavier hand.

But there was more to it than that. Eberhard Kienle compares the process of selling state assets with that seen in many similar periods of economic liberalization elsewhere in the world. As elsewhere, there was much about this process for the public in Egypt to criticize, from the widening income gap between rich and poor to the obvious signs of elite corruption, in which state assets were sold off at less than their value to close associates of the Mubarak family.[13] To be sure, the regime itself was careful to maintain food and other subsidies against World Bank advice, and to try to ensure that privatization did not lead to high rates of unemployment. But this was not enough to deflect the strong criticism leveled in the media against some of its most influential supporters.[14]

President Mubarak himself, though, remained a less dominant figure than his powerful predecessors, content to rule by an intraelite consensus until various factors, which can only be guessed at, began to push him toward the much more monarchical style of presidency that announced the third stage of his rule in the late 1990s. One factor must have been pressure from the cronies and others who now had what was a huge stake in the continuation of the regime without further change at the top. Another may well have been family considerations, particularly those relating to his eldest son, who had important business interests of his own. Then, too, as Mubarak grew older, without ever having nominated a vice president to succeed him, the question of how to prepare for his own demise must have begun to present itself. Given the fact that, in his view, he represented the last generation of leaders who derived their legitimacy from the 1952 revolution, it would have been natural for him to look toward someone much younger, perhaps born many years after Gamal Abdel Nasser's death.[15]

In the absence of hard evidence, what can be usefully done is to construct a chronology designed to serve as a general pointer to the main chain of events. This would begin with the return in 1995 to Egypt of the president's second son, Gamal, an investment banker, presumably at his father's request, a process reminiscent of Bashar al-Asad's enforced return to Syria the year before. The next key date is 2000, when evidence of the NDP's poor procedure for choosing candidates for that year's election created the possibility of a central political role for Gamal. He was soon named head of the party's powerful Policy Committee, where he could demonstrate his policy skills.[16] And then there was the president's "fainting episode," which took place while he was addressing the People's Assembly in 2003, an event that Larbi Sadiki calls a "strong reminder of the urgency of the succession issue."[17]

Beyond the construction of a chronology, the best that can be done is to suggest what one might, in theory, think must have been needed to make the president's son a viable candidate for succession given the fact that Egypt was not only a republic but also a country in which there had been only military presidents since 1953. It must necessarily have involved a period of testing to see whether Gamal was up to the job. It must also have involved building up support for him, especially among the military, while trying to neutralize those groups and forces that either considered one of their number better suited to the job or objected strongly to Gamal on any number of possible grounds: his age, the character and interests of his own close supporters, his political skills, and so on. And then there is the obvious surmise that, as this strategy continued year after year, the particular relationships among the president himself, his own close advisers, and his most powerful supporters in the military and the security services might have become subject to change, perhaps even to a decision to postpone the whole business until after the president's death.

In the light of all these considerations, my own interpretation of the process goes as follows. First, during the early years of the twenty-first century a number of signs pointed to a vigorous preparation for a Gamal Mubarak succession. These include not only his role in the NDP but also efforts to win the support of the leaders of the military and security, for example, seating him among the generals during his father's annual address to the army in 2005 and persuading Omar Sulieman, the head of the security services, to act as a witness at his wedding in 2007.[18]

Perhaps even more importance was the decision to allow Gamal and his team of young technocrats both to organize the 2005 elections and then to use them as a showcase for the promise of new policies of greater political and economic openness. Unfortunately for the Mubaraks, however, serious problems arose after two rounds of voting, when it was suddenly realized that the opposition Muslim Brotherhood might be about to win a dangerous number of seats. This apprehension led the police to close many of the polling stations during the third and last phase to prevent them from achieving further gains. (The elections were held, unusually, in three stages to allow supervision by members of the judiciary.)

Worse for the regime was to follow, with the Brotherhood using their expanded parliamentary presence to press for a program that included limiting the power of the president, as well as calls for greater accountability, particularly as it related to the corrupt practices of many people close to the regime.

Thus began a presidential retreat from further openness that can readily be interpreted as a criticism of Gamal's own overly optimistic agenda. This included a series of constitutional amendments in 2007 that, though dressed up as reforms, made it more difficult for anyone to stand in elections against a sitting president, while reiterating the ban on parties of a religious nature. Rules governing the conduct of future elections were also changed to allow the process to be overseen by "independent committees" that were even more regime dependent than the members of the judiciary who had been in charge of the process before. Accompanying these changes was a fierce campaign against the Muslim Brotherhood, along with pressure on the organization's media and economic interests.

It is not difficult to see the heavy hand of the security service behind this change of political direction, as well as, more speculatively, that of the older cronies in the military and elsewhere who feared that their monopolistic economic practices would be at risk from the globalizing policies of the Gamal Mubarak team. It is also possible to imagine renewed pressure on Hosni Mubarak himself to stay on as president in order to protect the country from the new dangers that the Muslim Brotherhood seemed to pose. The fact that the Bush administration changed its policy from one of democracy promotion in the Middle East to one of an alliance against "terrorism" in 2006 was no doubt another important ingredient in the new mix. So too the president's quite extraordinary physical revival after an operation in Germany in the spring of 2010 when, contrary to all public expectations, he appeared far more alert and vigorous than he had before.

Matters became still more uncertain after the national elections of 2010, masterminded by Gamal Mubarak and his close associate, the steel magnate Ahmed Ezz. As a result of two overlapping goals—the elimination of most of the opposition and the revivification of the ruling party, the NDP—the elections turned into an unsavory struggle between members of the political elite, all scrambling to get into a parliament that was guaranteed either to reelect the president or to elect his successor while passing a large number of important bills designed to reshape working practices and to provide access to government resources. Worse still were the revelations of ballot stuffing. This, together with the fact that opposition groups received only 3 percent of the seats, drastically reduced the efficacy of the election as a legitimating device for the regime, a factor that may have had something to do with stimulating the storm of public protest that led to the sudden demise of the whole Mubarak regime in February 2011.

Tunisia

In several ways, Tunisia's narrative is similar to Egypt's. But it sets itself apart in that the country's first president was also the first in the Arab world to announce that he intended to remain in office for life.

Tunisia gained its independence from France in March 1956, and became a republic after the abolition of its hereditary monarchy in July 1956 under the presidency of the veteran nationalist leader Habib Bourguiba, then fifty-four years old. Bourguiba took some years to establish himself firmly in sole power. His main instrument was the party he had founded in 1934, the Neo-Destour. Before independence, this party had practiced a considerable degree of institutional pluralism, supporting different notions of leadership and of the policies of economic and social development to be followed. Bourguiba's main rival at this stage was his former colleague Saleh Ben Youssef, who had been expelled from the party in 1955 and became a significant focus for opposition until his assassination in 1961. After 1956, other rivals were retired from office to be replaced by younger party activists, to ensure, as Clement Henry Moore puts it, the president's own personal power and to give an image of youth.[19]

As Bourguiba's power expanded, so too did his popular adulation as the "supreme leader" in a cult of personality supported by a series of five yearly presidential elections, beginning in 1959, in which he regularly received over 99 percent of the vote. Equally telling is his 1964 reply to a question about his role in the Tunisian system of government: "System, what system, I am in the system."[20] A decade later, in 1975, he insisted that he be proclaimed "president for life." Such were his authority and his control over the single party that he hardly needed to rely heavily on other props, such as the secret police.

Leader of a small country with a small army, Bourguiba required considerable skill to negotiate the difficult Arab and international currents of the early postindependence period. He was aware of the dangers of Nasser's powerful influence, on the one hand, and the spillover effects of the fierce struggle between the French and the Algerian nationalists, on the other. Hence he took good care to maintain friendly relations with the United States, from which he obtained significant aid, and with Europe, presenting himself as a secular modernizer with a particular concern for the rights of women enshrined in the 1957 Personal Status Law, as well as a moderate as far as Israel was concerned.

As time went on, Bourguiba experimented with various exercises in allowing the appearance of a carefully managed opposition. He invited political actors to submit a list of candidates for the 1981 national elections provided that they did not draw support from outside the country, did not advocate class struggle or sectarianism, and agreed to avoid criticism of the "president for life"—a list of requirements that owed a great deal to Egypt's electoral law of 1977. Nevertheless, no candidate who put himself forward was able to obtain enough votes to surmount a minimum threshold of 5 percent.[21]

Like many other Third World countries, Tunisia experienced considerable economic difficulties in the late 1960s. It was the first of the Arab regimes to begin the turn from statism to a more decentralized system of economic management, a redirection that occurred after the sacking in 1969 of the country's leading exponent of "socialism," Ahmed Ben Saleh. Political and economic problems returned in the late 1970s and early 1980s as a result of the country's growing external debt and the consequent need to curtail public services. This led to demonstrations and serious rioting in 1984.

Bourguiba's political difficulties then intensified because of the appearance of a more sustained internal opposition from a radical Islamic movement, the MTI (the French acronym for the Islamic Tendency Movement), founded in 1981 and led by Rachid al-Ghannouchi. The MTI's escalation of its struggle against the regime in 1987 encouraged Bourguiba to rely more and more on his minister of the interior, Zein El Abidine Ben Ali, whom he unwisely made prime minister in September of that year, only for Ben Ali to oust him two months later on the constitutional grounds of "incapacity."[22] There seems to have been little domestic opposition to the move. Bourguiba's increasingly erratic behavior, and his arrogance, egotism, and general unwillingness to listen to advice, posed an obvious danger to strong government at a time of great national tension.[23]

In the event, it appears that Bourguiba himself had paid little attention to planning a smooth succession. There had been a brief moment in the 1960s when he had thought about changing the 1959 constitution to provide for a possible successor, but he soon dropped the idea. As far as can be ascertained, he showed no sign that he considered his son, Habib Jr., who had entered the political bureau of the ruling party in 1964, as someone who might one day take his place. Knowing what we now know about the personal psychology of elderly Arab presidents such as Qaddafi and Mubarak, it seems likely that, as he got older, Bourguiba's desire to hold on to office only increased, fed as it was by unchecked power, by the support of his family and close advisers, and by what he fondly imagined to be the eternal adulation of his people.

Ben Ali, a young man of relatively humble social origins, had been chosen by the Neo-Destour Party as one of the young officers to receive French military training after independence. He was then sent on to the American Security and Intelligence School in Baltimore, Maryland, which provided him with invaluable links to the military and security services of Tunisia's two major foreign allies. Back home again, he rose through the ranks of the domestic security organization that monitored the loyalties of the officers in the Tunisian army.[24] In this and then in other, more senior posts he supported all the repressive measures of the Bourguiba era.[25]

Ben Ali used the 1988 Neo-Destour Congress to invest himself with complete control of party and state. He also employed it to ease out many of Bourguiba's main supporters, some of whom were arrested on charges of corruption. In a further effort to stress his own personal authority, he had the name of Bourguiba's Neo-Destour changed to the Constitutional Democratic Rally (RCD in French). Like many new arrivals in the office of president—for example, Sadat and Asad in 1970—he took good care to distance himself initially from some of the harsher policies of his predecessor, freeing thousands of prisoners, encouraging political exiles to return, renouncing the notion of presidency for life, and promising a revival of political pluralism. In all this he paid particular attention to Rachid al-Ghannouchi, not only letting him out of jail but also inviting him to take part in discussions leading to the signing of a new National Pact.

There were limits, however, to such a display of inclusiveness, as the conduct of the 1989 elections soon revealed. Ben Ali was the sole candidate for president, as a result, in part, of a constitutional provision that made it virtually impossible for anyone to stand against him. Meanwhile, the electoral law, though amended in places as a result of opposition criticism, still maintained the party list system that granted all the seats in any particular constituency to the party that won most of the votes, allowing the RCD to obtain all the seats in parliament on only 80 percent of the total. Token opposition was provided by six other party lists, including the Islamists, running as "Independents."

Altogether the whole exercise was a good example of the type of political management Ben Ali exercised for the rest of his rule, using an appearance of openness and willingness to listen to criticism to legitimize each new set of elections and so encouraging oppositional candidates to stand without hope of election except for seats especially reserved for them from 1994 onward. The fact that similar practices—the use of a National Pact and an election law to define "legitimate" opposition, as well as decisions as to roughly how many opposition candidates might be allowed to "win"—were to be found in Egypt, Jordan, and, later, Morocco is testimony not just to an Arab demonstration effect but also to the perceived utility of practices that combined regime security with an opportunity to scare local populations with the threat of what might happen if Islamic parties were allowed to contest every seat. Underlining this threat was the victory of the Islamic Salvation Front (FIS) party in neighboring Algeria in the elections of 1991 and the army coup that followed.

Elections for president and parliament in Tunisia followed every five years, always subject to some slight tinkering with the rules to meet internal and external criticism of the country's lack of pluralism, but with little, if anything, left to chance. They were managed closely by the Ministry of Interior, without foreign observers. And the exact date was

announced only two weeks or so in advance to keep whatever oppositional campaigns were permitted to a minimum.

In 1994, Ben Ali was the single candidate for president. In 1999, two
token opponents were allowed to stand against him, and together they
obtained just 2 percent of the vote. Elections continued after a 2002
constitutional amendment removed the previous term limit—two with
the possibility of a third—cleverly permitting the ruler to stand for an
indefinite number of future elections without actually going so far as to
name him president for life.[26] From then on, the electoral process itself
became part of his growing personality cult. Youthful-looking pictures
of him appeared everywhere and all party headquarters were decked
with flowers and photos like some personal shrine. As before, token oppositional candidates were allowed to stand against him. The four who
opposed him in 2004 together received less than 5 percent of the votes.
Five years later, in 2009, of the three candidates who were permitted to
stand, one claimed to have had his electoral manifesto censored (for its
reference to "persons well-connected with the regime" having made fortunes in recent years) while also being prevented from distributing leaf-
lets and posters.[27] Such theater was obviously used to create a sufficient
appearance of competition to ensure that Ben Ali could no longer be
accused of obtaining an absurd 99 percent of the vote.

As for the parliamentary elections that always took place on the
same day as the presidential one, opponents wishing to play by the regime's rules were guaranteed an increasing number of seats: nineteen in
1994, thirty-four in 1999, thirty-seven in 2004, and finally fifty-three in
2009 (in a slightly enlarged chamber of 212)—or 20 percent of the total.
The creation and co-option of a malleable opposition was also accompanied by paid allowances for its newspapers.[28] Highly managed though
it was, this proved just about acceptable to Tunisia's European partners,
who were anxious not to disturb the many arrangements for economic
and security cooperation between the European Union and its southern

Mediterranean partners, not to speak of Tunisia's role in checking illegal migration by Africans trying to cross the country from the south.

The truth behind the pretense of pluralism was, however a tightly managed police state run for the benefit of the president, his close family, and a small circle of friends and advisers. The president himself exercised absolute control over the party, over the state, and over the machinery of repression. According to Beatrice Hibou, writing in first decade of the twenty-first century, estimates of the number of police ran between 80,000 and 133,000 for a country of ten million people, a ratio of police to citizens many times larger than that in France, in addition to an army of informants.[29] As a result, employment in the security services may have sustained something like 10 percent of the population.[30] Meanwhile, the RCD itself, with its 7,500 local branches, acted more like a "security apparatus than a party."[31]

Huge domestic power of this type allowed members of the presidential family—beginning with Ben Ali's second wife, Leila Trebelsi—and their associates to use the cover of liberal economic reform to make huge fortunes for themselves. This proved to be a form of cronyism more typical of Syria than of Egypt, and was in marked contrast to the Bourguiba era, when members of his close family were only peripherally involved in economic activity. Typical methods of enrichment included the privatization of state assets such as hotels and manufacturing; the transfer of public land to private ownership; the granting of licenses to operate major public services, such as cell phones, airlines, international sea transport, Tunisian cruise ships, and TV and radio stations; and, on some occasions, the forced sale of private assets such as banks and newspapers. State resources were also used as a source of selective patronage both for members of the crony business community and individual members of the security services, while credit was freely provided for many privileged members of the new middle class, allowing them to buy houses and cars but leaving them deeply in debt and so enmeshed in a system of relations that it prevented them from criticizing or opposing the regime.

Needless to say, most such activities remained shrouded in the greatest secrecy, and any public mention of them could result in imprisonment or exile. Meanwhile, according to Hibou, domestic competition was enormously restricted, entrepreneurs outside the president's family circle being forced to keep their businesses small and diversifying their activities as much as possible to avoid possible seizure.[32]

Ben Ali's style of rule can be characterized as one of careful, methodical planning ahead, of political micromanagement, and of an often-vindictive punishment of critics, particularly those who published their criticism abroad. A good example of the first characteristic is provided by the way in which he introduced a new article into the constitutional law of 1994 allowing the president to submit proposals for the revision of the constitution to a referendum, a procedure he did not make actual use of until 2002 when he finally obtained the popular consent that allowed him to stand for further terms in office.[33]

Examples of Ben Ali's micromanagement are harder to find, but can probably be seen in the techniques employed to shield himself and his regime from criticism by finding ways to imprison journalists on trumped-up charges that had nothing to do with what they had actually written. An example is the case against Toufik Ben Brik, who was jailed on an assault charge after an alleged altercation with a woman in the street who accused him of damaging her car.[34] The use of extreme forms of political vengeance is easier to document. The case of Mohamed Bouabdelli, the founder of Tunisia's Free University, provides an excellent example. Bouabdelli's long dispute with the Ben Ali family culminated in a book critical of the regime published on the Internet in 2010. Ben Ali's response: the closure of the university (containing some 1,500 students) and the suspension of all teaching for three years.[35]

Syria

Unlike many of the other Arab countries, Syria started its independence in 1946 as a republic. Nevertheless, in spite of experiencing the region's first post–World War II military coup, it took many years before it established a strong presidential system. It also experienced inconclusive periods of civilian and military government in between, as well as three years (1958–1961) of union with Egypt under the presidency of Gamal Abdel Nasser.

The reasons that the country took so long to come to a strong presidency were many and various. Syria was much less socially integrated than other Arab countries, with many more local and ethnoreligious divisions than either Egypt or Tunisia. It possessed a small but well-entrenched landowning, banking, and commercial elite. It was also subject to a struggle for influence between various outside forces: the United Kingdom and the United States versus the Soviet Union, on one level; Egypt and Iraq, on another. Developments were further affected by a series of military defeats by Israel, including the loss of the Golan Heights in the south of the country in 1967.

In these circumstances, what proved to be a winning formula was some time in the making. One part of the process was the reduction in the power of the old-guard politicians as a result of land reform. Another was the nationalization of the banks and other commercial enterprises during the union with Egypt. Yet another was the alliance between the fledgling Ba'th Arab socialist party and a group of Ba'thi army officers belonging to the small, socially disadvantaged Alawi community, whose strong personal links allowed them to hijack the party in 1966 and establish their own, army-backed regime.

At the center of this last development was the uneasy partnership between two senior Alawi military figures, Hafiz al-Asad, who became minister of defense in 1966, and Salah Jadid, who, though he took no formal post, used his control over the army to act as the new regime's strongman until he was ousted by Asad in an internal coup in 1970. The loser's fate was to be placed in Damascus's Mezze prison until he died in 1993.

Hafiz al-Asad proceeded carefully to build up his own personal power, not actually becoming president until February 1971, after staging a referendum in which he obtained over 99 percent of the votes. Then, like many other aspiring Arab heads of state, he initiated a brief period of economic openness in which, in contrast to the inward-looking policies of international isolation and control instituted by Jadid, he encouraged joint ventures between foreign and local investors in selected sectors of the economy such as tourism and the import of agricultural machinery.

This self-styled "corrective movement," though of only marginal economic importance given the overall pattern of state management and control in association with Ba'th Party unions of industrial and rural workers, laid the basis for a set of business partnerships between mostly Alawi senior military officers and mostly Sunni members of the urban business community that was to form the basis of a particularly Syrian form of crony capitalism that has dominated the economy until the present day. Family members who also benefited from the limited economic opening of the 1970s to build huge fortunes were Asad's brother, Rifaat, and his brother-in-law, Muhammad Makhlouf.[36]

One of Hafiz al-Asad's first major acts was to increase the powers of the presidency in the new constitution of January 1973. This then formed the basis of what Raymond Hinnebusch as early as 1990 was already calling a "presidential monarchy" supported by the three essential components of Asad's rule: the army, the security services (including rival intelligence services and a huge army of informers), and the Ba'th Party from which was drawn a tame cabinet of ideologues and technocrats.[37] Meanwhile, as is usually the case with similar authoritarian regimes, all independent institutions such as the press, the judiciary, and the universities were placed firmly under government rule.

The president himself—a secretive, extremely hard working, austere, and, on occasions, ruthless man—proceeded to create a personal system of management based on personal aloofness (his main form of communication was the telephone), an intimidating manner, and a complicated balancing act between the representatives of the different institutions and components parts of his new regime. It was, and is, a system usefully described by Bassam Haddad as a kind of personalized corporatism in which only the president and a few close advisers know all the key relations between its component parts.[38]

To make matters more complicated, Asad opted to maintain a large and expensive military machine, both for self-protection and also to magnify Syria's strategic importance as a way of extracting resources from the Soviet Union, Saudi Arabia, and, from the 1980s onward, the revolutionary regime in Iran. This too required very careful handling. For one thing, Asad was running the risk of a preventative war by Israel at a time not of his own choosing. For another, military initiatives such as Syria's 1976 invasion of Lebanon against the Palestinians and their leftist allies proved unpopular enough to promote a domestic backlash led by the local Muslim Brotherhood, first in the form of assassinations of Ba'th Party officials, then of an uprising in the city of Hama in 1982 that was only crushed after days of brutal fighting during which, at a conservative estimate, at least 5,000–10,000 people were killed.[39]

On top of all this, Hafiz al-Asad had major problems with his health. Notably, in November 1984, at the age of fifty-three, he suffered a serious illness that, in turn, provoked a major clash with his brother Rifaat, who was emboldened to use his control over a large military force known as "the Defense Companies" to support his own claims to the succession. Months of tense confrontation were only ended in March 1985 by a dramatic meeting between the two brothers at their mother's house in Damascus at which Rifaat was persuaded to back down. He was then rapidly removed from his command and, after a short while, sent into exile in Europe.[40]

The affair was to have lasting consequences. Senior members of the elite appear to have agreed, if they had not before, that the most serious threat to what all perceived as an Alawi-dominated regime was a split at the top. The result: the Alawi generals, the Alawi heads of the security agencies, and, no doubt, Hafiz al-Asad himself came to believe that their own positions and that of their community in general could only properly be protected by keeping the presidency in the hands of one of their own, preferably the Asad family itself. It is also possible to conjecture that it was at this same moment that Asad first began to consider his eldest son, Basil, who was then in his early twenties, as a possible successor.

It would also be characteristic of the president's cautious approach to major decisions for him to take his time to think the matter through, paying particular attention to the question of how his own very personal style of political management could first be studied and then passed on to someone of, as yet, unproven skills and abilities. It is this cautious, community-led approach that makes the question of the Syrian presidential succession so different from that which was later to exist under Ben Ali in Tunisia, Mubarak in Egypt, and elsewhere. Whereas Asad had the future of a whole Alawite minority community to think about, the others were much more simply focused on purely family concerns.

The matter of succession presented itself openly again when Basil al-Asad, now thirty-three, was killed in a car accident while driving to Damascus Airport in January 1994. Much was made at the time of the fact that he, now an army officer and commander of the Presidential Guard, was being "groomed" as the president's successor. No doubt in some general sense he was. But we can also surmise that Hafiz al-Asad still had other options in mind, while remaining unsure about how to mastermind such a family transition given the existence of Ba'th Party republicans who wished to have their own say in the matter, as well as senior Alawi generals worried about the choice of an unproven young man.

Once again Asad behaved with great caution. On the one hand, he summoned his second son, Bashar, now a twenty-eight-year-old ophthalmologist, back from his studies in London to join the army, a hugely significant act. On the other, he does not seem to have made active preparations for the transfer until he was ill again himself in 1998. This had the obvious advantage of preventing the Syrian political process from being dominated by the succession issue, while simultaneously allowing time for Bashar to prove himself. But it also had the countereffect of preserving the hopes of other members of his inner circle who felt that they had a better right to succeed Hafiz than his young son, as well as of encouraging quite reasonable worries among some of the older members of this group that, given the fact that Bashar would certainly come to power with a younger team, they would quickly be sidelined and some of their power and influence, perhaps even some of their wealth, removed.

The Asads' campaign seems to have begun with a publicly announced drive against "corruption" in which, according to Bassam Haddad, it was only well-known opponents of a Bashar succession who were found guilty.[41] Other possible opponents of Bashar were stripped, piecemeal, of their particular responsibilities. And others again, such as senior generals and security chiefs whose loyalty to Bashar's succession was deemed suspect, were retired at the regulation age. This was not the case, however, for the equally elderly Field Marshal Mustafa Tlas, who was kept on to play what looks like a key role as facilitator in the days just before and after Hafiz al-Asad's eventual death in June 2000. No such finesse was shown, however, in the case of potential supporters of a Rifaat al-Asad candidacy, hundreds of them being placed under arrest in Damascus and Latakia in February 1999. Viewed as a whole, the process itself could well be regarded as Hafiz al-Asad's final lesson to his son about the proper management of the Syrian political scene.

Even so, there were some obvious hiccups. Although many things could be planned in advance—for example, getting the Syrian parliament to amend the constitution article regarding the minimum age of a president from forty to thirty-four—others had not had time to unroll before Asad Senior's death. For one thing, he died before a crucial meeting of the Ba'th Party's Regional Command Council at which the party apparatus itself was supposed to be subject to strong criticism and then reform. For another, there was the obvious problem facing a personalized political regime that relied for part of its legitimacy on an incoherent body of laws and precedents in that the various bits and pieces could not be easily made to fit together in a relatively short space of time. To take just one example, Article 85 of the 1973 constitution provided that it was the first vice president, Abdul-Halim Khaddam, who was to succeed the president on his death. Yet, though this caused a certain amount of confusion for a few days, it was soon clear that Bashar had become the majority's favorite candidate and that no alternative candidate was going to risk opposing him for fear of losing all.[42]

Given what was known about events following the death of great leader presidents—in Egypt in 1970 and, more significantly, in Tunisia in 1987—it was reasonable to suppose that Bashar al-Asad would undertake two initial initiatives: first to get his own more youthful team in place as quickly as possible, and second to make promises and announce measures designed to convince doubters that he was his own man, that he recognized that times had changed, and that he was going to do away with some of the most-criticized and irksome practices of his father's rule. What should also have been predictable at the time was that popular enthusiasm for something that was inevitably going to be characterized as a Damascus "spring" would soon begin to threaten the basic interests of Asad family rule, including those of the military and economic elite who depended upon it for their personal and political well-being.

Expectations of change were immediately raised by the new president's inaugural speech, in which he talked of a softening of the one-party state and of bringing Syria into a new age of information technology.[43] Other moves soon followed: an amnesty for a significant number of political prisoners, a substantial rise in the wages and salaries of public-sector workers, and promises to reactivate the role of the National Front, a defunct seven-party coalition led by the Ba'th. Even an apparently much less important announcement, that pictures of the president would be removed from nongovernmental buildings, seemed to suggest a reversal of the cult of personality that had been allowed to develop under Bashar's own father.

Emboldened by such measures, groups of intellectuals began to call for the end of the forty-year-old state of emergency and for the rights of free assembly and uncensored expression. Their protests then found institutional expression in the creation of informal discussion forums. But no sooner did these small but significant local initiatives begin to attract attention from abroad than the regime clamped down again, closing the forums, arresting dozens of those who had signed petitions, and dispersing public meetings and sit-ins by force.[44]

All that remained of the initial period of openness and talk of reform was a willingness to continue to discuss possible solutions to the huge problems the country continued to face. Of these, the most pressing was a dire economic situation made worse by dwindling resources of oil and water augmented by the inability to obtain fresh aid or even private investment from abroad because of Syria's continuing alliance with Iran, its occupation of Lebanon, and its close relationship with groups labeled terrorist by the United States and its allies. Like all such regimes, that of Bashar al-Asad was looking for workable proposals that could be implemented without threatening its own hold on power. This is not to say, however, that it was not serious in its search for acceptable remedies, nor that some of the ideas put forward, particularly in terms of a more liberal approach to economic management, were not stored up for later use, for example, the creation of new sources of vital credit by permitting the opening of private banks.

Showing much of his father's caution, Bashar also took five years to create a new leadership team. He used the Tenth Regional Conference of the Ba'th Party in 2005 to replace some, but not all, of the older members of the Regional Command. Then, in the immediate aftermath of the conference, he confirmed his brother-in-law Asaf Shawkat as head of Military Intelligence and his brother Maher as one of the two heads of the Republican Guard.[45] Slowly, too, he began to establish his own style of government, although, according to a report by the International Crisis Group, it took him many years to develop the confidence to dispense with some of the elaborate sets of checks and balances among the several power bases at the regime's inner core that he had inherited from his father. By 2008, according to the same report, he was "displaying greater decisiveness," willing to take risks and to stand by the consequences.[46]

Part of Bashar's confidence came from the success of a limited economic liberalization. This involved a series of necessary but unpopular reforms, such as the ending of all food and heating subsidies that affected not only the Syrian lower classes but also powerful business groups that had been able to profit from the old order. Where this left the old crony elite is unclear. But it seems likely that it created a divide between an inner core, which continued to benefit from monopolies they had obtained over many parts of the domestic market, and the more entrepreneurial figures who found places in the Syrian Business Council, established in 2007 to encourage investment by both local and foreign capital.[47]

One of the obvious contradictions between the two groups was nicely revealed in 2008 when the United States eased some of the economic sanctions imposed by President Bush and the U.S. Treasury, which had forbidden American firms from dealing with Rami Makhlouf, Asad's cousin, on the grounds that his mighty tourist and telecommunications empire was tainted by corruption.[48] As in Egypt, the stage now seemed set for a long struggle between the well-established crony monopolists and those members of the business community who wanted to benefit from opening up to the global economy, with all the demands for transparency and regulated competition that this would very likely involve.

Algeria

The Algerian republic, born out of a fierce anticolonial struggle against the French, was managed and controlled by two major institutions: the National Liberation Front (FLN), which was the official party; and the military. Both were used to build up an authoritarian system of government in which the state administration, fed by revenues from oil, occupied a central position.

It was no doubt inevitable that the first president, Ahmed Ben Bella, a civilian, was overthrown in 1965 by the first of a long series of military men, Houari Boumedienne, an austere, reserved figure who managed the complex task of uniting the scattered forces of the Algerian military—some of whom had fought against the French inside the country, some from outside—into a single cohesive national army. Surrounding himself with loyalists, he used his growing power to push through state-driven development policies aimed at rapid industrialization, very much in the style of Egypt and Syria. As with similar regimes, rule was by decree, there was little popular discussion of its policies, criticism was suppressed, the media spoke with one voice, the intelligence and security services clamped down on any opposition, and the single party was used more as an instrument of control than a vehicle for debate.

Things began to change only in the years preceding Boumedienne's untimely death in December 1978 at the age of forty-six. Efforts were made to revivify the FLN. Consultative assemblies were established at various levels, and then, after a period of managed but relatively open debate, a new constitution was introduced to be ratified later by public referendum. Like many such constitutions, it gave something in the way of greater political freedom—notably the creation of a 261-member popular assembly—while offsetting it, just in case of some unforeseeable and unintended consequence, by legitimating the president's existing powers and then specifying new ones, such as allowing him the right to issue decrees when the assembly was not in session.

Quite accidentally, the new constitution also prepared the way for the smooth transfer of power to Boumedienne's successor, the minister of defense, Colonel Chadli Bendjedid, a compromise candidate who emerged out of a contested election during the FLN congress held in January 1979. The other major candidate was Boumedienne's longtime foreign minister, Abdelaziz Bouteflika, who, twenty years later, was to become president himself, in 1999.

Bendjedid's presidency was the occasion for two abortive attempts to inject civilian authority into the regime by the creation of nonmilitary institutions. The first of these occurred in 1979 when the FLN was provided with a political bureau, a representative central committee, and various policy commissions. This process was almost immediately halted by an outbreak of serious unrest among the Berbers of the Kabyle Mountains that was worrying enough for the army commanders to return control over the party to Bendjedid himself and then, in 1984, to reestablish the army's general staff (abolished in 1967) as its own alternative center of power. The result, as Hugh Roberts has trenchantly observed, was that the president was now "formally accountable to nobody but informally accountable to the army commanders."[49]

The second attempt to reduce the power of the military was the result of Bendjedid's own response to the severe economic unrest produced by the huge fall in oil prices in the mid-1980s: the introduction of a new constitution that allowed the formation of parties other than the FLN. Among the groups to benefit from this provision was the Islamic Salvation Front, which was able to take advantage of the widespread popular discontent to win more than half the votes cast in the municipal elections in June 1990, and then a quarter of those in the first stage of the national elections held in December the next year. Faced with this huge threat to their own positions, the senior commanders ordered the president to dissolve the National People's Assembly, then to resign, replacing him with a five-man Council of State that immediately canceled the second round of the elections, igniting a ferocious uprising by groups of Islamic militants and ushering in another decade of direct military rule.

Armies involved in a prolonged struggle against domestic opponents tend to become politicized themselves. Algeria was no exception. As the 1990s progressed, a significant division occurred between those senior commanders who wished simply to eradicate the militants and those who wished to negotiate, making it convenient for them to support a compromise civilian candidate in the 1999 presidential elections, Abdelaziz Bouteflika, and then help him to an overwhelming victory. Bouteflika immediately demonstrated considerable political skills by supervising a successful program of national reconciliation, as well as by creating a power base wide enough to allow him, for the first time in Algerian history, to achieve civilian ascendancy over the military. Other successes included the renewal of good relations with Algeria's major Western allies, France and the United States, along with the use of a fortuitous increase in oil revenues to pay off much of the country's international debt. Reward came in the shape of Bouteflika's victory in the 2004 presidential elections, where he defeated five opposition candidates and obtained just under 85 percent of the vote.

By this stage the president had built up a powerful position for himself as what Roberts calls "the supreme arbiter of policy debates and conflicts of interest."[50] As with other Arab presidencies, the endurance of his power depended on a strong centralized state and powerful security apparatus combined with an appearance of political openness while cracking down hard on criticism or dissent. Wide use was also made of state resources such as contracts and privatized assets to reward and so maintain the support of the many and varied interest groups or individuals on which any authoritarian president must partially depend.[51] Most important of all, the president established what Isabelle Werenfels likens to a "shadow cabinet," based on thirty or so advisers, containing two members of his family (his brothers), as well as men with significant regional knowledge and influence.[52]

Nevertheless, management of an expanding elite of individuals and collectivities must have required considerable skill, even if Algeria's natural fragmentation—based as it was on family, tribal, and regional loyalties and preexisting patterns of recruitment—made it more difficult for its component parts to coalesce behind one particular policy. As Werenfels explains in an interesting section on continuity through change, the elite's continued fragmentation not only "reflected longstanding and deep divisions with Algerian society as a whole" but was also reinforced by the oil rent, which "helped the core elite to finance a costly divide and conquer strategy."[53]

In these circumstances, and given the prevailing trend in the neighboring Arab republics, it was only natural that Bouteflika, no doubted egged on by his own entourage and others who benefited from his rule, should begin to think about running for a third term, even though this was expressly prohibited by a 1996 constitutional amendment. Given the usual secrecy that surrounds such matters, the exact chain of events is unclear, the more so as, whatever the context, moves of this type are almost inevitably subject to opposition somewhere within the regime. Nor can it be ascertained whether a health scare in November/December of 2005—when Bouteflika spent three weeks in a French hospital reportedly suffering from what may have been a gastric ulcer hemorrhage, but which many believed was cancer—had anything to do with fresh anxieties about the country's political future, whether with or without him.

At any rate, it was in Bouteflika's Independence Day speech in July 2006 that he first revealed his plan to reamend the 1996 constitutional amendments on the grounds that, as they had been pushed through during a civil war, they were now out of date. This could be taken as code for his desire to remove the clause setting a two-term limit on the presidency. Two years later, in November 2008, with the end of the president's second five-year term fast approaching, the country's tame, FLN-dominated parliament adopted a set of amendments removing these limits, it is said, with "minimal debate."[54]

Bouteflika's regal speech announcing his candidacy in February 2009 is a wonderful example of the rhetoric of a man who half-believes—perhaps more than half—what he is saying:

> From the four corners of the country, and from all layers of the population, appeals were addressed to me to carry on my mission. . . . Everyone understands that I cannot remain oblivious to such pressing calls. . . . Refusing to run would be painful for me, and not moral vis-à-vis the people, who gave me their trust and support in four universal suffrages, the presidential elections of 1999 and 2004, and the referendums on civil concord (1999) and national reconciliation (2005).[55]

Bouteflika duly won the April 2009 presidential elections with, allegedly, 90.2 percent of the vote. What mattered just as much was the official figure for the all-important voter turnout, which was put at 74.3 percent of the electorate.[56] Given the president's age (seventy-two) and the fact that he did not appear to have a son, popular speculation turned at once to the likelihood that one of his several brothers would be groomed to succeed him, something that rapidly became known as "the Cuban option" or "the Cuban scenario," referring to the key relationship between an ailing Fidel Castro and his younger brother, Raoul.[57] Particular attention was paid by some journalists to the extra duties said to have been given to Bouteflika's brother, Said, a personal adviser on political and security affairs.[58] As in all such situations, it is natural for opponents of the president to want to cast the succession question in the worst possible light. It is equally natural for the regime either to say nothing or to deny everything. And so, in spite of the many signs of popular discontent with the president's rule, it remains until the present day.

5 Presidents as Managers in Libya, Sudan, and Yemen

The power structures of the three remaining republics with presidents for life—Libya, Sudan, and Yemen—evolved differently from those of Algeria, Egypt, Syria, and Tunisia as a result of the existence of a number of significant features that are generally associated with the more fragmentary nature of their societies. While these are generally identified with the existence of so-called tribes, as Mohammed Bamyah has pointed out to me, it would be incorrect to describe the state systems themselves as tribal, because a tribe is not a state and cannot be used as a model of state governance. Rather, what is being described is a method of political management that involves a constant manipulation of a variety of subnational solidarities and allegiances which act centrifugally to divide the people into separate social, ethnic, and religious groups recognized by the ruler as significant political actors in their own right. And though, for the purposes of simple exposition I refer to all these subgroups as tribes, it must be recognized that this is a very plastic term for a reality that may exist as much, if not more, in the ruler's mind than as a set of observable collectivities on the ground. Note too that, as also happened in the colonial period, it is sometimes enough for those in power to treat certain groups as having tribal features for them to assume a solidarity that they might not otherwise have possessed. Even so, it would seem that it was rare for the members of such groups to demonstrate an unconditional loyalty to their leader. One result, among many, has been the practice of providing weapons to these leaders in order purchase their support, thus ensuring that practically the whole population is armed.

The social fragmentation that gives rise to such tribal polities is underpinned not just by their large size but also by the presence of mountainous and desert areas containing heterogeneous, often nomad, populations used to an autonomous way of life. Historically these peoples have been difficult to bring under the direct control of a central administration by military or other means. In the case of Yemen, for example, the country consists of some 150,000 tiny settlements, many of them hardly accessible from the capital, Sana'a. It also has more arms per capita than almost anywhere else in the world.[1] By the same token, it has always been relatively easy for more aggressive neighbors to interfere by taking up the cause of one rebellious local group or another.

Hence, rather than relying on a well-developed state apparatus and long traditions of political obedience, the successful presidents of such tribal republics have been forced to play the role of an arbitrator and distributor of resources as much as one of a single enforcer of a single policy based on the formal institutions of a strong government. Here the ruler's personal memory of each local group's history, of its strengths and weaknesses, and of the price its leaders can exact for obedience, is more significant than a set of well-kept files. Here too the army has remained of continuing importance both as an instrument of domestic control and as an institution that is itself "tribally organized," in Sheila Carapico's phrase, and largely commanded by members of the president's own tribal relatives and close followers.[2] Meanwhile, the post of president remains a dangerous job, one often threatened by coups and threats of assassination. It is a situation well captured, for me, by the sight of an antiaircraft gun guarding the presidential palace just outside Sana'a when I drove past in the mid-1990s.

Historically, such states have also suffered from an inability to tax as well as from a lack of taxable resources. But even when oil came to play a much more important role, as it did in Libya in the 1970s and Yemen and Sudan in the 1990s, presidents were still encouraged to continue their old role as managers and brokers, using their new resources to co-opt support along traditional geographical and tribal lines. This, in turn, made them more vulnerable to oil shocks such as those of the mid-1980s, opening them up to increased foreign pressures and forcing them into short-term and often hasty adaptations as far as economic and political policies were concerned.

In each case—in Sudan after the military coup of 1958, in Yemen after the Egyptian-supported coup of 1962, and in Libya after the overthrow of the monarchy in 1969—the initial drive to modernize was pursued in rough imitation of the Nasserite Egyptian revolutionary state. But, over time, a lack of central power combined with various forms of local opposition forced presidents in all three countries to alter their methods in the interests both of maintaining themselves in power and of achieving some part of their original social programs. Their own developing political skills were part of this process. So too was the fact that the different members of each country's elites—including tribal leaders—tended to live close together in the capital city and to interact with each other socially even when they disagreed politically. One important result: as the presidents' positions strengthened, most regionally based opposition movements, though sometimes threatening to secede in order to obtain more resources, became less and less likely to do so.

Libya

Libya as a modern state was created de novo by the United Nations in 1951 out of three more or less independent entities, Cyrenaica in the east, Tripolitania in the west, and the Fezzan in the south. Although administered briefly as a single entity by the Italians after 1911, its different parts had been shaped by different histories and different patterns of social organization. Hence the new king, Idris, was led to administer the country by a mixture of personal patronage and kinship, using as his resources first the tiny revenues derived from foreign aid, then the much larger sums derived from concessions to foreign oil companies followed by the country's share in a growing export trade, which had reached some three million barrels a day by the end of the 1960s. As in other oil-producing states like Iran, all political activity was banned and systematically repressed, leaving a vacuum to be filled by the young officers led by then-Captain Muammar Qaddafi, who made the military coup of 1969.

Taking Nasserite Egypt as their model, these officers formed a Revolutionary Command Council and attempted to create an "Arab socialist" one-party authoritarian state. As in Egypt, their leader was quick to develop into the charismatic director of their revolution, dismissing those of his brother officers who disagreed with him while building up a strong personalized power base.[3] As in other Arab revolutionary states, this also involved an increase in the size of the bureaucracy and the creation of a set of overlapping intelligence services—for example, the Intelligence Bureau of the Leader created in early 1970s and an enlargement and "reshaping" of the armed forces to prevent further coups. Perched more and more securely at the top was a small core of loyalists that included old army colleagues, tribal leaders, and members of Qaddafi's own family and tribe, who, together, managed and controlled the various institutions of the state.[4]

Initially, there was some debate within the ruling group about the proper use of the country's growing oil revenue after the nationalization of the industry in 1971. But this was soon won by Qaddafi himself, who forced the more technocratic members of his team to allow him to distribute the new wealth to key groups of supporters in the form of jobs, loans, subsidies, and concessions, while also using it to promote a series of experiments in popular democracy designed to force Libyans to participate more directly in their own modernization. Whereas other Arab rulers chose to take their time over what they believed was, inevitably, going to be a lengthy process, Qaddafi, conscious of Libya's small size, scattered population, and almost complete lack of an educated, professional class, seems to have felt that he had no choice but to resort to more direct methods not to be found in other models. Hence his proclamation of Libya as a "state of the masses"—in his Arabic neologism, a *Jamahiriya*—in 1977.

It is here that serious problems of analysis begin. Given Qaddafi's powerful, flamboyant, energetic, and seemingly eccentric personality, it is difficult to separate out the extent of his own personal role in promoting the series of social experiments that followed from those of his close colleagues. Nor, without insider knowledge, is it possible to understand the balance between the quixotic and the inspirational, on the one hand, and the shrewd, realistic assessment of how far it was possible to transfer power—first to a nationwide system of popular congresses and then to revolutionary committees—on the other. In the almost total absence of the necessary information, a good guess might be that the core members of the regime allowed the man known as "The Brother Leader"—never "President"—to make whatever radical innovations he might choose, provided their own vested and institutional interests were not under any serious threat. Indeed, it might further be argued that this process could be regarded as more reciprocal than most conventional accounts allow, a notion based on a supposition of the way the elite's early recognition of the Leader's own megalomaniacal delusions about the extent of his own power to do good to his people encouraged its members to construct a kind of mirror state that reflected back to Qaddafi just what he wanted to see while allowing them to pursue their own personal interests to their own particular advantage.[5]

Two insights can be used to support such a hypothesis. First, as Libya's few political historians agree, the creation of the new committees was never allowed to interfere with key bureaucratic institutions of the regime: the oil industry, the army, the security service, or the Leader's own control of foreign policy.[6] Second, the period of experimentation lasted less than a decade, leaving Libya with a set of formal and informal institutions that have remained, more or less unchanged, from the late 1970s to the present day.

It was the regime's almost total reliance on oil revenues that both allowed it to function in this way and, in the 1980s, posed the greatest challenge to its system of political management. Dirk Vandewalle's analysis of the pattern of resource distribution closely resembles those to be found in the Gulf States: a large proportion of the population was on the government payroll and much of the rest was supported, directly or indirectly, by monopolies established over the import of scarce goods, with everyone in receipt of subsidized or free welfare services and basic foodstuffs.[7] The result, as is also well known, is that such systems are not only particularly vulnerable to oil price shocks of the kind they all experienced in the mid-1980s, but also particularly resistant to change. This is well illustrated by Qaddafi's response to the dramatic fall in oil prices in 1986, a type of Libyan *infitah*—liberalization or opening up—by which in 1987/1988, and again in 1990/1991, the state sought to divest itself of some of its economic burdens, such as subsidies, while empowering the small private sector to play a larger role as far as freer imports were concerned.

As might easily have been predicted, the result was fierce opposition from many powerful vested interests within Libyan society, particularly those led by vocal and well-connected members at the regime's core. Of particular significance were the managers of highly protected state companies, the technocrats who managed the oil industry, and an assortment Qaddafi's former military colleagues.[8] Hence, in a very short time, much of the strength of the new measures was watered down and the economy returned to its old form of statism, helped by the recovery of world oil prices in the early twenty-first century. More or less the same thing happened as a result of a third attempt at an *infitah* in 2003 that, though resulting in some privatizations of state assets, still had much of its impact blunted by the usual opposition from the usual powerful political and economic interests.[9]

As for Qaddafi himself, he apparently came though these various crises with much of his old self-confidence in his ability to manage an ever-increasing coalition of different, sometimes incompatible, interests more or less intact. Nevertheless, the energy and attention involved must have taken its toll, the more so as the number of groups—including tribes—to be placated and managed inevitably increased in line with the growth in incomes, opportunities, and education. There was talk of "illnesses" in the 1990s, when the Leader was in his fifties, and further talk of his wanting to prepare his eldest son, Saif al-Islam (born in 1972 to his second wife), to succeed him. But, as usual, these were rumors rather than well-established facts.[10] The best that can be said is that, soon after Saif had finished his studies at Libya's Tripoli University in 1994, he either offered himself as an envoy and troubleshooter for his father or he was encouraged to do so; probably a bit of both. As a result, Saif became increasingly active toward the end of the 1990s, establishing his own foundation, the International Charity and Development Association, and helping to lead Libya out of the diplomatic isolation imposed as a result of its role in the destruction of a Pan American plane over Lockerbie, Scotland, in 1989. He also used his Truth for All campaign to try to curb the arbitrary excesses of the Revolutionary Committees. According to Larbi Sadiki, his father liked this campaign because it absolved the senior Qaddafi from personal blame. Nevertheless, there were limits, as Sadiki also notes, and Saif was "unlikely to touch persons" close to the Leader himself.[11]

There is a variety of evidence to suggest that not only were Saif's efforts considered harmful to the basic interests of some of the older members of the regime's inner core, but that they were also sufficiently dangerous to disqualify him from the succession itself. It also seems likely, although very difficult to prove, that other members of the Qaddafi family—notably Saif's younger brothers, Muttasim and Khamis, who between them ran Libya's security and military apparatus—may have had ideas of their own.[12] Certainly they appeared be a serious obstacle to a Saif succession if they should decide to pool their resources against him.

Meanwhile, for reasons already alluded to in other parts of this book, it is possible to suggest that the Leader himself was, and remains, in various minds about the whole situation: testing Saif's candidacy against the waters of elite opinion, sometimes wanting to appoint a successor before he dies, and sometimes thinking that he should leave it to the veteran revolutionary institutions to decide after he has gone.

There were, and are, formidable practical problems as well, most notably the fact that Qaddafi the father has no well-defined position to hand on and works through no clear set of governmental structures. The one solution proposed was that a new organization, to be called the Popular Social Command, should be created to run the state in place of the now defunct Revolutionary Command Council, something Qaddafi himself announced in a 1996 speech. Its functions, as outlined in another speech in March 2000, would be to act as an umbrella over the General Secretariat of the General People's Congress (commonly thought of as the parliament), the General People's Committee (the government), and the security services, with its general coordinator—presumed to be Saif at this stage—to become the Leader's successor as the Head of State.[13] As Rachid Khechana pointed out, if this proposal were actually implemented it would have combined the present roles of leader and executive head of government in one person, in charge of both domestic and internal affairs.[14]

Saif himself, sensing opposition to such a formal role, had not, as of the end of 2010, accepted the role, preferring, he said, to wait on the sidelines until Libya had adopted a whole series of democratic institutions:

"I will not accept any position unless there is a new constitution, new laws and transparent elections. Everyone should have access to public office. We should not have a monopoly on power."[15]

Then, in December 2010, it was reported that Saif and his charity were withdrawing from political activity concerning reform and human rights entirely in the interests of its "core duties" of humanitarian work and development.[16] The situation was obviously one that called for hesitation, and when Saif hesitated, potential supporters must have hesitated too, fearful of finding themselves on the wrong side of what they might easily suppose to be about to became a bloody, and possibly fratricidal, struggle. The growth of popular opposition to the regime in the first months of 2011 only made the problem of succession more pressing but also more opaque.

Sudan

Colonial-period Sudan was governed by the British as two distinct entities—the Muslim north and the Christian and pagan south—a division that produced a civil war in 1955 in anticipation of independence the following year. Military rule then became the norm, accompanied by attempts to create a viable modus vivendi between the two regions, notably the Addis Ababa agreement of 1972. But this agreement ended abruptly in renewed fighting in 1983 when its progenitor, President Gafar Nimeiri, unwisely attempted to impose Islamic law on the south. A second major influence on the country's political fortunes has been its proximity to the much more powerful Egypt, whose postrevolutionary trajectory many Sudanese presidents tried to emulate while keeping Cairo's political and military presence to a minimum.

Nimeiri himself was overthrown in a coup in 1985, in the midst of growing economic difficulties that he was unable to contain. After a short period of civilian rule marked by an increased emphasis on Islam, the present Sudanese president, Omar Hassan al-Bashir, seized power in 1989, suspending political parties and establishing the Revolutionary

Command Council for National Salvation, with himself as head of state, prime minister, and minister of defense. Four years later, in 1993, he increased his great powers still further by personally appointing himself president, disbanding the Revolutionary Command Council, and concentrating all executive and legislative powers in his own office. This last move was then ratified by a national election for the presidency in 1996, giving him a five-year term of office.

For the first ten years of his rule, Bashir worked in close association with Dr. Hassan al-Turabi, a charismatic Islamic activist who acted as chairman of the ruling National Congress Party and speaker of the new National Assembly. The two fell out, however, for a number of reasons, including Turabi's support for a parliamentary bill aimed at limiting the president's powers once it became clear that Bashir planned to run again for office in 2001 in spite of the agreed-upon one-term limit.

It can be assumed, however, that this dispute was symptomatic of something deeper. It was not just Bashir's growing unwillingness to share power with the leader of the country's most popular religious organization, the National Islamic Front, but also his opposition to the ideological limits this imposed on his own flexibility of action at a time when he was contemplating sending troops into the restive Darfur region, an action Turabi opposed, regarding it as his own political bailiwick. The result was a dramatic palace coup in which Bashir sent troops and tanks to oust Turabi from his office, and then dissolved the parliament and declared a national state of emergency.

President Bashir's decision to intervene in Darfur follows a pattern of action well described by Alex de Waal as "counter-insurgency on the cheap."[17] After years of governmental neglect, a coalition of groups came together in 2003 to take up arms as a way of calling attention to their many local grievances. With the national army stretched and underresourced after so many years of fighting against the rebels in the south, Bashir chose to counter the demands of the growing Darfuri opposition by unleashing a group of mounted nomads known as the Janjaweed. It was the unusual cruelty of their violent, scorched-earth attacks on civilians, particularly women and children, that internationalized the conflict to the extent that the International Criminal Court levied accusations of war crimes and crimes against humanity against Bashir himself in 2008.

In spite of the international notoriety, Bashir is, in many ways, a typical modern leader of Sudan. He is someone who, again in Alex de Waal's words, acts as less of an autocrat than as a "chairman of a board," managing an unruly coalition of "Islamic ideologues, party bosses and security chiefs, each of whom has his own fiefdoms and funds." Hence the skills required are those of patronage politics: the ability to weigh up the price at which each of his key partners can be kept in line and then find the resources to do so in terms not just of tangible financial assets but also of a set of political supports and threats including the go-ahead to plunder either the state's resources or those of some other group within the larger society.[18]

Such are the skills that have allowed Bashir to rule Sudan for over twenty years. And such are the skills that have allowed him, for the first time in Sudanese history, to propose a way to cut the Gordian knot binding the North and South under the 2005 Comprehensive Peace Agreement, allowing the south to vote for its own secession in January 2011, followed by an orderly transfer of power.

Whether it will work without leading to yet another civil war is another matter. Meanwhile, Bashir himself has moved to secure himself more firmly in power, building on the local, national, and Islamic support for him that was generated by the International Criminal Court's international arrest warrant, removing some of his most dangerous critics, and in April 2010 winning new presidential elections with an official figure of 68 percent of the vote.

Born in 1944, Bashir leads a vigorous public life away from his palace, showing particular enjoyment at large public rallies. His popularity is helped by the country's strong, increasingly oil-based economy. And he enjoys the additional benefit that his main domestic rivals distrust each other more than they do him.[19] It may also be that, for the time being at least, his colleagues think it wiser to wait and see whether the difficult business of splitting the country in two can be carried out successfully before making a move.

Little is known about Bashir's domestic circumstances, however, other than that he is married to a widow with children but has no children of his own. As a result, the succession question has not openly presented itself so far. But it surely must as Bashir gets older or experiences a period of serious ill health.

Yemen

Yemen, like Sudan, consists of two distinct parts, uneasily united in May 1990. Before that time, the north and south had had quite different political histories: the south was under British and then local communist rule; the north became independent from the Ottoman Empire in 1918 under hereditary imams until a revolutionary movement toppled the Imamate in 1962. This event triggered a long civil war in which the new republic came under a pervasive Egyptian influence, aspects of which remain in its bureaucracy, its educational establishments, and its military until the present day. Furthermore, many parts of the united country still remain outside governmental control, necessitating much the same process of negotiation, accommodation, bribes, and threats as in Sudan. In Yemen, however, the periods of the use of actual armed force have proved much shorter, the most notable being a brief and bloody campaign to prevent a southern succession in 1994.

Yemen's present president, Ali Abdullah Saleh, is a professional military man who seized control in the north in July 1978 at the age of thirty-two. He then went on to become the president of a unified Yemen in 1990, and continues to derive considerable local legitimacy from his rule as unifier and nation builder.[20] Certainly his most significant innovations have been in the area of creating institutional administrative structures to help govern the country. The first of these is the General Popular Congress, established in 1982, which brought together a thousand "prominent" supporters of the regime from all parts of Yemeni society, including most of its more powerful tribes.[21] This congress was then transformed into something more like a political party for the 1993 general elections, and was used by Saleh as a way to encourage southern participation by including them as members of a new ruling coalition.

Saleh went on to establish greater power for himself when he stood in the first direct presidential elections in 1999, obtaining over 90 percent of the vote against a former party colleague running as an independent. This was followed by the establishment of an appointed 111-member council of advisers with legislative powers, a kind of second house.

Events leading up to Saleh's decision to stand for a second term in 2006 were surrounded by much the same type of uncertainty and, possibly, bad faith as those present in other Arab presidential regimes. To begin with, he announced that he would not contest a second election, giving hope to the opposition by saying that he hoped that all the parties would "find young leaders to compete in the elections because we have to train ourselves in the practice of peaceful succession."[22] This was in 2002. Four years later he had changed his mind, saying that he was bowing to "popular pressure and appeals of the Yemeni people," words similar to those used by the presidents of other Arab states such as Bouteflika in Algeria. Perhaps he intended to stand all along, as opposition figures suggested.[23] Equally possibly he was persuaded to stay on by a combination of his own family and crony followers, as well as by international pressures and promises from the United States and Saudi Arabia, anxious that he continue his role against al-Qaeda and other Yemeni-based terrorist organizations. This time he won just over 77 percent of the vote against a southern rival, Faisal bin Shamlan.

It should also be noted that, by 2006, after fifteen years in office as president of a united Yemen, Saleh and his family and associates already controlled most of the top positions in the army, often combined with ownership of, or partnerships in, the many contracting, trading, and manufacturing companies that had sprung up as a result of the wealth produced by the oil and gas finds of the early 1990s.[24] As of 2000, those who commanded the army, air force, special forces, republican guards, and special guards included one of the president's sons (Ahmad), three of his half brothers, and three of his nephews. This is unusual for the family of an Arab head of state but not, as Sadiki points out, peculiar in the northern part of Yemen, where there is a long tradition of nepotism and of public posts that are generally passed on from father to son.[25]

Nevertheless, in spite of such family support, governing Yemen remains a difficult task that requires not only great skills as a mediator but also the financial and other resources necessary to feed the elite patronage networks that, in turn, distribute money and opportunities to those lower down in society. This is a complicated enough activity at the best of times. But it became even more difficult during Saleh's second term as the central government was forced to deal with a series of challenges to its authority—challenges that were often followed by attacks against oil pipelines or police stations—stemming from complaints about the lack of jobs and services. Another complicating element came, in 2004, from an escalation of fighting against the Houthi religious rebels in the north. Some suggest that this last event was the result of a misplaced confidence on Saleh's part based on an increase in American military support as part of the war on terror.[26] Others assert that he started the campaign in order both to bolster his own crumbling authority and as part of a plan to secure the succession for his eldest son, Ahmad.[27]

Problems intensified further when southern grievances against northern rule solidified into an organized protest by retired army officers, who were joined by state officials and unemployed youths, including some elements who wanted the south to secede from the union.[28] To this was added the further complication of the establishment of an active al-Qaeda branch in the south followed by various attacks on some of its members by both U.S. drones and Saudi special forces. If war on two fronts was not enough, Saleh now had to engage in the difficult balancing act of satisfying American demands in order to obtain much-needed military and financial assistance without arousing still more internal opposition.

By 2009/2010, the country's internal divisions, coming at a time of a reduction in the oil revenues that provide some 90 percent of its income, were also reflected in a stalled political process. Elections were postponed until February 2011, after an agreement between the government and the opposition parties grouped together in a coalition called the Joint Meeting. What remained was an extremely difficult task: all the parties needed to form a 200-man committee—half from Saleh's General People's Congress, half from the opposition—for national dialogue, with the goal of agreeing on constitutional amendments designed to pave the way for political reforms.

Intercutting with all this and making the whole situation more complicated still was the question of the presidential succession. This could, in theory, be subject to political agreement, but rumors continue to involve Ahmad, rumors that appeared to be given more weight when he was given the nonmilitary task of heading an investment committee aimed at finding new resources to revive the ailing economy.[29] Nevertheless, Ahmad's succession will not be easy. He is still young. And there are other senior commanders in the army who apparently resent his rapid promotion and special status. Meanwhile, there are also the younger members of the family to consider—including the president's other sons—leading to the possibility of coalitions both in support of Ahmad's succession and against it. Last, to complicate the whole matter still further, there is the Yemeni version of the popular wave of revulsion against presidential families that rocked the Arab world early in 2011, encouraging Saleh to promise a number of concessions concerning his own continued rule, without convincing the protesters that they would actually be implemented if he managed to keep his power intact.

THE THREE STATES I HAVE grouped together under the general rubric of "tribal republics" share a style of government which has a family of resemblances that separate them from their stronger, more centralized republican neighbors. Rulers are required to manage systems that possess relatively weak armies and bureaucratic institutions, significant internal divisions, and, at least in their early stages, insufficient resources to buy off all of their populations. All have also had to overcome significant opposition both from local elements and, over time, from members of a growing urban professional middle class—including the military—which disputed their right to speak in their name and to direct a large share of revenues and business opportunities to their own family and a few well-placed cronies.

Nevertheless, styles of management have differed in significant ways as well. Some have depended on the rulers' perceptions of the social makeup of their own various constituencies and the degree to which such factors as kinship and clan, tribe and locality can be used to divide, to balance, to manipulate, or to create new loyalties. Others involve the ways in which each ruler has presented his country to the outside world. In the case of Qaddafi, for instance, as Almawludi Al Ahmar has noted, he has used his country's vast oil wealth to try to create a picture of a Libya that has no internal problems except those created by outside meddling.[30] However, Ali Abdullah Saleh has generally adopted exactly the opposite strategy of using the specter of domestic division and external threat to garner military and financial aid from both the United States and Saudi Arabia.

Last, the threats that each ruler has faced have generally been quite different in character, with Qaddafi facing a series of inside or palace coups, while for Omar al-Bashir the main danger came from secession and for Saleh from concerted tribal rebellion. That is, until the uprisings of 2011, which revealed that there were regions of Libya—in the east and in the Nafusa mountains south of Tripoli—where local resentments were still strong enough to fuel protracted armed opposition, while much of the opposition to Ali Abdullah Saleh in Sana'a came from the educated youth protected by dissident tribal and military forces within the capital itself.

Arab leaders joking together during photo opportunity at Khartoum summit, March 2006. From left to right, Omar Hassan al-Bashir of Sudan, Ali Abdullah Saleh of Yemen, Émile Lahoud of Lebanon, Abdelaziz Bouteflika of Algeria, Bashar al-Asad of Syria, and Muammar Qaddafi of Libya.   (AP Photo/Nasser Nasser)

Middle East leaders at the White House summit on Israel/Palestine, September 2010. This photograph gained notoriety after it was manipulated by the editor of Egypt's *Al-Ahram* newspaper in order to place President Hosni Mubarak (extreme left) to the front and right of President Barack Obama. (AP Photo/Pablo Martinez Monsivais)

Youthful-looking Arab leaders relaxing at Baghdad summit called by Saddam Hussein in November 1978. (© Jacques Pavlovsky/Sygma/Corbis)

Arab first ladies at Lebanon's presidential palace, March 2004. From left to right, Suzanne Mubarak of Egypt, Andrée Lahoud of Lebanon, and Asma al-Asad of Syria. (AFP/Getty Images)

Andrée Lahoud and Asma al-Asad walking in step through downtown Beirut before the Arab Women's Summit in 2004. (Getty Images)

Mural of Syria's "Holy Family," showing Hafiz al-Asad and his two sons, Basil (left) and Bashar (right), September 1999. (Time & Life Pictures/Getty Images)

Tunisia's new president, Zein El Abidine Ben Ali, after he had replaced his predecessor, the ailing Habib Bourguiba, in November 1987. (AFP/Getty Images)

Presidents Jacques Chirac of France and Abdelaziz Bouteflika of Algeria stand at attention during the playing of their national anthems in Algeria, March 2003. (Gamma-Rapho via Getty Images)

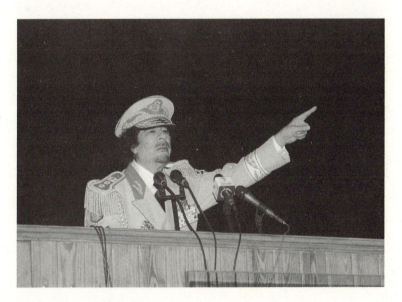

Dressed in a Ruritanian costume of his own devising, Libya's "Brother Leader" Muammar Qaddafi makes a point while celebrating the fortieth anniversary of the ejection of U.S. troops from his country in June 1970. (AFP/Getty Images)

Sudan's Omar Hassan al-Bashir at a "Meet the People of North Darfur 'Event'" in Khartoum, August 2010.   (AFP/Getty Images)

King Abdulla of Saudi Arabia and Muammar Qaddafi relax after a session of the Arab League Summit, Doha, March 2009. (EPA Images)

Egyptian Americans' posters comparing Hosni Mubarak to Adolf Hitler, a dumb cow, and the devil at a New York protest in February 2011. (AFP/Getty Images)

An Egyptian in Alexandria tears down a poster of Hosni Mubarak with the words "Yes to Mubarak the future," January 2011.   (AFP/Getty Images)

Tunis on fire in protest against President Zein El Abidine Ben Ali's defiant speech of 14 January 2011.   (AFP/Getty Images)

A protester outside Tunis's Criminal Court holds a poster declaring Zein El Abidine Ben Ali "Wanted for Dictatorship" as the exiled president is tried in his absence, June 2011.   (AP Photo/Hassene Dridi)

Protesters erect a poster of Hosni Mubarak looking very much like a female pharoah with the words "Put Egypt's Pharoah on trial," Tahrir Square, Cairo, May 2011.   (AFP/Getty Images)

Patriotic Yemeni protester uses hands painted in national colors to demand that the "hunted prey," President Ali Abdulla Saleh, "Get out, get out," Sanaa, April 2011.   (AFP/Getty Images)

6 Constrained Presidencies in Lebanon and Iraq after Hussein

The emergence of strong presidents for life in the Arab world has been historically constrained in two countries with sectarian systems of representation and their necessary corollary, the coexistence of weak, inclusive central governments that, by incorporating the leaders of all major communities, seek to prevent any one of them from being in a position to dominate the others. There is something paradoxical about this in the Lebanese case, where the powers granted to the president at independence in 1943 have been described as being those of a "republican monarch."[1] Yet there have always been sufficient counterbalancing forces, both inside the presidents' own confessional communities and outside, to ensure that, with only one exception, in the 1940s, whenever a Lebanese president tried, or was even thought to be trying, to change the constitution in such a way as to allow him to run for a second six-year term in office, he was prevented from doing so.

In Iraq, the sectarian divide was transcended for a long period after nominal independence in 1932 in the interests of a Sunni-dominated national unity. After the overthrow of the monarchy in 1958, this allowed republican presidents from Abd al-Salam Arif (1963–1966) onward to create and then to maintain strongly centralized security states in which sectarian interests were largely subordinate to national ones. In this interesting case, sectarianism became an important force constraining presidential action only after Saddam Hussein's system of personalized presidential government was overthrown in 2003, to be replaced by an institutionalized political sectarianism where parties were organized and governments formed along largely confessional lines. Then, at once, a more "Lebanese" logic obtained in the country, where presidential power was limited so as not to overshadow a relatively weak, inclusive, and multisectarian coalition cabinet.

What also links the two countries' postindependence political experience is a confessionally divided national society in which the initial dominance of members of one confession—in Lebanon the Maronite Christians, in Iraq the Sunni Muslims—was both vigorously contested and then variously accommodated in an uneasy set of institutionalized arrangements subject to regular challenge from within the system as well as from outside it. On the one hand, there has been intense political competition among the elite of the ruling sect; on the other, opposition, sometimes armed, from sections of those religiously or ethnically defined communities that felt politically, and often economically, disadvantaged by the existing balance of power.

Meanwhile, in Lebanon since its creation, the system has worked to contain the development of a secular-minded middle class, making it difficult for those wishing to obtain popular support for nonsectarian political movements or to break the hold of the ethnically and religiously based communities over the education, health, and personal lives of their adherents, including their insistence that there could be no system of civil marriage. Much the same system was institutionalized by Iraq's 2005 constitution by which, after more than fifty years of a form of secular universalism that placed all Iraqi citizens under the same national regime, the disappearance of most of the country's secularist and modern-minded middle class and the policies of the American occupier combined to allow control over personal status to be transferred to the Muslim clergy and the Kurdish tribal leaders.

In exploring these and other similar issues I have been much influenced by two sets of theoretical interventions by Sami Zubaida. One is his observation that, although ethnic and confessional identities were certainly in existence in the early modern period, from a political point of view what matters is the question of how and under what conditions they have been politicized and in what manner.[2] The second concerns his deployment of the notion of political communalism to describe the condition in which religion as a marker of identity becomes subordinate to the larger fear that a community's special institutions and beliefs, and sometimes its very existence, are at risk.[3]

Lebanon

Modern Lebanon was established under the French mandate as a republic. The country obtained its first constitution in 1926, giving it a strong presidency, a single chamber, and the makings of a confessional system by way of its provisions that government and administrative posts were to be distributed fairly among the various Christian and Muslim sects, and that control over the personal status of individuals was to be relinquished to the heads of its religious communities. A few years later, it was agreed that election to the Chamber of Deputies should also be organized on a sectarian basis.

The country's first president, a Greek Orthodox, was elected by the deputies in 1926 for a single four-year term, which was then raised to six years in 1929. His time in office concluded in a period of great political confusion due to the French high commissioner's 1932 suspension of the constitution in order to block the presidential candidacy of a Muslim notable, which, he feared, might cause the office to pass out of Christian hands. Constitutional life was restored only in 1936 when the first of a long series of Maronite Christian presidents, Émile Eddé, took office. His electoral success was made more significant by the fact that the 1931 census, the only one ever held, seemed to show that the Maronites were the country's largest Christian sect.

The whole episode was also of major significance for two other reasons as well. First, it provided a vivid demonstration of the importance attached by the Maronite elite to their control of the office of president, with a fiercely contested election in which Eddé obtained only one more vote in the chamber of deputies than his bitter rival, Beshara al-Khouri. By the same token, leading members of the same elite also had a strong interest in ensuring that none of them served for more than a single term so as to give the others a better chance of obtaining the same high office. The second reason is that, whatever presidential powers the constitution provided, they could always be set aside by the French, backed, of course, by their army of occupation. Further proof of the strength of this constraint came in 1939 when the French again suspended the constitution at the start of World War II, dissolving the chamber and then, in 1941, dismissing President Eddé himself.

Political life resumed in 1943 under British pressure, with elections leading to a victory for Beshara al-Khouri as the president of a now almost independent Lebanon. Shortly before the election, Khouri had come to an unwritten agreement, the National Pact, with the leading Muslim politician, Riad al-Sulh. The pact enshrined two major cross-confessional understandings. The first was that the president and the commander of the army should both be Maronite Christians, the prime minister a Sunni Muslim, and the speaker of the chamber a Shi'i Muslim. The second laid down that, in the case of the Chamber of Deputies, as well as the award of most administrative posts, there should be a 6:5 Christian-to-Muslim ratio.

One major result of the first of these provisions was, as Fawwaz Traboulsi points out, that the power of the president was to some extent constrained by his political relationship with his Muslim prime minister.[4] Traboulsi might also have added that to make the army commander a Maronite as well opened up the possibility of having a military president, as was to be the case in 1958, and again in 1998 and 2007.

The evolving Lebanese political system now possessed three main features. The first was the necessity of maintaining a weak state and a small army, the logic being the desire to avoid the danger that any one sectarian group would use these structures to dominate the others. The second followed from the first, ensuring that the country lacked any real ability to defend itself against its more powerful neighbors, Syria and Israel. As for the third feature, this confirmed the leadership of a self-reproducing business and commercial elite that used access to the presidency and control over the political process to create and maintain policies expressing its own interests in economic openness, free trade, minimal legislation, and low taxes, while restricting the provision of what few social services existed to the separate sectarian communities. In Traboulsi's argument, this oligarchy, when solidified at independence, consisted of some thirty families with, at its center, a "consortium" consisting of Beshara al-Khouri's two brothers, his sons, and a dozen related families holding monopolistic control over the "main axes" of economic power.[5]

The significance attached by the elite to these structures was made further apparent by the fierce competition among the Maronite leaders themselves, one of whom, Beshara al-Khouri, managed to obtain a temporary amendment to allow him to stay on in office for a second term. But this was only achieved by fixing the 1947 election in such a blatant way as to unite so much of the country against him that he was finally forced to resign in 1952 when the army, under its well-respected commander, Fuad Chehab, refused to support him against the more militant of his opponents. Khouri was succeeded by Camille Chamoun, whose authoritarian style and plans to obtain an illegal second term aroused even more opposition, culminating in a mini–civil war that resulted in the emergence of General Chehab as the country's first elected military president in 1958.

Chehab, though well respected by the public at large, soon ran into troubles of his own.[6] Anxious to reform the country's institutions and to bring state services to the poorer communities outside Beirut, his policies of increasing centralization soon succeeded in offending much of the sectarian leadership whose positions he seemed to threaten, both in terms of their own locally based power and, in the case of the Maronites, their own desire for office as well. The result was yet another political crisis, diffused only by Chehab's announcement that he intended to abide by the constitutional provision limiting him to one term, and then by resigning at the appointed time.

Whether or not this actually served the national interest is another matter. Chehab's hand-picked successor, Charles Helou, not only lacked his own popular base but was also faced with the formidable challenges posed by the suspicious collapse of one of the country's main banks in 1966, the impact of the Arab defeat in the June war of 1967, and the subsequent emergence of the Palestinian armed resistance movement based partly in camps on Lebanese soil.

Worse was to follow under the successive presidencies of Sulieman Frangieh (1970–1976), Ilyas Sarkis (1976–1982), and Pierre Gemayal (assassinated in 1982). The crude partisanship of these three presidents in favor of the Christian forces against the Muslims, the leftists, and the Palestinians was one of the main causes of the long civil war that broke out in 1975. Continued partisanship was also partly responsible for the war's longevity, encouraging it to rage off and on until the leaders of the exhausted parties came together to sign the Taif Agreement in Saudi Arabia in 1989.

Although the main aim of this agreement was to reconstruct the sectarian system in such a way that political cooperation among the sects could be restarted, there were also those among the signatories who hoped that it might also pave the way for a national politics that could transcend these same sectarian divisions. But this was not to be the case. For one thing, the civil war itself, fought along largely sectarian lines, had not only caused a wholesale relocation of much of the population into still more intensely communally organized and protected enclaves, but it had also encouraged the rise of powerful local sectarian militias, the most important being the one associated with the Shiite political movement Hizbollah, with considerable material support from Shiite Iran. For another, it could be argued that the Taif amendments to the constitution, ratified by the members of the Lebanese parliament in 1991, made agreement on national aims even more difficult than before by reducing the powers of the Christian president to the advantage of the Sunni Muslim prime minister and the Shiite speaker of the national assembly. Not only could the president no longer preside over cabinet meetings, but he also lost the all-important right to dissolve the assembly.

Presidential authority was further reduced when successive presidents became something approaching puppets of the Syrian military occupation of the country that lasted until 2005. Their subservience was underlined by the fact that, on two occasions, in 1995 and 2005, the Syrians pushed amendments to the constitution through a captive parliament, prolonging the president's term of office from six to nine years.[7] It is also worth noting that, since the Taif Agreement, two of the three presidents—generals Émile Lahoud and, after 2007, Michel Suleiman— were military men. Yet even after the Syrian withdrawal, their powers were held fiercely in check by the fact that the country was now divided in half by two rival political and military coalitions, one largely Shiite, the other a combination of Sunni and Christian groups.

The fierce fighting that broke out in May 2008 is a perfect example of both the resilience of the revived sectarian system and the weakness of the central government led by President Suleiman and the army. The conflict began in response to what Hizbollah and its allies regarded as the unacceptable demand to close its private telecommunications network as illegal. The fighting then quickly escalated to encompass most parts of the center and north, and was only brought to an end when the government agreed to rescind its original decision. Suleiman's two contributions to the settlement of the conflict, first to use the army only to try to separate the warring parties, not to enforce the government's will, and then to insist that the government itself back down, while subject to much criticism, represented the most a president could do in such circumstances: finding a formula to preserve domestic peace while preventing the army from being drawn into a fight in which it would have been, inevitably, seen as acting on behalf of one group of citizens against another.

The lessons of this crisis are clear. One concerns not just the resilience of the sectarianism system but also the way it strengthens itself when faced with threats to its existence, whether those threats come from civil war or from Taif-like attempts to create stronger national institutions to replace it. Indeed, one can observe something like a vicious circle at work, in which, as sectarian organizations become stronger, the central government weakens in terms of uncollected taxes and the ability to provide local security. This, in turn, promotes even more reliance on the sectarian leadership for support. The other major lesson is that Lebanese presidents are systematically unable to build up their own power. This leaves them with no alternative to the very difficult diplomatic task of trying to defuse tensions where they can in the interest of preventing yet another round of civil war.

Iraq

Iraq became a republic as a result of the abolition of its monarchy in a military coup in July 1958, its new prime minister, Brigadier Abd al-Karim Qasim, being one of the coup's main leaders. As in Egypt, the coup very soon became a "revolution" with all the usual revolutionary symbols and practices, including public celebrations in the renamed Liberation Square, show trials of leading members of the old regime, the abrogation of the defense treaty with Britain, and a series of populist measures that included a sweeping land reform which eliminated most of the large rural estates.

Yet, even more rapidly than in the Egyptian case, its leader "drifted" into a personal dictatorship, firmly convinced, as Charles Tripp points out, first that a degree of direct control was necessary for his own survival, and then that he represented all Iraqis and that he alone could define the common good.[8] An important part of this process, as Tripp also notes, was Qasim's discovery of the "ease of patronage in a system already geared to central, hierarchical control."[9] Unfortunately for him, this concentration of power isolated him both from the popular forces that had initially supported him and from the Arab nationalist officers in the army, who felt he no longer wished to promote the idea of a union with Egypt and Syria. He was assassinated during a military coup in February 1963, after which his body was displayed on Iraqi television to convince any doubting supporters that the "Sole Leader" was really dead.

Neither of Iraq's next two presidents lasted very long. The first, Abd al-Salam Arif, was killed in a helicopter accident in 1966. And the second, his brother and successor, Abd al-Rahman Arif, was deposed in 1968 by another military coup led by General Ahmad Hassan al-Bakr in association with a small number of members of the Iraq Ba'th Party, including Bakr's young relative, Saddam Hussein. For a few years it was Bakr, now the new president, who enjoyed the greatest power. But as the 1970s continued, he was gradually eased out of power by Hussein, who used the party to create a new base for himself that was sufficient, by the late 1970s, to control the army and then, after he had deposed the sixty-five-year-old Bakr in a palace coup in July 1979, the state. His passage from party apparatchik to national leader is nicely illustrated by his change of costume, from pinstripe suit and tie to a variety of ever more colorful costumes designed to emphasize his role as the leader of all the classes, professions, and groups that made up Iraq's diverse society.

Saddam Hussein's own presidency can be chronologically divided into three periods: the long war with revolutionary Iran (1980–1988);

the brief period of postwar reconstruction (1987–1990); and, finally, the period of international isolation and sanctions following the Iraqi occupation of Kuwait in 1990, which culminated in the overthrow of his regime as a result of the Anglo-American invasion of 2003. It can also be looked at as a particular exercise in the creation of a strong presidency for life with its own combination of centralized power, a well-organized but wholly subservient party, an idiosyncratic personal style of rule, and a set of crony-confidants, all underpinned by large revenues from oil and their use to create a vast web of patronage that embraced most of the population in a system of rewards for the few and horrible punishments for those who tried openly to oppose it.

Had Saddam Hussein better understood the threat he faced after the World Trade Center attack on the United States from the senior members of the George W. Bush administration, he might well have continued as president for the remaining decades of his life, to be succeeded either by one of his sons or, just as likely, by a close colleague able to mobilize the support of the Ba'th Party. As it was, he was overthrown at the age of sixty-five to make way for a totally different type of regime, though one of which he was, in some ways, the unwitting creator.

Although there can be little doubt that President Hussein was an out-and-out secularist himself, some of the policies he pursued—notably his war with Iran and the decade of international sanction that followed—had the unintended consequences of undermining the position of the nationally minded and secular middle class. At the same time, these policies excited well-justified concerns among sections of the Shi'i community about the dangers he and his regime posed to their religious practices, their links with Iran, and so their general well-being.[10] While large numbers of the old urban professional classes fled, many of those Iraqis who remained began to develop sectarian networks of their own, either simply to survive the harsh economic conditions of the 1990s or, in the case of some Shiite sections, to form a combination of popular and religious organizations to oppose him.

So it was that when Coalition Provisional Authority under Ambassador Paul Bremer began its work of national reconstruction and democracy building in Baghdad in May 2003, it seemed natural to establish a system of political representation more on sectarian, ethnic and religious than national identity, with membership on the first Governing Council based on a formula of fourteen Shiite members, five Kurdish members, and four Sunni Arab members.[11] The fact that Saddam Hussein's banned Ba'th Party was conceived of as largely a Sunni organization; the important role given to the Ayatollah Sistani in managing and directing Shi'i opinion; and the presence of influential Shiite exiles such as Ahmad Chalabi, who had no local constituency of their own, only a general Shiite one, all encouraged the same mind-set and the same process. So, too, did the special alliance between Washington and the Iraqi Kurds and the American willingness to allow them to be represented in Baghdad by their two traditional leaders, Massoud Barzani and Jalal Talabani.

The politicization of sectarian difference found another significant expression in the drafting of the new constitution in 2005, with a drafting committee chaired by the outspoken leader of the military wing of the Islamic Supreme Council of Iraq, one of the two main Shiite communal organizations. Relations with those Sunnis who agreed to participate were tense and, in the end, only three out of the fifteen Sunni committee members attended the signing ceremony, with not one of them being actually willing to sign.

According to the new constitution, the divided nature of the country's population was recognized in two introductory articles. Article 1 referred to the country as a "federal state" and Article 3 defined Iraq as a country of "many nationalities, religions and sects."[12] The notion of federalism, opposed by many Sunnis, was a concession to the Kurds as a way of allowing them to maintain their laws, rights, and customs that had developed separately from those in the rest of Iraq. The recognition of sectarian difference can be seen not only as the recognition of Shiite demographic dominance—conventionally viewed as more than twice that of the Sunnis and Kurds combined—but also as a step toward the creation of separate jurisdictions and practices with regard to the regulation of personal status. This latter move was immediately criticized by feminist activists as moving the women of Iraq from the previous national and uniform system of jurisdiction to a divided one controlled by the religious leaders of the separate communities, as in Lebanon, Israel, and India.[13]

Just as important for my argument, lurking somewhere in the background was, and perhaps still is, a wish to borrow some aspects of the Lebanese model, but without going so far as to spell it out in any great detail. This can be seen, for example, in Article 9 of the constitution with its reference to an army created with "due consideration" for the sectarian "balance." It can also be seen in the very obvious subordination of the president to the prime minister who, given the electoral power of the Shiite community, was almost certainly going to be a Shi'i himself.

What was totally lacking, however, was reference to the set of practices regarding the division of office and administrative posts between the sects that had developed in Lebanon over the years. Thus the politicians were left with a huge task when it came to the allocation of posts after the March 2010 election had produced a stalemate between the Iraqiya list of Ayad Allawi with its mix of Sunnis, Shi'is, and others and the more solidly Shiite list of the outgoing prime minister, Nouri al-Maliki. To make matters more complex still, the resources controlled by the government and the separate ministries were far, far greater than those in Lebanon, and so even more contentious, involving as they did access to considerable revenues from oil as well as management of a very large army and an even larger force of policemen and other security personnel. No wonder the process proved to be so long and so acrimonious, with over eight months of bargaining over detailed items of control, influence, and budgets, and then (as of January 1,

2011) still no appointment to the key defense, interior, and national security ministerial slots.[14] No wonder, too, that some of these negotiations depended on further borrowing, for example, a plan involving the obviously Lebanese formula of combining a Kurdish president with a Shiite prime minister and a Sunni speaker.

Turning last to the role of the president, this has been twice limited so far, first by making him a Kurd, second by giving him only limited constitutional power along with a limit of two four-year terms. Nevertheless, the man himself, Jalal Talabani, elected first by the new parliament in 2005 and then reelected in 2010, has demonstrated some ability to try to find a way through the sectarian deadlock, offering useful advice and, on occasion, making suggestions about how best to divide the key ministries between them.[15]

Whether such an arrangement can last is another matter. Perhaps fortunately for Iraq, the commander in chief of the army is a Sunni and therefore not a viable candidate himself for the presidency. Nevertheless, it is possible to imagine a future commander, or even a powerful Shi'i politician, deciding to use the country's oil and other resources to install himself as a strong president, using methods that will, inevitably, be reminiscent of those employed by Saddam Hussein.

THE POSTINDEPENDENCE EXPERIENCE OF LEBANON has yielded a model of political sectarianism which, in some major respects, has been replicated in post–Saddam Hussein Iraq. This involves developing a system of representation along largely sectarian grounds managed by a relatively weak president in tandem with a relatively strong prime minister, and depending upon a system of rules and practices designed to facilitate accommodation while limiting obvious sources of tension such as the presence of armed militias. As history also shows, such systems take several decades of trial and error to perfect themselves as they seek to limit secular forms of expression while avoiding the danger of sliding into a paranoid form of communalism in which differences are exaggerated for the purposes of popular mobilization as much against "moderate" leaders as against the perceived sectarian "other."

Contemporary Iraq, as has been seen, is still very much at the beginning of a version of the same process with a weak presidency but, as yet, no well-established practices of power sharing among its confessional leaders. To make matters more difficult, it contains features not to be found in Lebanon, notably a large and battle-tested army and the prospect of very large revenues from oil once production returns to its late-1970s peak. And though, initially, the use of these powerful resources for political purposes was limited both by disputes among the major Shi'i leaders and by the army's role in confronting a common terrorist enemy, it is possible to imagine the emergence of a powerful Shi'i prime minister like Nouri al-Maliki, who used the huge resources at his disposal—including his role as commander in chief and his personal control of at least two intelligence services—to create a dual system of centralized government in which he, effectively, rules Iraq in association with a weak president who is also one of the de facto rulers of Iraqi Kurdistan.

7 The Monarchical Security States of Jordan, Morocco, Bahrain, and Oman

A report issued by Beirut's Center for Arab Unity Studies in the early 1990s observed that the Arab monarchs who had survived military coups "adopted the pattern of the military-technical elite in many respects."[1] This characterization calls proper attention both to the similar trajectories pursued by the leaders of the republics and the monarchies, and to the way that the latter—notably the kings of Jordan and Morocco—replicated many of the practices of the former simply in order to survive. Kingship bestowed only a little extra by way of legitimacy in the Arab world and had to be propped up by use of an omnipresent security service, a tame military, and managed elections. These monarchies also shared many of the same strategies found in the republics, notably the enormous effort put into creating the impression of a basic constitutional legalism.

This leaves the issue of succession as the only major difference between kings and presidents for life. Kings seem to have something of an advantage in this regard, the training and acceptability of their sons as future monarchs raising many fewer problems than in the republics. The kings are also more likely to make sure that they have sons in the first place by marrying early, unlike, say, Ben Ali or Bouteflika. Yet we should also note that, even for the kings, last-minute changes of mind and sudden substitutions are possible. Whereas passage from father to son proceeded without incident in Morocco, in Jordan, Abdullah's eldest son, Talal, was passed over on the grounds of incompetence in favor of his grandson, Hussein, in the early 1950s. Nearly fifty years later, Hussein, in his turn, made a deathbed decision to appoint his own son, Abdullah, to the throne, rather than his brother, Hassan, the long-serving crown prince.

Other factors that point to some differences between Arab monarchies and republics include the greater protection kings seem to have had from accusations of personal corruption, and their ability to maintain the traditional loyalties built up among sections of their populations by their royal predecessors, notably among certain tribes.

Arab monarchs learned to mimic the practices of legitimation developed by their presidential neighbors. Most notably this includes the use and misuse of constitutional legality and the employment of elections to fill parliament with their supporters, with all that this entails in terms of the problems raised by denunciations of mismanagement, exclusion, and bad faith.

The Hashemite Kings of Jordan

The state of Transjordan was created in 1922 as a fief for the Amir Abdullah, a member of the Hashemite family of Arabia who had fought with the Allies against the Ottoman Turks during the later stages of World War I. The state was administered under the general aegis of the British Mandate for Palestine, but was deliberately excluded from the area devoted to the establishment of a Jewish national home. It became an independent monarchy, still under Abdullah, in 1946. And, in 1950, it obtained international recognition for its government over the part of pre-1948 Palestine now known as the West Bank.

Given its origins, King Abdullah and his successors, Hussein (1953–1999) and Abdullah (1999–), had to contend with a special set of problems stemming from their country's geographical position, squeezed as it is between Israel, Iraq, Syria, and Saudi Arabia, as well as its almost total lack of economic resources. These problems included the presence of a sizable population of Palestinian origin, tensions with its Arab and Jewish neighbors, and the fact that Jordan depended, and continues to depend, on large amounts of aid and outside assistance.

Yet the regime survived in spite of King Abdullah's assassination in 1951 and an unsuccessful military plot to overthrow King Hussein in 1957. That the regime endured was the result of solid domestic support for the monarchy from the army and from the tribal south, as well as an informal alliance among Israel, the United States, and America's Arab allies based on their mutual concern that Jordan should not be allowed to fall into either radical Palestinian or radical nationalist hands.

Two other factors were also of great relevance. One was the greater concentration of Jordanian royal power stemming from a series of amendments to the 1952 constitution. This did much to alter the balance of power between the king and his cabinet vis-à-vis parliament and the judiciary. A particularly good example is the 1984 amendment granting the monarch additional authority to suspend parliamentary elections.

A second factor was the skill shown by King Hussein in managing a set of often contradictory imperatives. He proved exceptionally dexterous at walking a tightrope among Israeli, Palestinian, Arab, and Western demands, on the one hand, and those of the various segments of his own people on the other. At some times he ruled with a parliament, at others without. In 1967 he joined in an Arab war against Israel, to disastrous effect (losing the West Bank in the process); in 1973 he did not. And at one time or another he obtained aid from the Arab League, the Arab oil states, the British, the Americans, and the International Monetary Fund. Other benefits derived from the remittances sent back from Jordanians working in the Persian Gulf. Meanwhile, he was always working hard to make Jordan as internationally useful as he could, setting it up as a training ground for Arab soldiers and policemen, a refuge for Arab exiles and refugees, an intermediary in regional disputes, and a valuable ally.

If one can see a turning point as far as this general strategy is concerned, it is in the late 1980s and early 1990s when Hussein was forced to respond to a new set of powerful challenges that posed a grave threat to the oil-financed equilibrium he had managed for the previous ten years. These challenges included the collapse of oil prices in the mid-1980s; the end of the Cold War; the Iraqi invasion of Kuwait, in which he chose to support Saddam Hussein against the American/Arab coalition; and the run up to the Israeli-Jordanian peace treaty of 1994. His strategy: to use the emergence of what American and Israeli boosters were then calling the "New Middle East"—with its promise of open borders and intraregional cooperation—to restructure the Jordanian economy in the direction of a greater self-sufficiency based on encouraging foreign investment and private initiative, in other words, a type of latter-day *infitah*.

The problem was that this new strategy not only involved returning to a form of managed parliament in an effort to obtain public support for his new policy—including a peace treaty with Israel—but also presented a huge threat to the interests of all those who had obtained easygoing jobs either in a bloated public sector or in an army the country could no longer afford. As in Mubarak's Egypt or Yeltsin's Russia, King Hussein was creating a new parliamentary and electoral platform for people to voice their opinion of government policies at just the same moment when those policies contained much they wished to criticize.

Difficulties intensified further after 1996 with the advent of a new and more hard-line Israeli government followed by the outbreak of the second Palestinian Intifada in 2000. They were then made worse by a second fall in oil prices in mid-decade. Opposition to Hussein's method of rule mounted, not just from among Islamists who boycotted the 1997 election in protest against the peace treaty with Israel, but also from those hurt by the economic downturn. Per capita income fell 13 percent in 1993–1996, and people became more and more worried about public-sector layoffs, something of particular concern to members of the king's base of support in the tribal south.[2]

Hussein and his cabinet responded with a curb on press freedoms, and backed them up with an extension of powers of the General Intelligence Directorate. What followed was an increase in his control over the opposition and a greater management over the electoral process, including targeted support for certain favored candidates, and then continuing influence over their votes in parliament.[3]

The king's many absences from the country toward the end of the decade as he went off in search of treatment for his cancer can only have made the situation more dangerous. No doubt his fatal illness also affected his last-minute decision to name his son—a man of the army and of the intelligence services—as his successor rather than his more cerebral brother Hassan. At any rate, Abdullah came to the throne in February 1999, determined to reassert royal authority. His primary target was the Islamists, who, in his eyes, posed a threat to his desire to strengthen Jordan's alliance with the United States anchored by his ostentatious support for the war on terror declared after the World Trade Center attacks in 2001. But he soon had to face down an even more influential array of critics, who were threatened by his renewed drive for economic development and its associated administrative reform.

To make his task more difficult still, Abdullah, like all his republican Arab neighbors, felt it expedient to make a show of his democratic credentials. Efforts in this direction soon collided with certain basic features of his father's electoral strategy that had been designed to reduce the weight of Palestinian and other urban critics of his policies, while overrepresenting those of his traditional and mostly rural supporters. No doubt well aware of the problem, Abdullah twice postponed the national elections due to be held in 2001, using the absence of a working parliament to issue some 200 royal edicts, mostly concerned with controversial matters of security and economic restructuring.[4] Then, when the elections were finally held in 2003, the number of Islamists in parliament was reduced to sixteen. The 2007 elections were even more highly managed, with the result that the Islamist presence dropped to six, with no other party represented in parliament at all.

Problems continued to mount, however. The new parliaments, dominated by the leaders of important tribal families, became deeply unpopular with the public at large. They also contained numerous critics of the king's economic policies, as well as of the business technocrats who filled the cabinets charged with implementing them. The social tensions this released gave rise to a sporadic set of popular demonstrations and protests that grew in intensity through 2008 and 2009. Some were aimed at government policies; others involved often violent clashes between tribal elements vying with each other for seats in parliament that were seen, correctly, as the best way to obtain access to schools, jobs, and economic opportunities in such difficult economic times.[5] Still the king pressed on with his attempt at economic reform, postponing the 2009 elections until 2010, dismissing parliament halfway through its four-year term for not moving fast enough on reform, and, once again, ruling by decree.

The election, when it finally came in November 2010, proved to be a lackluster affair, boycotted by the Islamists and largely ignored by the rest of the voting population. It produced an entire parliament of men— two-thirds of whom were first-time members from tribal families— who, although nominally the king's supporters, remained as suspicious of his economic programs as they had been before their election.[6] Almost immediately, the regime itself was forced to recognize the existence of yet more public discontent triggered by the steep rise in the price of food (particularly of tomatoes) and of fuel, by putting back some of the subsidies that the free marketers had recently removed.

This tactic then had to be repeated in January 2011, as the number and the size of the demonstrations swelled in response to the Tunisian example and included a "Day of Rage" in Amman when members of the crowd chanted, "The Jordanian people are on fire."[7] Clearly the Arab monarchs were not exempt from the pressures that were besetting their republican counterparts. Nevertheless, it can also be argued that their somewhat more exalted position put them above the political fray, and so better able to shift the blame to their cabinets and away from themselves. Only time will tell.

The Royal Line in Morocco

Unlike Jordan, Morocco had had many centuries of independent rule until the French established a forty-four-year protectorate in 1912. Its sultans, and then kings, also had a better claim than the kings of Jordan to monarchical legitimacy as long-recognized descendants of the family of the Prophet Muhammad. Nevertheless, as in Jordan under King Hussein, the first king after independence, Muhammad V, took great care to establish himself as the leader of the nationalist movement. He was helped in this effort by the fact that he was briefly imprisoned by the French, which gave the usual boost to his credentials. Nevertheless, this strategy quickly brought him into conflict with the secular nationalists led by the Istiqlal (Independence) Party in a struggle that continued after his death in 1961.

Matters deteriorated further under his son, Hassan II, in spite of the fact that the new king managed to engineer a split in Istiqlal's ranks that led to the creation of the UNFP (National Union of Popular Forces). Economic difficulties helped to make the situation worse, and there was a brief period—following the two assassination attempts on Hassan's life in the early 1970s—when it looked as though the monarchy might not survive.

That the monarchy did in fact manage to weather the storm can be explained largely by two factors. One was the great amount of highly personal centralized power built up by both Muhammad V and Hassan II. This allowed them to establish, and then to maintain, control over the different parts of the state administration, backed by the use of the family's own personal wealth to create an elite of "king's supporters" who had a large personal stake in the regime's success. The other factor was the organization of the "Green March" begun in November 1975, a carefully orchestrated event in which a large crowd was assembled along the country's southern border in order to participate in a mass crossing into the disputed territory of the Western Sahara previously ruled by Spain. This proved a master stroke from the king's point of view, making him once again the leader of the country's nationalist movement, shrouding the whole process in popular religious symbolism, and binding the military commanders to what they had no difficulty in believing was a matter of Morocco's national honor and national security.

Staying in power was one thing; finding a formula for a stable political system was another. It took a long process of trial and error to proceed from the highly managed elections of 1977 and 1984 to a point in the 1990s at which King Hassan II felt secure enough to allow opposition politicians the possibility of a small share in government. Indeed, the turning point did not really come until 1997 when, after an election contested by a large number of parties, he asked the veteran politician Abder-Rahmane Youssefi to form a cabinet representing a seven-party coalition.

Hassan II died in 1999 and was replaced by his son, Muhammad VI. Muhammad VI was a man of the same age as Jordan's new king, Abdullah, but he had received a great deal more royal training, as he had been well educated in Morocco and France, and then had undertaken a number of important duties under his father's watchful eye. Muhammad also differed in style and approach from the Jordanian king. While Abdullah was immediately anxious to assert his own personal authority and to push his country hard in one particular direction, Muhammad presented his people with a long political "spring" that he used to repair some of the harm done to the reputation of the monarchy by his father's repressive ways. Most notable was his creation of a program called l'Instance Équité and Réconciliation, based on the ideas behind the South African Truth and Reconciliation Commission, which paid financial compensation to over 11,000 victims of wrongful imprisonment and other harsh measures. Meanwhile, the 2002 election was contested by twenty-six parties spanning the whole political spectrum from left to right, from which was drawn a cabinet representing very much the same wide range of political opinion.

Muhammad VI also proved better able than Abdullah to find a way of incorporating the various politically organized Islamic groups into his system of national representation. This ability became particularly important after a series of bombings attributed to radical Islamists rocked the city of Casablanca in 2003. On the one hand, he dismantled some fifty Islamic groups, while in 2004 presenting a new parties law (based very much on Egyptian lines) outlawing parties based on religious, as well as ethnic, linguistic, or regional sentiment. On the other, he went to considerable lengths to nurture a moderate Islamic party, the PJD (Justice and Development Party), which won the second largest number of seats in the 2007 election.[8] The king also benefited greatly from the fact that having Islamists as candidates raised public enthusiasm for the election, increasing the turnout to a respectable 37 percent while leaving him with no obligation to include any of their leaders in government.

The same balancing act can be seen in Muhammad VI's promotion of the political rights of women. First came a reform of personal status in 2004 by which women were no longer viewed as minors, followed by the creation of a special constituency by which women elected a fixed number of female representatives to their own section of parliament. Both measures were bitterly opposed by members of the senior Islamic clergy, the *ulama,* and so had to be pushed through using the special authority that the Moroccan king obtains from his traditional role as Commander of the [Religious] Faithful.

Nevertheless, there were limits to his policy of greater openness and inclusion. As far as political management was concerned, he had not felt compelled to surrender any of the monarchy's considerable power, and he continued to fill the most important posts in government—foreign affairs, interior, defense, and Islamic affairs—with his own associates. As for meaningful economic reform, although some steps were taken in the direction of greater transparency, members of the elite were generally as unwilling as those in Jordan to support measures that would threaten their own privileged positions.[9] Again as in Jordan and elsewhere, this same elite included a set of businessmen with close ties to senior army officers and ex-officers who were not only well looked after with generous pensions and the provision of personal staff, but were also encouraged to set up defense contracting enterprises of their own.

Given these constraints, it was fortunate for the king that he was able to do enough in terms of reforming public enterprise and of privatization to promote a more diversified economy capable of attracting considerable amounts of foreign capital. Jordan's performance also included a reasonable rate of growth and, at least until the world food crisis of 2009/2010, low inflation. All this was to prove of the greatest advantage when it came to weathering the economic and political storms that began to affect the rest of the Middle East and North Africa in late 2010.

Bahrain

Unique among the ruling families of the Persian Gulf, those in Bahrain and Oman have adopted a system of primogeniture, passing on rule to the king's or sultan's eldest son. This, in my estimation, makes them one with the republican *gumlukiyas* described in earlier chapters, sharing many of the same features in terms of the possession of large security apparatuses and strategies for legitimation based on their constitutions and, in the case of Bahrain, some form of electoral process.

Bahrain became independent from British semicolonial protection in 1974 with a constitution that provided for a parliament and a system of regular elections. It also inherited a well-developed system of internal security with a General Directorate of Security, managed initially by a senior British intelligence official. To this was added, in 2002, a National Security Apparatus containing a paramilitary security force drawn largely from foreign nationals that was used repeatedly to control and subdue Bahrain's restive majority Shi'i community chafing at its lack of representation in a state run by a Sunni elite.

Bahrain's original constitution was suspended in 1975 in response to outspoken criticism by parliamentary opponents of the ruling family, the Al Khalifas. The ruler, Sheikh Isa Al Khalifa, then governed alone and by royal decree, further proof of the continuing difficulties of establishing a system of constitutional monarchy in states such as those of the Gulf where the ruling family not only ruled but occupied all the most important ministries of state as well, thus opening itself up to embarrassing public questioning by commoner critics in the assembly. In 2005, for example, members of the Al Khalifa family held over half the cabinet-level posts including all the important ones connected with the interior, justice, and defense.

After almost thirty years, the constitution was revived in February 2002 by the new ruler, Shaykh Hamad Al Khalifa, who had succeeded his elderly and long-lived father in 1999. Interestingly, he also used the occasion to proclaim himself king, perhaps in an effort to institutionalize the system of primogeniture that he had come to regard as giving the ruler some distance from the advice of his cousins and uncles.

The move is also generally interpreted as a response to a period of considerable unrest among the Shiite population. It involved the same kind of political spring that was occurring in Morocco and then Syria at the same time, with a release of political prisoners, attention to the political rights of women, and, in the case of Bahrain, the creation of a bicameral legislature with an elected lower house and an appointed upper *shura* council. Parties were not permitted, however, allowing the election in 2007 of a group of "king's men" as independents to offset the voting power of any Shiite bloc. The elections of 2010, held at a time of greater Shiite unrest, produced much the same result. Meanwhile, as in Morocco and Jordan, it was the king who appointed the cabinet regardless of the composition of the lower house.

There were fewer problems in Bahrain, however, where the rulers have been able to use a relatively rich set of resources to maintain a high standard of living for its citizens, including the opportunity to import big quantities of largely cheap foreign labor. Although its limited supplies of oil ran out early, it obtained significant assistance from the oil provided by its Saudi neighbor while pushing forward with a successful diversification of its economy by building its own aluminum plant (using oil as inexpensive fuel) and growing its own banking and insurance industries. The country was the first to provide such services for the Saudi market, then to the rest of the world. However, as pointed out above, this was not enough to overcome the grievances of most of its poor Shiite rural population, whose repeated political demonstrations were a feature of the first months of 2011.

Oman

Modern Oman, formerly the Sultanate of Muscat and Oman, has been ruled since 1970 by Sultan Qaboos, who came to power after he had overthrown his father, Said Bin Taymour, with British help. In an Oman political spring he opened up his previously isolated country to foreign capital and removed many of his father's tight restrictions on personal liberty. He also created a highly centralized administrative structure, with himself as prime minister.

As for government, and lacking both siblings and a son with whom to share rule, he placed himself at the head of the ministries of foreign affairs, finance, and defense. The remaining members of the council of ministers, in effect the cabinet, were (and are) also appointed by the sultan. A system of limited elections was added in 2000 with the creation of a two-council system, an elected *majlis al-shura* (or consultative council) balanced by a *majlis al-dowla* (state council) with all its members appointed by the sultan.

Oman lacked a written constitution until November 1996. What was then produced was a document of little substance, as it contains few details about the organization of government, leaving all specifics to be decided by individual laws. It would seem that its major purpose was, and is, to deal with the difficult question of succession, given the fact that Sultan Qaboos has no male heirs. Of particular importance is Article 6, which states that if the ruling family council cannot agree upon a successor within three days of the sultan's demise, the defense council will confirm the appointment of the "person designated in the letter to the family council" by the dead man. It is firmly believed in Oman that this letter has already been written, although few know what it actually says.

In spite of huge powers allotted to the sultan and the general lack of popular representation, there were few signs of overt opposition to the Omani regime before 2011. This was the result, it can easily be argued, of respect for the sultan's traditional authority, augmented by his possession of enough revenue from oil to provide jobs and services for the majority of the people. Nevertheless, such was the power of Arab example that sporadic demonstrations against the sultan's policy began in February 2011.

KINGS RULE LIKE PRESIDENTS BUT from a somewhat different set of palaces and with somewhat different skills, training, priorities, and authority. They share the same concerns about security as presidents, and the same strongly personalized power based on a set of strongly centralized governmental structures. They also have much the same interest in developing extra forms of legitimation based on constitutions, elections, and the provision of economic well-being in order to impress both their own populations and the international community. Last, just because there are so many similarities between systems of government across the Arab world, Arab monarchs are in a position to borrow useful methods of organization and various institutional practices from their republican colleagues, just as they can also provide helpful examples of particular techniques themselves.

Where they differ is that, by definition, monarchies are hereditary forms of government while presidencies are not. This position gives monarchs a different authority, one that is independent, it would seem, from whatever claims they might make concerning their families' traditional and religious right to rule. Once they had distanced themselves from the close association with foreign rule that had been the main cause of the overthrow of the kings of Egypt and Libya, the survivors were able to establish a sense of permanence and of being above the political fray that protected them from much of the inevitable opposition that arose from time to time to their policies and their shortcomings. This protection gave them a reserve of respect that presidents had a much greater difficulty in obtaining. It is to be seen, most notably, in the way they have been largely exempt from criticism of their own personal wealth and of how it was obtained. And as David Mednicoff suggests, it has also allowed them to act as a "calming buffer" between popular demands and state institutions.[10] Popular respect and the quality of being slightly above the fray was to serve them well when the storm broke over the heads of the Arab presidents in January 2011. Nevertheless, in the case of both Jordan and Morocco continued popular pressure forced both to promise to devolve some of their powers to a prime minister who represented a majority in parliament, a step that if taken seriously would push them more toward a European-style constitutional monarchy.

8   The Politics of Succession

The few republican presidents who died in office were generally succeeded by a previously designated vice president, for example, in Egypt.
A few others were pushed aside toward the ends of their lives by an
ambitious subordinate. In the 1990s, Hafiz al-Asad was the first to open
up the notion of a family succession.

In what follows, I use material from Syria and Egypt, then from
Libya, Yemen, Tunisia, and Algeria, to develop two linked arguments.
One is that, in all these countries, the expectation of a family succession affected every part of the political process. The second is that the
choice of a family member, usually a son, although designed to produce
a sense of security and predictability for important sections of the elite,
proved quite capable, if mishandled or if it was simply allowed to go on
too long, of promoting exactly the opposite: an atmosphere of anxiety
and uncertainty exacerbated by increasing popular hostility to the ruling family itself.

The reasons for such anxieties are quite clear. The special case of
Syria apart, the Arab republics lacked, and still lack, any well-established
model for a family succession. For one thing, the necessary procedures
cannot, as Anthony Billingsley points out, be set out in specific detail

in a republican constitution.[1] Nor can succession follow conventional practice in the Arab monarchies where primogeniture is now the well-established rule. Moreover, for these and other reasons, republican successions are likely to be disputed. To speak in the most general terms, Arab security states contained at least two influential groups of people: those who had a vested interest in persuading the ruler to appoint a family successor, and those who did not. For the latter, familial succession was seen as a threat either to republican legitimacy or to their own particular interest, perhaps as rival contenders for the presidency, perhaps as members of some major institution—the military, the security forces, the ruling party—with interests of its own.

All this contributed to creating a climate of secrecy, rumor, and uncertainty, a mirror perhaps of the very real uncertainty in the mind of the ruler himself when it came to working out what was best for himself, his family, and his own concept of the national interest. Hence too, a general tendency to hedge bets about who might actually succeed, creating further uncertainty in an atmosphere of watching and waiting.

Syria and Egypt

Family succession in Syria had much to do with the particular position of the Alawi minority in that country, as well as the particular situation inside the Asad family itself, notably the rivalry between Hafiz al-Asad and his younger brother, Rifaat. Like everything to do with Hafiz al-Asad's style of government, the process was well thought through with a characteristic combination of thoroughness, attention to detail, and caution, proceeding one step at a time.

It was also, as must always be the case, accompanied by many of the vicissitudes that personalized rule must bring. Not only did the plan have to be substantially reworked after Basil al-Asad's untimely death, but Hafiz al-Asad himself died before he was able to complete his term of presidential office.[2] Nevertheless, even by 2000, the process of grooming Bashar, that is, of giving him vital on-the-job training and then of having a smooth, one-day transition program in place, was sufficiently well advanced and sufficiently watertight to survive any accidental interruption.

What are the major lessons to be learned from the Syrian example and how easy might it have proved to replicate in Egypt and elsewhere? From a comparative point of view, these lessons can be summed up in terms of a political process involving a number of key components. They must include the process of identifying a successor, presenting him to the elite and the public, testing his popularity and observing any negative responses to him, grooming him by giving him gradual access to real power, ensuring his acceptance by allies and helpful Arab neighbors, and finding one or more senior persons to shepherd the son instantly into the presidency once the current president died.

Beyond these requirements, there was also the question of how much else could be determined in advance by a ruler, aware that there would have to be change after he is gone and also aware that his son was younger and different from him, more "modern" in his approach to technology and probably to the management of the economy, and likely to be advised by people of much the same type. For one thing, there was almost certainly going to be some kind of political spring in which the new ruler announced himself, tried to ingratiate himself with a wide spectrum of the population, and, very likely, came up with some new or revised formula for regime legitimation. For another, something would have to be done about the major black spots of the father's regime: its human rights abuses, its lack of transparency, its tolerance of high-profile corruption. In the Syrian case, there is something that could be seen as almost poignant in Hafiz al-Asad's attempts to lay out a new agenda toward the end of his life, not only to help his son but also, one might surmise, to protect, or perhaps even embellish, his own legacy in Syrian eyes.[3] Yet all the time he would have to have known in his heart that, with his death, his own direct influence over future policy would come to an end.

Three other aspects of the process are also worth noting, in ascending order of importance. The first is the notion of the "files" that Bashar was given as he got closer to power, such as the very important "Lebanese file" that he took over in the late 1990s.[4] Note that in contemporary Arabic usage, the word "file" really means a personal responsibility for the management of and control over a whole major area of Syrian policy, subject, of course, to the overall supervision of the president himself. As such, it was a clever way not only of giving Bashar significant administrative experience, but also of providing a public gauge of just how important his growing influence had become. Other Arab governments that operated on different administrative principles, such as those in Egypt or Tunisia, might well have had difficulty in employing this particular mechanism as part of their own succession process.

Second, and more important, there are the lessons to be learned from the deliberate mystification that accompanied Bashar's grooming. For example, as late as 1998, his father stated categorically that he did not want his son to succeed him.[5] Why he should have said this cannot possibly be known for sure. It may have been a temporary response to a special political challenge. It may have represented a moment of doubt and indecision. Or it may have been a tactical move, designed to muddy the political waters, to keep possible opponents off balance or to mislead a particular group of either internal or external observers. Yet, at a more general level, it can also be seen as part and parcel of the tactics forced on Asad himself, and then onto other republican presidents as well, by the fact that by grooming his son as his heir, he was doing something that some of his own people regarded as illegitimate, and possibly harmful to the wider national interest.

Third, and most important of all, is the emergence during the Syrian succession process of the notion of the existence of two separate groups within the elite, soon identified as the old and the new guards, with different and sometimes even contradictory interests. It might well be argued that if Asad had stuck to the formal rules concerning the age for military and bureaucratic retirement, as well as taking better care to create a well-defined career ladder for younger talent, it might not have become such a problem. Equally, though, one can argue that this division within the elite was an inevitable development on the part of a system of personal rule exercised by one man over several decades and of the way such a system nurtures many conservative tendencies like sticking to the tried and the well known.

There are peculiarly Syrian factors at work here as well. Notable among these is the military character of an embattled regime with its ranks of elderly generals, many of whom had significant financial relationships with leading Sunni businessmen that they wished to preserve. Further justification for such concerns came from the fact that these relationships had also become one of the central mechanisms for bridging the gap between the small community of Alawi rulers and the vast majority of the country's other Muslim inhabitants.

One final lesson trumps all the others in impact and influence. This is the fact that, both before and after Hafiz al-Asad's death, whatever the problems involved in moving to a system of family succession, they seemed to be able to be overcome by a combination of political skill, judgment, fine tuning, accommodation, and only a small amount of luck. On the one hand, the Syrian example seemed to provide the other Arab presidential republics with the assurance not only that a roughly similar process could actually be carried out in their own countries, but also that some of the stigma attached to it by republican purists had already been removed. On the other hand, political opponents of similar processes elsewhere now possessed the ability to draw public attention to an alarming list of the negative costs involved in family successions, for example, in terms of continued corruption and of the obstacles these successions posed to meaningful political and economic reform.

Turning now to the somewhat different political and historical context to be found in Egypt, the first thing that many Egyptians will tell you is that their country is so different from Syria that comparisons are quite beside the point. There is certainly some truth in such assertions. But in the particular case of the factors affecting presidential successions, the differences were not as strong as such critics would like to believe. I will lay out what I take to be the major differences between Egypt and Syria before returning to the continuing significance of the notion of Syria as a template and the way in which, *grosso modo*, the Syrian experience could have been seen as a useful box of political tools for employment elsewhere.

First and foremost, the Syrian state under Asad was run in a much more centralized way than that of Egypt under either Sadat or Mubarak. This is partly a reflection of different Syrian presidential practices, encouraged by the way that the solidarity of the small Alawi minority binds the generals and the leaders of the security services in a common interest in mutual survival. This set of circumstances does not exist in the same way in Cairo. Indeed, it would have been unthinkable that the head of the Syrian armed forces could have brought tanks out into the street, as happened after Mubarak's 2003 fainting fit, and then use them to prevent Gamal Mubarak from getting through the cordon to his father's side.[6]

By the same token, Asad's regime dispensed almost entirely with the use of elections as a means of regime legitimation, thus making their good management a minor aspect of presidential practice, not a major one as it has been in Egypt. Other significant differences include the cult of the whole Asad family and the very close relationship between the Asads and the Hashemite rulers of Jordan. This relationship was expressed after 2000 in the almost parallel style of public activity of the two "first ladies" as well as, more importantly, before Asad's death, by the influence on Asad exercised by King Hussein in his capacity both as a military leader and as a guide to the succession practices of monarchical family rule.

Nevertheless, there were many signs that pointed to a Mubarak seeking to follow in Asad's footsteps, at least until Gamal Mubarak's mismanagement of the 2005 elections. These included bringing Gamal back to the country from abroad, exposing him to the public eye, creating an influential new post for him, sending him to Washington on a number of occasions to encourage American support, and, in general, putting him through his paces while ensuring that he also got married and started a family of his own. Then, too, Gamal was encouraged to develop a close relationship with the longtime minister of defense and chief of the army, Field Marshal Muhammad Hussein Tantawi, and the director of national intelligence, General Omar Sulieman, one or other of whom seems likely to have been asked to play the Mustafa Tlas role as mentor and facilitator for a Gamal Mubarak succession.[7]

Where the two processes seem to have parted company is in the way in which the testing of Gamal demonstrated both flaws in his own management skills and a growing apprehension among the generals about his ability to meet the challenge posed by the Muslim Brothers in particular, as well as a whole list of institutional interests in general. The result was a situation of confusion and uncertainty, fed by questions about his father's health and intentions, and the rumors and leaks that these inevitably encouraged. One can even speak of a mild public hysteria in the summer of 2010 after President Mubarak's three-week stay in a German hospital for what was described as gallbladder surgery, followed by three weeks of convalescence. At one stage, the Egyptian share price index dropped 2.4 percent in a single day. And it subsequently took a very vigorous public relations campaign to convince people that, contrary to appearances, the elderly president was still on top of his job.

Nevertheless, and all this notwithstanding, there is still good reason to argue that the Syrian model was still in play until the enforced ending of the Mubarak regime. There was the almost daily repetition of the official story of an ineluctable timetable leading up to Mubarak Senior's reelection as president in 2011, after which, as many pointed out, he would have been free to appoint his son as his own vice president if he so chose. One can also easily imagine the existence of a Syrian-like plan in which, should the president die before then, the same speedy transition would have been announced in time for that evening's TV news. By the same token, there were the enthusiastic activities of minor regime supporters pathetically anxious to display their support for Gamal Mubarak's succession in advance of the event, and also the counter-activities of the regime's most vocal opponents. These opponents continued to criticize a family succession and were, it must be assumed, ready to use any post–Hosni Mubarak Cairo spring to press for a whole host of immediate reforms.

The lessons from both the successful Asad succession and the problems with the Mubarak one must have been painstakingly analyzed in Libya, Tunisia, Algeria, and elsewhere. There is the obvious point that the longer the process continues, the more difficulties are likely to arise, resulting perhaps from the secrecy involved, perhaps from a lack of real urgency, and perhaps because it offers greater opportunities for changes in the details of the plan, for opposition, and for mistakes. The Syrian example also provides a better sense of the pros and cons of a sitting president refusing to give up office before he dies rather than seeing his son into power himself. The same example also throws light on the general problem of having to deal with a set of popular anxieties and concerns about a process that, after a president reaches a certain age, simply cannot be avoided.

Libya and Yemen

Though nothing like as advanced as they were in Egypt, the politics of succession have already begun to play a role in both Libya and Yemen, where the presence of a longtime president with grown-up sons encouraged both speculation and opposition to what the ruler might be planning. In each case, there is a sense of a family dynasty being formed, although exactly what shape it might take was, and still is, open to question. Furthermore, in Libya at least, there is a significant story to tell. It starts with the aging leader's obvious desire to take a less active role in government, yet being unable to find a comfortable spot as some type of elder statesman. The story goes on with his eldest son, Saif, standing in the wings, having been twice repulsed in his attempts to act as his father's right-hand man. Clearly there are many lessons to be learned from this tortuous process, and there would have been many more before it could be considered complete.

Using the chronology established for Libya in Chapter 5, we can discern a process composed of three important features. First, there was the health of the leader himself along with his apparent concern to hand off some of his duties to someone he trusts, who also seems to have the sophisticated modern skills that a wealthy, oil-rich country needs to flourish in a globalizing world. Second, there was Qaddafi's attempt to create a coherent political and administrative structure for his successor to inherit, a problem peculiar to Libya with its long history of administrative experiment, and one not faced quite so starkly in the rest of the Arab world. This began, as I have already suggested, in 1996 with the creation of a putative new organization, the Popular Social Command that, as announced four years later, was to act as an umbrella over the General People's Congress and the General People's Committee and would include a "coordinator" who might one day, presumably after Qaddafi's death, become both the country's inspirational leader and its official head of state.

Third, as a consequence both of his position as eldest son and of his high-profile activities, it was natural that speculation about Saif's future role should intensify when he completed his first degree in 1994, at age twenty-one, and then again after his return from graduate work in London in 2008. Given his developing views about the importance of human rights, of transparency, and of using a revived civil society as a basis for a new style of democratic practice—not to speak of the support his ideas seemed to have found in Europe and America—it was also natural that opposition to his succession should manifest itself in many sections of the elite including from within the Qaddafi family itself. For some, it must have been concerns for their own financial well-being; for others, worries that Saif posed a threat to the legitimacy of the regime itself and its practices of administration via the various layers of revolutionary committees. And who, deeply embedded as most of the elite were in a pervasive system of secret practices and arbitrary decisions, would not have been alarmed at the implications of Saif's powerful slogan, "Truth for All"?

Without being able to learn much about the details, it would seem possible to discern a process by which the senior Qaddafi, uncertain about the succession, instituted a policy of testing the waters, of waiting to see how Saif and his prospective reforms were locally received, while at the same time remaining unsure of how much of his own power he wished to relinquish. And all the time, he was subject to conflicting advice from his family and colleagues about how to proceed. Whatever the exact causes, the result was that Saif himself made a series of tactical withdrawals in 2010, moving from an initial position of saying that he would not "accept any position unless there is a new constitution, new laws and transparent elections" to the much weaker one in which he announced his decision to withdraw his charity from political activity concerning reform and human rights in the interests of focusing on its "core duties" of humanitarian work and development.[8] Whether this was simply a device to lull opposition or represented a major setback to his and his father's plans remains to be discovered.

The uncertainty produced by the struggle over the succession in Libya must have consequences for future planning at both the individual and the state levels. This was a matter of particular consequence in a country so rich in oil, with so many large infrastructural projects in the works and so many major acts of privatization—for example, the telecommunications and steel industries—in the works. It certainly worried potential foreign investors, for whom the possibility that fighting over the succession might lead to an internecine civil war seems to have become a real concern.[9]

Events in Yemen have not proceeded nearly as far. The intentions of President Ali Abdullah Saleh toward the succession can be only inferred from various steps he has taken to promote his eldest son, Ahmed (born 1970), first within the military, then to posts in the administration. It has also been inferred, both inside and outside Yemen, that these moves have been met with opposition from some of the senior military commanders, perhaps on account of Ahmed's youth, or perhaps out of fear that he might undermine their own authority. Once again, it is possible to discern a process of testing and perhaps even grooming at work. Given the fact that the president himself was in his late fifties in 2000, when he appointed Ahmed head of the Republican Guard, he does not need to make any irrevocable decisions for some years to come. Nevertheless, at the beginning of 2011, Ali Abdullah Saleh still faced the same uncomfortable decision as Muammar Qaddafi: whether he should try to establish his son's succession during his own lifetime or leave it to be fought over by members of the elite after he has gone.

Algeria and Tunisia

The presidents of Algeria and Tunisia were not only relatively elderly, in their seventies, but they also lacked grown sons who might possibly succeed them, facts that make the politics of succession in these two countries somewhat different from those of the Arab republics elsewhere. True, there was in Tunisia, and still is in Algeria, the same obsession with presidential health, vigor, and looks. In Algeria at least, the same worries exist about the impact of Bouteflika's death upon the economy. True, too, there was a huge amount of speculation, both inside both countries and among the North African commentators in urban centers such as Paris, about who was supposed to come next. In Algeria, the speculation still centers on President Bouteflika's younger brother, Said, who is his personal physician and close adviser. In Tunisia, by the end of 2010 the frontrunner seemed to have been the president's son-in-law, Sakhr al-Materi, who was busy carving out a position in business, as a member of the ruling party, and, perhaps even more important, as a political presence via his ownership of a radio station (Radio Zitouna, established in 2008), his establishment of an Islamic bank (also called Zitouna) in 2010, and his sponsorship of several private development projects in the agricultural sector.

Nevertheless, as of December 2010 there had been no sign of an official process of grooming in either Algeria or Tunisia. Questions about each president's intention continued to be met with official silence or by a standard reference to the appropriate provisions within the constitution. The result, not surprisingly, was a general anxiety about the future combined with a deep-rooted popular suspicion about each president's intentions. In such cases it is only natural that opposition criticism should focus on the activities of a greedy family dynasty as a proxy for all the other ills from which they believed their country suffered: arbitrary rule, exemplified by a lack of transparency, bad economic management, heavy-handed policing, and the tendency to see everything in security terms.

To make matters worse, there was no reason to suppose that matters would get any better over time as both presidents moved toward their eighties. And yet both would have had to deal with a fixed political calendar, in which 2014 would have seen both of them come to the end of yet another term in office. By then Bouteflika will be seventy-seven and Ben Ali would have been seventy-eight, a suitable age, it might be supposed, at which to reveal something definite about their future intentions. One significant moment as far as Ben Ali was concerned was whether or not preparations were being made for yet another constitutional amendment, in this case one to get around the provision stating that the country's president must be under seventy-five.

We can also be sure that, somewhere inside each elite, there were more active discussions leading to more concrete preparations for the future. In Tunisia, of course, Ben Ali's precipitate flight in January 2011 made all such discussions moot. In Algeria, continuing discussions must also involve senior figures in the army, including an influential group of retired generals, as well as the leaders of the government party, the FLN. If similar situations elsewhere are anything to go by, as they surely are, the process will inevitably be accompanied by rumors, speculation, and leaks to the press, as well as, behind the scenes, the emergence of one potential successor to the exclusion of all possible rivals.

WHAT I HAVE DESCRIBED IS a process that was going on within the Arab republics long enough to have many readily identified features. On the one hand, there was, and in some cases still is, a set of elderly presidents trying to keep the appearance of old age at bay. On the other, an understandably anxious population, facing an uncertain future after the death of someone who, for the majority of them, was or is the only leader they have ever known. To make matters more uncertain still, the presidents themselves, Hafiz al-Asad apart, proved enormously reluctant to name their successor in advance for reasons outsiders can only guess at. For some it may involve cold calculation in terms of a fear of arousing opposition to their plans or, perhaps, harming what remains of the republican revolutionary legitimacy they inherited from their predecessors. For others, one can imagine the presence of what might be called the "King Lear syndrome," in which old men cling to power, unable to face the consequences of being sidelined and forgotten after they have given it away. One thing is sure: they are all men who took good care to ensure that there was no one in their family or their entourage with enough influence and authority to tell them that it was time to go.

Filling the gap while the people waited, and in some cases still wait, to learn their leader's true intentions produced an uneasy combination of two very different discourses. One was the endless repetition of an anodyne official line to the effect that existing constitutional procedures would provide the answer when the time came. The second was a ca-cophony of rumor, deliberate falsehoods, and political gossip that each presidency did its best to control or often to suppress. In Egypt, to take just one example at random, four newspaper editors were jailed in 2007 for speculating about the president's health.

Meanwhile, the longer all this went on, the more momentous the process of succession seemed to be. Sons, where they existed, could not be like their fathers however much they may have been trained by them behind the scenes. As Sheila Carapico notes, the former are likely to be more liberal, better educated, more widely traveled, and more willing to open up.[10] Clear to all was that the new rulers, however they came to power, would usher in a period of great change that would last much longer than any brief, liberal spring. But how much, and in what ways this period would affect the different institutions of state and the differ-ent groups within the elite remained worryingly difficult to determine in advance.

9 The Question of Arab Exceptionalism

Are the Arab states exceptional in having possessed so many presidents for life with monarchical tendencies? This is a question that requires some care in answering. For one thing, similar tendencies either exist, or have existed, in other parts of the former colonial world, including Central Asian states that became independent after the breakup of the former USSR. For another, the notion of exceptionalism itself can easily be misused, either to justify a particular national narrative—for example, that of the United States or nineteenth- and early twentieth-century Germany—or to call it in question. Such notions of exceptionalism become even more problematic when supported by the employment of essentialist argument, for example, that Germans—or in the Middle Eastern case, Arabs—have a peculiar predilection for a particular type of dictatorial rule.

Given these problems, the question is best answered by employing a comparative framework and with proper attention to chronology and periodization. I argue that there is, indeed, a case to be made for a type of Arab exceptionalism between 1970 and 2010, and, further, that this is best explained by what I call an "Arab demonstration effect" stemming from developments in the specially close ties that have united the Arab world since at least the end of World War II. I will also say something about how this impact of a mutual "Arabism" affected both support for and the leadership of a putative Palestinian state as well as the significant role played by Saudi Arabia in supporting its own concept of an Arab political order.

An International Comparison

First, a reminder of the numbers. As of the end of 2010, and just before the sudden fall of Tunisia's Ben Ali, the Arab world contained nine republics including the Libyan Jamahiriya, all but two of which were ruled by men who showed every intention of staying in power until the end of their lives. In most cases, this process had involved either some amendment to an existing constitution to remove a term limit or, in the case of Yemen, an expression that this was what the president wished to do. Furthermore, in the seven states with presidents for life, one (Syria) had seen a successful succession from father to son and another five (Algeria, Tunisia, Libya, Egypt, and Yemen) showed signs that a family succession was being actively contemplated.

How does this compare with the situation to be found in the other parts of the non-European world? The question is a difficult one: what exactly is to be compared with what? For one thing, should we be concerned just with the forty years in question, or also with the sudden collapse of much of the same system in early 2011 and the reasons for it? Then, too, how much importance can we attach to plans for a presidential family succession when, as of the end of 2010, only one such transfer had taken place, and that in Syria for particular reasons which were not to be found elsewhere in the Arab Middle East? Last, there is the question of the coexistence between monarchical presidents for life and both kings and other forms of absolutist family rule, something unique to the postcolonial world.

Nevertheless, if we just concentrate on the system of presidents for life as typical of a particular stage in Arab political development, which had its origins in the coup-proof regimes that began to be established in the 1950s and 1960s and reached its culmination in Bouteflika's abolition of the two-term presidency in Algeria in 2009, we can talk of a distinct form of personal rule that, I would argue, can be compared with similar structures and processes in other regions of the non-European world.

Following on from this, a general look at the literature on the subject would seem to suggest two hypotheses. One is that the presence of presidents for life was, while it lasted, more common in the contemporary Arab world than in Africa, though not in parts of post–Soviet Central Asia. The second is that the structure of political power in Arab North Africa and the Arab East was, for a long period, more stable than that in sub-Saharan Africa.

The only worldwide statistical survey I know of that touches on some of these subjects is Jason Brownlee's analysis of a set of 258 of what he terms "Post–World War II non-monarchical autocrats" who ruled for more than three years.[1] The data Brownlee presents suggest a high turnover of presidents around the world, with those making it past their sixties constituting just over a quarter of the total.[2] Moreover, when broken down by region, these data also show that the presidential experience in the Arab world between 1970 and 2010 does not look so exceptional when set against some other areas, such as the Caribbean/ Central American region, some few decades ago. What Brownlee's data do not show, however, is whether the global rate of turnover of presidencies was getting faster or slower over time, or whether proportionally more presidents are managing to stay on for life.

As for family succession, Brownlee also puts forward some interesting hypotheses regarding the circumstances that encourage a hereditary succession, notably a combination of the political (or, in his terms, "staying power") and the biological ("having an adult son available"). But here the Arab sample, with only one hereditary succession in Syria, is too small to allow an international comparison.

Turning now to some nonquantitative comparisons, a reading of the sub-Saharan African material suggests a number of tentative conclusions. Hence, although the political history as analyzed by someone like Jean-François Bayart looks very similar to that north of the Sahara and is marked by much the same practices—for instance, what he calls the invented "fairy story" of democracy for the purposes of internal and external legitimation—the creation of a set of strong, centralized states in sub-Saharan Africa has not been achieved to the same extent, or even close to the same extent, as in the Arab world. True, there are a number, for example, Museveni's Uganda, that are run like family enterprises. Nevertheless, as a rule, African armies have remained more powerful independent actors than in the Arab world; Africa's tribal leaders remain strong, and African elections can still lead, on occasion, to the defeat and resignation of incumbent leaders.[3] Then, too, at least until 1994, the fourteen former French colonial possessions of sub-Saharan Africa remained much more subject to French interference and control than either their local British counterparts or their neighbors in North Africa, with their presidents usually protected but occasionally replaced on orders from Paris.[4]

There is also a useful comparison to be made with the five Central Asian successor states of the former Soviet Union: Kazakhstan, Uzbekistan, Turkmenistan, Kirgiz Republic, and Tajikistan. Here all the new presidents inherited strongly centralized administrations, faced many of the same challenges that the new Arab presidents faced, and very soon established themselves as presidents for life using referenda, managed elections, and enforced changes to the initial postindependence constitutions to do so. Since then, two have died (Aliyev of Azerbaijan in 2003 and Niyazov of Turkmenistan in 2006) and one has been overthrown (Akayev of Kirgiz Republic in 2005) by a challenger (Bakiyev) who was himself pushed out of office by the "Tulip" popular revolution in 2010. As in the Arab world, there has as yet been only one, highly controversial and last-minute, transfer from father to son, that of Heyder to Ilham Aliyev in Azerbaijan.

Comparisons with the Arab states are obvious, although there are some obvious differences as well. First, the sample is smaller, there being only five states in question in Central Asia with systems of presidents for life that go back only to the early 1990s. Second, these presidents came to power in a context of much less regional violence than in the Arab Middle East.[5] Third, as a consequence of their own long, and often mutually supportive, struggle for independence, the new Arab governments inherited a strong history of cooperation, which they formalized into a set of shared institutions and practices that, in turn, fostered further sharing and influence including, as I have argued earlier in this book, a tendency to have the same type of institutions and, of course, the same type of presidencies.

On the basis of this limited comparison, it would seem possible to argue the following: that political conditions in a group of Arab republics (Egypt, Tunisia, Libya, and Yemen) were unusual in being able to support the emergence of a small number of presidents for life beginning immediately after the creation of each republic, in some cases over fifty years ago. Also, over time, conditions changed enough in a second group to allow the same process to take place in the 1970s for Syria, the 1980s for Sudan, and the 1990s for Algeria. From this it can readily be concluded that republican presidents for life soon became a more universal phenomenon in the Arab world than in other regions of the non-European world, with the exception of former Soviet Central Asian republics.

Furthermore, the process itself can be best explained not by reference to some essentialized component of the Arab or Muslim "character" or "culture" but, rather, in terms of three historical factors. One was the greater centralization of Arab security state structures, including their regimes' greater ability to put an end to the military coup. And the second was a set of common challenges—oil, Israel, outside interference—along with the development of the practices of cooperation and of pooling of information that these regimes then employed to meet them. As for the third, the particular character of the Arab world in the context of world regional history, this is important enough to demand a special section to itself.

The Special Character of the Arab World

The notion of the Arab world as a specific geopolitical region of the world was formed in the early part of the twentieth century by the interaction of two sets of forces, one internal and one external. As far as the former was concerned, the Arab sense of unity was based primarily on a common language and on a largely common religion, reinforced by the common historical experience of being subject to a growing European influence over their politics as well as their major economic assets, notably oil. It was further nourished by an intellectual elite producing books, films, music, journals, and later television programs in Arabic, encouraged by a host of pan-Arab institutions designed to promote an interactive cooperation beginning with the Arab League (more properly the League of Arab States) established in 1945 and going on through a variety of schemes for a free trade area, a common market, and other forms of unity and united action such as the Organization of Arab Petroleum Exporting Countries (OAPEC).

Driving much of the process of creating more uniform Arab institutions and common practices was the enormous influence exercised by the Egypt of Gamal Abdel Nasser and Anwar Sadat. Not only was Egypt the largest and militarily most powerful Arab state, with the largest number of well-educated professionals, but it was also, in the Nasser period, concerned with the direct export of its own revolutionary institutions to neighboring states such as Sudan, Libya, Syria, and North Yemen. This included all aspects of what Kirk Beattie calls the model of the "military transitional authoritarian regime," ranging from the transition from rule by members of a revolutionary command council to rule by a single leader to such particular niceties as the exchange of uniforms for civilian clothing by the president himself, accompanied by those officers who chose to accompany him back into civilian life, or the renaming of the central square in Baghdad and Sana'a after Egypt's Tahrir (Liberation) Square in Cairo.[6]

The developing practices of the Nasserite revolution also came to exercise a more general influence over the management of government in Iraq and Algeria, as well as the leadership style of Yasser Arafat's Palestinian government in exile. In some cases, it was the Egyptian approach to land reform or to the nationalization of large parts of the private sector; in others, it was such initiatives as the insistence that at least half of the members of any representative assembly be workers or peasants.

A second wave of influence followed, as the steps taken by President Anwar Sadat toward economic liberalization, as well as the more tentative ones toward a multiparty system with managed elections, were both copied and echoed in one way or another across the Arab world, including in the monarchical states of Morocco and Jordan. Two examples are of particular significance. The first concerns the Egyptian Parties Law of June 1977, with its insistence that no party could be formed on the basis of ethnic, racial, geographical, or religious factors. The introduction of such categories was designed to prevent the opposition politicians from benefiting from their access to particular subnational political constituencies, and it has been repeated, more or less word for word, in similar laws passed in Bahrain and Morocco in 2005. The second is Sadat's creation of a partially elected *shura* council in 1980 to act as a second chamber to the existing People's Assembly with special powers of its own, allowing it to suggest new laws while acting, if necessary, as a check on measures taken by the elected parliament. This idea was even more widely copied, for example, in Saudi Arabia, Oman, Yemen, and Bahrain, with an equivalent institution in Tunisia.

External influence has always played an important, though I would argue subsidiary, role in the emergence of the notion of a unified Arab world during and after World War II. To begin with, this notion was largely the result of British and French, then Soviet and American perceptions of the Arab Middle East's geostrategic position. These views found official reflection in the creation of the Middle East departments in their rival foreign offices or of Middle East commands within their military. These offices and commands were then used to try to influence the policies of the Arab states in terms of building up offensive and defensive coalitions for and against other great power clients, including such immediate non-Arab neighbors as Turkey and Iran. Hence, at one time or other, both Cairo and Baghdad became the focus for efforts to extend foreign influence throughout the Arab world, with Beirut, Tunis, and Riyadh often playing significant supporting roles.

The result of the interaction of both these internal and external forces was to reinforce a sense both of Arab identity and of the particular interests of each particular state. Some followed the Egyptian example; others worked to reinforce opposition to Egypt's influence. The same occurred as far as outside influence was concerned, with some Arab states choosing to work with one of the world powers and others to work against it. This led, not surprisingly, to the appearance of competing forms of Arabism at the international level, even as the vast majority of the individual regimes worked to protect their own sovereignty while building up sufficient power to make themselves safe from both their enemies and the activities of overeager allies.

All this is well known. What is observed less often is the way in which both internalist and externalist influences helped to shape the emergence of strong personal presidencies sustained by a common set of structures and practices concerned with security and postrevolutionary legitimation. It was as a result of both internal and external pressures that Arab regime presidents felt the need to strengthen themselves against possible interventions coming at them from within the region and without. Not surprisingly, they also turned to each other for help, advice, and practical models when it came to the day-to-day business of what Larry Diamond has termed "authoritarian statecraft," that is to say, the patterns and institutions by which authoritarian regimes manage politics and hold on to power, not to speak of the finer arts of manipulation, persuasion, and propaganda.[7]

In this regard, the Arab states exhibit a pattern of close relations and mutual influence much more like that developed in Western Europe after World War II than the looser sense of association to be found in postindependence sub-Saharan Africa, Central and East Asia, and Latin America.

Intra-Arab Cooperation and the Demonstration Effect

Regime leaders in the Arab states are keenly aware of what is going on in the rest of the Arab world. They use this to try to improve their own strengths while anticipating problems that they observe across the border, for example, how to try to control food prices after nationwide antigovernment protests broke out in Algeria and Tunisia in December 2010. They have also been ready to borrow both discrete ideas and practices as well as more systematic structures in order to improve their chances of staying in power. I will begin with a survey of some of the institutional mechanisms involved before going on to evaluate the importance of some of the major initiatives they encouraged, particularly as they affect the presidencies of each republic.

The first, and still one of the major, frameworks for maintaining a structure of Arab meetings and regular exchange is the League of Arab States, with its many committees and subcommittees involved with such particular subjects as economics (The Economic and Social Council of the Arab League's Council of Arab Economic Unity); and the league's organization of Educational, Social, and Cultural Affairs (ALESCO). The league, too, provides an umbrella structure for the creation of more specialized pan-Arab institutions such as the Arab Interior Ministers Council, which was established in Tunis in 1982 with its annual meetings of the Arab ministers of interior themselves. Arab police academies form part of the same security-minded structure, providing training programs for both their local and visiting Arab police officers. So too are the regular meetings of the Arab chiefs of police with their exchange of information about innovations in police practice.

It should also be observed how the often unwieldy process of Arab League deliberations was circumvented by the summit meetings of Arab heads of state, inaugurated by President Nasser in 1968 and maintained on an ad hoc basis ever since. Summits allow the individual leaders to maintain regular contact, to get to know each other, and to conduct a personal form of high-level diplomacy that owes little to the initiatives of their respective foreign offices or other ministries, and of which phone calls and sudden visits form an essential part.

Also of importance are the mechanisms that have been developed to improve the practice of regime security at the regional level. One such consists of institutions such as the (Prince) Naif Arab University for Security Sciences (originally founded as a High College in 1983), with its many seminars and meetings on vital subjects, such as "Skills of Security Personnel and Their Relative Impact on Combating Terrorism." Another is the practice of gathering together specialist Arab ministers to create new forums to deal with the appearance of new threats. A good example is the Cairo meeting of ministers of information in 2010, which addressed a joint Egyptian/Saudi proposal for the creation of a regional office to supervise Arab satellite stations as part of a drive to ensure that these stations do not serve as a front for terrorist organizations.[8]

The appearance of long-serving presidents for life provided an extra source of emulation at the highest level. Leaving aside the question of those particular borrowings that went into the creation of each Arab security state, there was, and in some cases continues to be, a separate set of influences that both encourages the existence of this particular type of presidency and helps to shape the way it is conducted. One useful way to think about it is with the notion of an elite club of Arab leaders, both presidents and monarchs, who meet regularly enough and over a long enough period to become extremely familiar with each other and each other's ways. This point is made perfectly by the obvious intimacy on display in photographs taken of the 2010 summit hosted by Muammar Qaddafi at Sirte.

Membership in this exclusive club can be taken to have helped boost their own sense of legitimacy. It may also have engendered a special sense of camaraderie. Only these men can know what it is like to be at the helm of an Arab security state for many years. Only they have experience of the pressures involved. Only they can really imagine the debilitating fear that must been felt by President Ben Ali when he was suddenly faced with a popular opposition he could no longer control, the road to the airport his only, desperate, way out.

Something of the clubbiness of all this is apparent in the comments made just after the Tunisian president's fall by his next-door neighbor, Muammar Qaddafi of Libya. He was "pained" by Ben Ali's overthrow, he said, "and what for?... In order for someone to become president instead? I do not know these new people, but we all know Ben Ali and the transformation that was achieved in Tunisia. Why are you doing all that?"[9]

The Special Cases of Palestine and Saudi Arabia

Two cases that are both exemplary of the influence of the Arab order but also present special problems for analysis are those of the Palestinians under Yasser Arafat and the Palestine Liberation Organization (PLO) as beneficiaries of particular types of Arab support and inspiration, and the Saudis who, after the demise of the Nasser regime in Egypt in 1970, played an enormously significant role in supporting a regional status quo that eventually came to contain so many republican presidents for life.

First, the Palestinians, although never having an independent state of their own, adopted a republican form of government in those areas of pre-1948 Palestine where they were permitted to exercise a limited form of sovereignty as a result of the political agreement with the Israelis reached in 1994. This included an elected president who is subject, at least in principle, to the rules set out in an interim constitution that was supposed to guide the conduct of political life until a final settlement. Yet that notwithstanding, the actual exercise of political power remained very similar to systems that Yasser Arafat and his close colleagues had created in exile, and was run very much along the highly centralized lines they had observed in the major Arab states such as Egypt, Syria, and Iraq. As a result, and had he lived longer, there is little doubt that Arafat would have tried to amend the constitution to allow him to remain as president for more than his appointed term.

Had Mandatory Palestine actually been partitioned between an Israeli and a Palestinian state in 1947/1948 as the United Nations had intended, the history of Palestinian self-government might have been very different, even though the Palestinian leadership, like that of its Arab neighbors, would surely have been subject to strong pressure to create a strongly centralized administration under a military president. In the event, however, only the Jews obtained one (Israel), while a strong combination of political and military actors—the British, the Zionists, and the ruler of Transjordan—combined together to prevent the emergence of a Palestinian state that, in their eyes, would have acted as a destabilizing force in the region. Instead, the area allocated to the Palestinians under the UN resolution passed into the hands of the Jordanians (the West Bank) and the Egyptians (the Gaza Strip).

For the next twenty or so years, Palestinian politicians living in exile were kept firmly under the control of the other Arab states, which, though permitting the establishment of a symbolic body, the PLO, in 1965 made sure that it took no steps that might threaten their own security. Matters changed radically, however, after the total defeat of the Arab armies by Israel in the 1967 war. Out of the ashes came a new set of militant guerrilla leaders, personified by Yasser Arafat, and dedicated to the practice of armed struggle symbolized by one of the most popular posters of the time, an arm holding a raised AK-47 assault rifle. Within a year, Arafat's Fateh had taken over the PLO (including all its diplomatic and material resources) and began the long process toward obtaining sufficient international recognition to back the establishment of a Palestinian state on whatever part of old Palestine could be obtained by a combination of military and political means. Meanwhile, as Yezid Sayigh has demonstrated so well, the logic of the situation led to the creation of a statelike structure in exile, created by Yasser Arafat and a few colleagues, very much in the image of the authoritarian systems then to be found in Egypt, Syria, and Iraq.[10]

In Sayigh's analysis, a number of factors combined to shape the type of organization that Arafat was able to construct, including the need for a centralized administrative system to mobilize the manpower and resources of a dispersed refugee community, and also enough secrecy both to avoid assassination and to sustain a process of armed struggle violently opposed by Israel as well as, more covertly, by a group of Arab states on which the new PLO relied for official support. Of equal importance was the role of Arafat and his own Fateh group, mostly lower-middle-class young men who had benefited from the expanded educational opportunities established by the Arab populist regimes in Egypt, Syria, and Iraq. Then there was the particular character of Yasser Arafat himself, authoritarian and controlling on the one hand, secretive, suspicious, and distrustful on the other. He was constantly developing the skills necessary to co-opt or to destroy rivals, to build parallel and competing administrative structures, and, generally, to keep on top of the fractious world of refugee politics.

As Sayigh also sees it, the development of Arafat's personal control was also assisted by a number of highly contingent external factors. Among these were the enforced move of his headquarters from Amman to Beirut and then on to Tunis, shedding rivals along the way, and the growing international recognition of the PLO under his control as the sole viable negotiator.

Finally, the new regional context produced by the first Palestinian Intifada beginning in 1987, followed by the collapse of the Soviet Union and the 1990/1991 Gulf War, led to a serious international effort aimed at the settlement of the Palestinian issue. This attempt was then further encouraged by Israeli Prime Minister Yitzhak Rabin's conversion to the advantages of a clear separation between the Israeli and Palestinian populations inside pre-1948 Palestine, with the Palestinian portion policed, managed, and kept under control by an Arafat-dominated Palestinian Authority (PA).

The stage was now set for Arafat to bring his state-in-exile and style of leadership back to Palestine in 1994, and then to integrate them with the existing Palestinian leadership in the West Bank and Gaza. Not surprisingly, this move was carried out at great speed and without any real attempt to alter old practices in the light of the radically new circumstances on the ground. As a result, locally resident politicians and notables were quickly integrated into the system, creating a single elite based on the use of patronage derived from the new international funds at their disposal. And although elections were held in 1996 for a presidency—won easily by Arafat himself—and for a new legislature, neither this incipient pluralism nor the associated demands for transparency made much headway. Very soon the critics were overwhelmed by the entrenchment of the now-well-established PLO practices of "patronage, purchasing loyalties and administrative and financial corruption" identified as early as 1997 by the Palestinians' own Palestinian Legislative Council as responsible for the loss of over 20 percent of the PA's budget.[11]

Responsibility for this unfortunate state of affairs can be assigned to two interlocking and reinforcing sets of forces. One was the authoritarian structures developed under Arafat's control in exile. The other, the huge imbalance of power between Israel and the PA, made everything subject to powerful Israeli interests—usually backed by the United States and often by the European Union—of which security and containment were far and away the most important. So Arafat remained a potent political as well as economic force for the Palestinians even after the Second Intifada broke out in September 2000, leading to the reoccupation of the West Bank and Gaza by Israeli forces and his virtual imprisonment in his Ramallah compound until his death in 2004.

Arafat was succeeded as acting president by his deputy, Mahmoud Abbas, a process legitimated by an election the following year in which he obtained nearly two-thirds of the vote in an almost 100 percent turnout. As in the case of his predecessor, his real power to manage Palestinian affairs was strictly limited by Israeli control over the borders of his ministate, over its economy, and over the many day-to-day concessions he was forced to make to maintain his position. By 2007, he found himself ruling the West Bank alone after a split developed with the Hamas movement that controlled the Gaza Strip. Paradoxically, however, this reduction in the area he controlled led to an increase in his own personal power, removing a potent source of criticism of his own authoritarian ways. It also provided him with the occasion to rule by decree for over a year in a way that was in clear violation of the Palestinian constitution, then to use his continuing control over Arafat's Fateh organization to exercise close supervision over his new prime minister, Salam Fayyad, appointed after the 2009 elections. Each needed the other for his own survival, Fayyad supporting Abbas in his unpopular policy of reconciliation with the Israelis and Abbas compensating for Fayyad's lack of a popular political base.

For the reasons just set out, the business of state building inside and outside Palestine provides a clear example of an exception that proves the Arab rule. It is clear that successive Palestinian presidents would, had they been able, like to have created a powerful security state like those of their Arab neighbors, and then to rule it for life. As it was, however, they were forced to operate in a context of limited sovereignty, forcing both of them to bow to internal Palestinian as well as international pressures for political pluralism. In these difficult circumstances, they exercised considerable skill in carving out a small and contested space for themselves, trading control over many normal aspects of government in exchange for support from the Israelis and the international community behind their efforts to subdue Palestinian militancy by the use of their own particular version of the stick (an armed police force) and a carrot (the distribution of international aid). This was just enough to keep them in power. But it was certainly not enough to allow them the luxury of trying to establish either their own dynasty or even of imposing a successor who was not himself popular with the people or the party, Fateh, that Arafat created and that Abbas still controls.

Whether they liked it or not, the Saudi regime was forced to support the successive Palestinian attempts to create both a government in exile and, after 1994, a new system of administration in Gaza and the West Bank. Lacking military strength itself, it was forced to use all its other resources—financial and religious—to try to create an Arab legitimacy for itself strong enough to protect it from predatory neighbors and from the revolutionary currents that were carrying away so many of the other monarchical regimes in the Middle East. The fact that it was so closely allied to the United States for strategic and other reasons only made the issue that much more pressing. Giving aid and encouragement was always one part of this process; support for a moderate, nonrevolutionary Arab political order another.

Naturally, the way this policy was conducted changed over time. While during the 1950s and 1960s the Saudi regime was very much on the defensive, after 1970 it proved resilient enough to try to create, and then maintain, a status quo composed of largely moderate, pro-Western regimes, while offering what were, in effect, financial bribes to those who might threaten such an order, like the Syrians. Central to this process over time were the presidents for life, known quantities to the Saudi leadership through regular meetings over many decades and always looking to Riyadh not just for subventions and profitable investments but also for access to the Saudi labor market for their own subjects. Further change came after the 9/11 attacks on New York and elsewhere, when cooperation between the Arab rulers intensified as they all sought to promote a brand of moderate Islam against the militant radicalism of al-Qaeda and its associates. Hence the very real sense of distress when some of these old friends like Ben Ali and Mubarak were overthrown by the popular uprisings of early 2011, followed by the offer of sanctuary to the former, and pressure on the Egyptian military not to allow the public trial of the latter in the summer of the same year.

THE DAY AFTER PRESIDENT Ben Ali's sudden flight from his country on January 14, 2011, two posters were held up by wildly demonstrating crowds, one in Tunisia and the other in Jordan. The first offered thanks to Al Jazeera, the Arab TV station based in Qatar in the Persian Gulf that was the first to report the country's nationwide protests and to help give them solidarity and coherence. The second, under a picture of a round piece of Arab flat bread, said simply, "Ayna anta ya Azizi"—literally, "Where are you O Azizi"—a name that can be translated as "my friend" but that also has something of the meaning of "Where are you when we need you?" This was a reference to the young Tunisian Mohamed Bouazizi, whose act of setting himself on fire in protest against his unemployment and his harsh treatment by the police had triggered the four weeks of increasing demonstrations that brought the Ben Ali regime crashing down.

But there is even more to this poster's pan-Arab character than that. There is also an allusion in the words to the genre of *latmiya* or funeral oration, for example, to the martyred leader Hussein, whose death in the late seventh century was one of the events giving rise to the emergence of Shi'ism as a different set of religious practices. Hence the cry "Ayna anta ya Hussein" or, in the same vein, "Ayna anta ya 'Umar" ("Where are you 'Umar?"), the first of the Prophet Muhammad's successors; or even "Ayna anta ya rasulullah" ("Where are you Prophet of God?"). Such signs provide striking testimony to the ties that bind the Arab world together and that allowed its people, at a particularly dramatic moment in Arab history, to think of themselves as one with a single individual in a country they had probably never visited and whose single life became "the measure of millions."[12]

The existence of such ties has affected the president-for-life phenomenon in a number of important ways. These rulers all promoted much the same policies "to manage and contain political opposition, fend off demands for political reform and respond to economic liberalization and technical change."[13] And when one of them failed in any of these particular tasks—whether in political management, like Ben Ali, or in the larger task of keeping a country together, like Bashir of Sudan—the shock they all felt was palpable and the lessons they knew they must learn from it were insistent. For as, one by one, they entrenched themselves for life, each of them must also have had a very real fear that, one by one, they might fall or be swept aside. The demonstration effect clearly works both ways.

But does this make the Arab world, as some have argued, "outside" history? That is, is the Arab world so special that it is entirely disconnected from the larger forces of market capitalism and political pluralism that are identified as central to modernity by writers from at least Max Weber onward? For a while it might have been possible to think so, possible to suppose that the Arab world constituted a peculiar backwater, untouched by the major world historical forces at work in the twentieth and now the twenty-first centuries. But even before the fall of Ben Ali—an event that was the result, in large measure, of a modern set of grievances connected to world food prices and middle-class unemployment, as well as of a modern set of political techniques approaching that of a popularly organized general strike—it was clear that the presidents for life shared much with other presidents outside the Arab world. They were clearly subject to many of the same global influences, such as political Islam, the stress on individual human rights, the revelations of

WikiLeaks, and the American-directed war on terror. It is only the presence of so many of these presidents for life in one region over the last forty years that is so unusual in global terms, something that has to be explained in relationship not to the exceptional character of the Arab peoples, but to material factors that exercise a greater-than-usual power in the Arab world, notably the intensity of the multiple ties that bind it together, Palestine and oil money included.

10 The Sudden Fall

On 31 December 2010, the Arab world contained nine presidents, of whom seven clearly intended to stay in office for life and six were over sixty—a veritable kingdom of the old. No one predicted, nor had the means to predict, what lay ahead. Egyptian newspaper columnists, for example, writing of what to expect in 2011 could see little significant on the political horizon other than continued speculation as to whether Gamal Mubarak would succeed his father, nothing more. Elsewhere, there was some question about opposition to President Ali Abdullah Saleh's plans for his eldest son. Meanwhile, academics were still writing about what Eva Bellin, in 2005, had called the "robustness of the coercive apparatus." And where they did address the question of the conditions under which regimes might fall, it was almost always argued in terms of possible weaknesses at the top, perhaps a fiscal crisis that could lead to a "hollowing out" of the coercive apparatus.[1]

Out of the blue, and beginning with what might otherwise have been a minor event—the self-immolation of Mohamed Bouazizi in the southwest of Tunisia—a spark was lit that caused popular feeling to explode across the Arab world, bringing the immediate downfall of two presidential regimes (in Tunisia and Egypt) and posing a substantial threat to three more (in Libya, Syria, and Yemen), forcing their leaders to confront the rebels in a series of increasingly violent confrontations. And though, in retrospect, it is possible to discern some of the material causes of these events, it is their existential quality that seems worthy of most notice, the fact that so many people in so many places were united in the desire to free themselves from a set of oppressive, arbitrary, corrupt, controlling, and incomprehensible regimes, all of which appeared as though they would last the length of their own lifetimes and beyond. To take just one telling example, a young Egyptian of thirty would only have known one ruler, Hosni Mubarak, and could expect to know only one more, his son, Gamal.

In the event, the most useful way of explaining these unexpected irruptions of popular grievance was provided by Timur Kuran in his seminal article "Sparks and Prairie Fires: A Theory of Unanticipated Political Revolution," based on a study of the French, Russian, and Iranian revolutions. Here he theorizes that in repressive regimes people conceal their true opinions but at considerable psychological cost. Then, in response to a slight surge in more open opposition, more and more individuals are emboldened to publicly express political dissatisfaction until there is a wholesale shift in "public sentiment."[2] A further elaboration is provided by Arne Klau, in which he notes that the coming of Facebook and Twitter allowed Tunisians and Egyptians to express their dissatisfaction to each other at very low cost—for example, without running the risk of attending public meetings—and so giving them a sense of their own large numbers even before the first demonstrations began.[3]

The revealed weaknesses of the Arab presidential regimes and the way that these weaknesses combined created a revolutionary situation that brought hundreds of thousands of people into the streets to try to complete the work of liberation first begun by the founders of the very same structures they were now trying to overturn.

The Weaknesses and Contradictions of Arab Presidential Regimes
To speak very generally, the Arab presidential regimes contained—
and those that remain still contain—five basic weaknesses:

1. The majority depended for their legitimacy on the appearance of
   constitutional legality supported by managed elections, both of
   which created problems of political management. Just why this was
   so remains something of a puzzle. On the one hand, the overman-
   agement of national elections like those held in Egypt in November 2010 can be shown to have contributed something to the final
   delegitimation of the Mubarak regime. On the other, as the political history of Asad's Syria or Qaddafi's Libya shows, the absence of
   such practices does not seem to have made their survival any more
   or less difficult, even if it did help to isolate them from much of the
   Western world for much of their political lives.
2. The Arab presidential regimes also depended on steady economic
   growth to provide jobs and goods and services for their populations, something that was made more difficult by the large crony
   sector within each economy that contained many more monopolists than free marketeers.
3. All the regimes in question failed either to incorporate the majority of their youthful populations into their systems of ideology
   and practice nor to provide them with employment, housing, and,
   even more important, any prospect of a better future. No wonder
   that such a high percentage saw their only hope in migration. No
   wonder that Mohamed Bouazizi became such a symbol of the
   hopelessness that so many of Tunisia's quarter of a million unemployed graduates experienced in their daily lives, including the
   huge problem of raising enough money to find somewhere to live
   after they had gotten married.[4]

4. The highly centralized nature of the systems and the consequent lack of coordination among the component parts of government and, in some vital instances, the armed forces meant that each regime's capacity to respond to domestic crises was limited, whether in terms of meeting sudden emergencies—for example, large rises in the price of food—or sustained civilian disobedience. By the same token, there was an absence of planning for worst-case scenarios and, in the case of the Egyptian army at least, a sense among the senior officers that they could not trust the lower ranks to obey if they ordered them to put down the demonstrations with force.

5. A preoccupation with stability, as I have argued, is part and parcel of authoritarian structures, which abhor controversy, division, and anything that is beyond state control. In the case of the Arab republics, one can easily infer that its purpose was to impress both their own populations and their foreign supporters—the superpowers, the Europeans, and usually the Saudis—with their reliability and predictability, an important substitute for the legitimacy that some of them seem to have felt they lacked. Hence also their constant appeal to the dangers of internal division—whether ethnic, geographical, or religious—dangers that, as argued in previous chapters, their laws governing the formation of political parties were specifically designed to prevent. Nevertheless, it should be equally obvious that this huge emphasis on an oppressive unity came at the expense of pluralism, openness, trust, and honest communication, not to speak of the handicap it placed on imagination, innovation, and invention.

Perhaps most important of all, all these weaknesses were becoming more dangerous to the regimes over time as corruption and repression got worse while there was every sign that the ruling families intended to go on ruling for ever. In some places, like Egypt, this produced a series of small opposition groups like the one protesting against a Mubarak succession, which named itself, significantly, as *kifaya* (enough). In Syria, there was a smoldering resentment among the many members of the Sunni population at rule by a tiny Alawi minority whom they regarded at best as a clique of exploitative usurpers and at worst as heretics pretending to be Muslims. Meanwhile, a more pan-Arab form of opposition could be found among the Arab bloggers calling attention to a police brutality so arbitrary that it could affect any one of them at any time. This could then be generalized within an all-encompassing narrative of an Arab backwardness enforced by oppressive regimes that was repeated with new examples day after day on Radio Al Jazeera.

The Spark

So much could have been known in the months leading up to Mohamed Bouazizi's incendiary act. What can only be understood in retrospect is the role played by the young revolutionaries in Tunisia and Egypt who used this single act to create a nonviolent protest movement that, within weeks, brought tens of thousands of people into the streets, not just in the capital city but in many others besides. Listening to their talk in the days after the various uprisings, two things stand out. One was a distaste mixed with incredulity at the speeches of the presidents and their colleagues: arrogant, patronizing, hypocritical, and just plain stupid. Second, they spoke a language of choice and freedom, practiced daily on the Internet, in which they argued, said what they thought, and selected this rather than that in ways that they believed to be their right. Their hostility was just as intense in the case of the ruler of their neighboring state, Colonel Qaddafi, whose rambling speeches presented a topsy-turvy world in which he was not the ruler and it was his loving people who were actually in charge.

As for what constituted the revolutionary moment itself, we know from the various reconstructions conducted by journalists of Egypt's

Al-Ahram Weekly that the first large protest in Tahrir Square was planned, about a week in advance, for National Police Day, 25 January 2011, which was habitually used by the hated minister of the interior, Habib El-Adli, to laud and to show off the professional skills of the equally hated State Security Police.[5] Within a few days large enough crowds had gathered, first to cow and then defeat the antiriot squads, then to persuade the leaders of the army to secure Hosni Mubarak's retirement and to act as guarantors of a staged move toward a more plural political system. As in other parts of the Arab world, those present appeared as demonstrators in a double meaning of the word, both as opponents of the regime and as apostles of a personal freedom that also included the practice of brotherhood and helpfulness, which reminded those who saw it of many of the other great revolutionary moments of modern history, beginning in front of the Bastille in Paris in July 1789.

In the event, as is well known, while some regimes surrendered easily, others, like those in Algeria, Libya, Syria, and Yemen, chose to fight back. In the case of Algeria this produced what one set of analysts identified as a "rebellion by installments" by which the ruler made certain concessions and the restive population, mindful of the brutal civil strife of the 1990s, remained content with regular demonstrations and sit-ins to express their grievances rather than pushing things too far.[6] But in Libya and Syria, and to a more limited extent in Yemen, resistance by the president and his family provoked what rapidly turned into violent civil wars with all the savagery that such internecine strife almost inevitably entails. In each case, too, old divisions were immediately revived, whether between the north and south of Yemen, the east and west of Libya, or, most potentially fearsome of all, between the Alawi rulers of Syria and many of their Sunni compatriots. Just how dangerous this last situation threatened to become was illustrated by an interview between an American National Public Radio reporter and an anonymous inhabitant of the embattled city of Deraa who referred to the soldiers in the regime's elite Fourth Brigade as "al-Munifiqun," or the hypocrites mentioned in Sura 63 of the Koran, who abandoned their belief in God.

The Arab kings also chose to dig in their heels, offering a few concessions to popular demands, including constitutional reform, but in no case moving very much in the direction of the constitutional type of monarchy many of their critics demanded. Furthermore, after a short period of tolerating unarmed dissent, all pushed back, some with the greatest possible violence, as in Bahrain, where not only protesters were killed and imprisoned but also some of the doctors who had had the temerity to come to their assistance.

Nevertheless, the Arab revolutionary movement rumbled on with a vitality that gave no grounds for imagining that it would end in months rather than years, while certain to produce profound changes even in states where the regimes survived more or less intact. It is difficult to imagine there being any more presidents for life, let alone any more military ones, and equally difficult to imagine any republican head of state trying to start or to continue a family dynasty, with Syria being the one possible exception. Once the process of revolutionary transformation had started, there could be no going back.

Unfolding Events after the Arab Spring

With the lid blown off, the modus operandi of these regimes could be observed with much greater clarity, together with the characters and political behavior of the presidents, both those who tumbled quickly and those who managed to hang on. Informed judgment too became a possibility, with enough data about secret prisons, mercenary practices, and the use of force to subdue restive populations to allow precise accusations of corruption, torture, indiscriminate killings, and even brutal and widespread crimes against humanity to be made against their perpetrators, like Muammar Qaddafi and his son, Saif, with the suggestion that they be sent for trial in the International Court of Justice in the Hague.

Some of the news reinforced an awareness of the revolutionary enthusiasm, of the tremendous courage needed to breach the wall of fear
on which the Arab dictatorships depended, and of the ever-more imagi-
native use of Facebook—now the name of at least one newborn Egyptian girl—to make political connections. But many items do not make
for comfortable reading. There was the news of Qaddafi's use of coun-
terviolence involving thugs and rooftop snipers as well as his threat to
send his men house to house in Benghazi to hunt down his opponents
"like rats." Reports circulated of much the same tactics being employed
by units under the command of Bashar al-Asad's younger brother, Maher, first in the rebellious southern Syrian city of Deraa, then in other
towns and city quarters up and down the rest of the country.

There have also been fresh revelations of Western complicity in support of Arab presidential regimes engaged in America's war on terror,
including the sending of captured Arab jihadis to be tortured in Egyptian and Libyan jails before being forcefully interrogated by American
agents. American information technology firms too were seen to be in
the forefront of providing despotic Arab regimes with the means to both
monitor and block domestic social networks.

Nevertheless, for the political historian this was a rare and wonderful moment. For many years I had followed the lives of the republican
presidents, talking and, latterly, teaching about them, wondering at
their public performances, being truly shocked on occasion by their
brazen disregard for the norms of good government, and, all the time,
trying to puzzle out what made them act as they did. So it was with
both pleasure and a sense of incredulity that I saw these once mighty
men put under huge public pressure themselves, with some running for
their lives and others, sensing that they had nowhere safe to go, making
a few belated concessions while striving to put down peaceful protests
with force. And all at a speed and intensity that not only made analysis
difficult but made useful prediction virtually impossible. As he or she
contemplated the series of revolutionary explosions, the wise observer

could only take refuge in the observation that, like the French Revolution of 1789 or the Russian ones of 1917, the whole course had many years still to run.

All that can sensibly be done is to continue to take stock of the rise and fall of this particular system of monarchical-republican government and to note that, even as it collapsed in some states and struggled on in others, there were always new lessons to be learned and new evaluations and judgments to be made. This was the more exciting as the effort to make sense of the fast-breaking daily developments now became something much larger than a merely private academic concern but a matter of compelling interest, not only to the inhabitants of the Middle East itself but also to many governments and officials in the rest of the world. As I struggled to understand the death throes of the Qaddafi regime, for instance, I was doing so at the same time as the American president and members of his State Department—and coming up, it seems, with very much the same conclusion: that its leader would most speedily be driven out of office by increasing the stress level on his somewhat unstable personality through precision bombings and other measures, while forcing him to face the fact that he was no longer in full control of a loving, docile people.

Meanwhile, as the months progressed, certain features of the presidential systems seemed to become clearer. The first was a key difference in the makeup and role of the presidential families themselves. As events unfolded, it seemed less and less likely that it was an accident that it was just those regimes where members of the president's own family occupied some of the highest positions in the military and the security forces, as in Libya, Syria, and Yemen, that chose to fight a bloody civil war rather than seeing their armies force them into flight, like Ben Ali, or to capitulate, like Mubarak. The second was the significant differences among those who chose to resist, with Libya opened up to foreign journalists and those using the social media, while Syria remained tightly closed.

Nevertheless, resistance to the revolutionary movements sweeping the Arab world was also to prove something of a gamble. The appeal to the need for stability and the avoidance of chaos obviously had its limits as the situation progressed from being "chaos or us" [the ruling family] to "chaos and us."[7] Moreover, with the death toll mounting, the use of force ran the risk of not only provoking the population to greater resistance—and so creating the very situation it was designed to prevent—but also encouraging outside intervention, as in Libya and, to some extent, in Yemen. Hence, even if militarily successful, it offered the prospect of a dangerous aftermath in which popular resentment would be linked with increasing economic distress, with little hope of immediate redress. Nowhere was this more apparent than in Syria, where all the pre–civil war problems posed by a growing budget deficit, a serious drought, and the depletion of its limited domestic oil resources were greatly exacerbated, first by the measures taken to try to calm a restive population, like an across the board pay raise for all civil servants, and then by the impact of the fighting itself on the vital incomes obtained from trade and tourism.[8]

A second area where greater clarity became possible was that of presidential responsibility. Whereas, before 2011, it might have been possible to wonder about the extent to which a ruler like President Hosni Mubarak knew, or had been told, about high-level corruption, subsequent revelations made it impossible to believe that he did not. As postrevolutionary investigations of the secretive deal to provide Israel with natural gas at lower than the world market price reveal, the deal itself was brokered by a longtime friend of the president, proof positive that Mubarak himself must have been well aware of what was actually going on.[9]

A third area concerns the particular version of the mirror state to be found in Qaddafi's Libya and, to a lesser extent, in Ali Abdullah Saleh's Yemen. In the former, the colonel's frequent interviews and televised speeches provided fresh evidence of his disturbed state of mind and of the role of his family and colleagues in keeping him from slipping off the rails. In one, he spent two hours reading from notes brought to him, one page at a time, by an assistant, before ending with a wild shout, "Why do you do this to me?," aimed at his local opponents. In another, he repeatedly looked up from his notes toward someone or something off camera as though wanting to check up on how he was doing or, perhaps, even how he was looking. Both can be taken as a sign that he and his close aides were worried about letting him ramble on, frequently repeating himself or losing track of what he was saying. Both suggested the presence of one of his most powerful underlying delusions: that he was not personally the head of government and that, having refused to style himself as president, he had no powerful position to leave.

Abdullah Saleh's own daily speeches, broadcast from his heavily fortified palace outside Sana'a, began to take on something of the same surreal quality as well, for example when he was inveighing against "Zionist instigators and fornicating demonstrators."[10] And while there were days when he agreed to step down within a short time, there were others when he demonstrated his defiance by breaking his word and then sending tanks and armed troops against the camps and sit-ins of his student opponents.

Two final areas in which more could be learned as the process of revolutionary change unfolded concerned the people, not their old or new rulers. One involved the progressive replacement of the daily demonstrations in public places like Cairo's Tahrir Square and the Casbah in Tunis by popular pressures expressed elsewhere within the newly evolving political system, such as strikes and workplace sit-ins. In the case of the former, for example, the Tahrir demonstrators deliberately suspended their protests for some weeks to give time for the new provisional Egyptian government to act on their demands. In the latter, the successful use of Casbah Square by a grassroots coalition of workers, leftists, human rights groups, and Islamists to demand the removal of all traces of the Ben Ali regime gave way at times to small groups of people making particular demands, like jobs, or to crowds of migrant workers forced out of Libya by the fighting just across the border.

The second involved fears about the effect of the popular revolutions on the substantial progress made under the previous regime concerning women's rights. These were felt with special emphasis in Egypt, where some of the more recent attempts to promote such rights were particularly associated with the name of the former president's wife, Suzanne, including the so-called khul law of 2000 that allowed a woman to divorce her husband without his consent provided she gave up any demand for financial assistance. It also extended to the special quota for women's seats in parliament, which had reached sixty-four by 2010.[11] In Tunisia, anxiety focused on the future of the even more substantial rights contained in President Habib Bourguiba's family status law of 1957. Elsewhere, members of minorities that had been afforded some protection under the presidential dictatorships had good reason to worry about their status if and when their erstwhile protector was overthrown. Clearly there were some areas, notably ones where the promotion of international norms could be effected without serious political risk, where rights were likely to be better established and maintained under the old order than during the first flush of popular government.

Revolutions involving the almost total overthrow of a long-entrenched political order encourage great expectations but also, as some of the harsh realities of their brave new world become apparent, give rise to some well-justified fears. As of early 2011 there was much reason to suppose that it would take many years for a new social contract, embodied in a new set of rules and institutions, to work itself out. There is an obvious sense that presidential monarchy is an easier concept to understand and to practice than popular republicanism. Transforming revolutionary enthusiasm into legitimate constitutional order was obviously going to prove much more difficult.

Possible Future Trajectories

Revolutions tend to thrive on two basic emotions: huge expectations and a fear of a counterrevolution that will sweep all the initial gains away. This does much to account for their speed, their confusion, and, in the case of Egypt and Tunisia, the insistent demands that all institutions of the old order be dissolved and its leading figures prosecuted for their part in its crimes. But what comes next? Fortunately, the revolutionary tradition also contains the beginning of an answer: a new constitution accompanied by new elections. For Egypt and Tunisia, it did indeed constitute what Bruce Ackerman and others have defined as a "constitutional moment" in which popular enthusiasm becomes deeply involved in deliberations about the public interest to the exclusion of more partisan concerns, and so providing a degree of popular legitimacy that all constitution-making processes must possess if the document itself is to provide both an acceptable blueprint for a new social contract and a workable system of allocating as well as constraining political power.

Yet it is during this moment, too, that the serious problems begin. Constitution making requires some machinery for general guidance as to the allocation of tasks, the ordering of priorities, and the establishment of a timetable according to which new institutional mechanisms are to be created and then legitimated by elections or referenda. It also requires a determined effort at involving the largest possible cross-section of the population in the discussion—and not just in the capital city—if it is to have the stamp of popular acceptance that the formula "we the people," used in the preamble to the U.S. Constitution, suggests.

Parties, too, have to be formed, representing particular constituencies with particular interests, and all this in the context of a prolonged absence of independent political activity under the old regime, unrealistic expectations among sections of the population combined with a desperate desire for a return to normalcy, among others, and, almost inevitably, the presence of a major economic crisis.

Guidance toward a new constitutional order was provided in Egypt by the Supreme Council of the Armed Forces, and in Tunisia by the 131-person Higher Political Reform Committee and its associated committees and subcommittees. Both were inevitably criticized for the way their members were selected, for their lack of accountability, and for the speed—or lack of it—by which they proceeded. Both could reasonably be accused of elitism and for failing to communicate their ideas fully to the waiting public.

Turning now to the question of parties and elections, although many commentators pointed to the problems posed by the lack of genuine political competition since independence, some of the ingredients for a popular politics did in fact exist in both Egypt and Tunisia. Both contained political groupings of one type of another, some, it is true, having been co-opted by the previous regime, but others more uncompromisingly oppositional, even if, as in the Tunisian case, they had been forced to operate mostly in exile. Both countries also contained a significant associational life in which it was generally assumed by both government and society at large that the population was divided into different groups—professionals, workers, women, students, and so on—with different corporate interests. And no one could deny the existence of such larger sectional interests as those of the rich and the poor, the rural and the urban, the young and the old, as well as those who identified themselves as practicing one religion or another.

It is out of these ingredients that one could reasonably expect parties with different appeals and different constituencies to arise. And this is, indeed, what began to happen in the first months after their respective revolutions, first with the need for men and women representing various movements of one kind or another to sit on committees or, in the case of Egypt, to negotiate with the military members of the Armed Forces Higher Council who held the political ring, then as protoparties, like the Coalition of the Youth Movement (CYR), with members identified by their activism or simply by their presence in a political leader's Facebook. Meanwhile, the first political programs began to appear, for example, the CYR's call for a national minimum wage, something that represented its close association with labor and the major strikes, which had been such a feature of the three years before the popular uprising itself.

Still, large questions remained. One concerned not only what parties would put themselves forward for the first free national elections in September 2011 but also what rules would apply regarding their registration, their campaigning, and their conduct on polling day itself. Second, what would be the relationship between the candidates who presented themselves for the first competitive presidential elections and the political movements and groupings that supported them? The question of religious political participation was also of enormous importance. In Egypt the first provisional parties law banned any group formed on a religious basis or on any form of discrimination between citizens, a ban that the Muslim Brothers initially planned to circumvent under the banner of a previously formed "Freedom and Justice" movement. In Tunisia it looked as though the leader of the Nahda Party, Rachid al-Ghannouchi, was thinking about just the same type of thing.

Two other questions loomed just as large. The first involved the future role of the military. Fortunately this was not a particular problem in Tunisia, where the commanders of what was only a relatively small army played no role in the revolution itself other than the crucial one of refusing Ben Ali's last-minute call to intervene. But in Egypt, where the army had always enjoyed a privileged position, its decision not to allow a military president left it with no formal mechanism for protecting its own interests other than, perhaps, claiming the Ministry of Defense.

The question of both countries' economic future was just as formidable. Both had experienced high levels of growth in the few years just before the revolutionary uprisings, based on outward-looking strategies involving lowering tariffs, reducing subsidies, and slimming the public sector, which would now prove very difficult to sustain in the face of even higher levels of unemployment. Both depended on an ability to attract foreign investment and tourism that was badly damaged by the insecurities of the revolutionary moment itself. Both could expect huge popular demands for more protectionist measures such as higher tariffs on local products and limiting the employment of foreign labor. And, as if this were not enough, there were other large problems involved in moving from a system of crony capitalism to one based on transparency and accountability. For a while at least, the fall and subsequent flight or imprisonment of the old economic elite led to an extreme shortage of capital due to old projects being put on hold as well as the general uncertainty produced by restrictions on capital flight and other activities, which saw overseas suppliers demanding cash in advance and many Egyptian and Tunisian businessmen waiting outside the country until they had a better sense of what the new economic order might be.

All was not necessarily doom and gloom, however. Large-scale economic assistance was on offer from the World Bank, the European Union, and, perhaps, the oil-rich Arab states of the Gulf. Enterprise could be expected to flourish more readily with the crony monopolists gone and tax revenues to be higher under a new and more democratic regime. And there remained islands of best economic practice that had flourished even under the heaviest of presidential hands, for example, Egypt's Suez Canal Authority and Tunisia's Ministry of Tourism—which were able to provide models for the management of other strategic sectors of the economy. Meanwhile, the prospect of enhanced public services held out the promise of both jobs and an improved quality of life. It would then be up to the politicians to create structures that allowed all of these putative advantages to express themselves to best effect.

The situation in the "tribal" systems of government is obviously different. No matter who is the ruler of Yemen, for example, he will have to operate the same system of management and negotiation within the same context of a lack of large state resources and of a fragmented and, often, well-armed population. Libya, too, will require careful management by anyone who succeeds Qaddafi although he will have more financial resources. Furthermore, each of the new rulers will be under pressure to get rid of the personalized patronage systems run by the former members of the presidents' families, as well as to ensure that state resources are much more fairly distributed than in the past. As for Sudan, where Hassan al-Bashir was under little pressure from his population during the first wave of protests elsewhere, even he felt it expedient to announce that he would retire when his current presidential term expires in 2015. Much can happen between now and then, but looked at from the vantage point of early 2011, it would seem reasonable to suppose that he would be succeeded by one of his military colleagues.

The Possibility of Counterrevolution

All revolutions face the possibility of a counterrevolution by disaffected members of the old regime. In Egypt, the first attempt came early, in the shape of a hastily arranged attack on the demonstrators in Tahrir Square by a motley collection of thugs, some of them temporarily unemployed tourist guides from the Pyramids riding their horses and camels. Its aim was obviously to make the country appear ungovernable, with the hope of persuading the army to clear the square. And though obviously a failure, it did much to persuade the young demonstrators that they had to try to root out all the members of the old regime and their state security allies before they were in a position to make a second attempt.

Counterrevolutions can also come in other forms. Some of the leaders of the youth rebellion feared that officials in the Mubarak regime's political party, the NDP, might use their skills to reenter parliament as elected members of some new organization. They also noted the continued practice of arbitrary arrests and torture by police officials who continued to be protected after the revolution by the Egyptian military. Lurking behind all this was a longer-term threat from the local equivalent of what in Turkey has come to be called the "deep state," that is, a network of officials and former officials with loyalties to the security services who have both the resources and the incentive to destroy an open postrevolutionary regime. Similar groups, known as the "silovaki," also exist in present-day Russia, consisting of anyone with a background in agencies that use force or coercion.[12] Clearly, the struggle to bring such groups under proper civilian control was going to take a great deal of time and effort by the newly elected governments that pluralism and political freedom were likely to bring.

HISTORICALLY, THE WORLD'S GREAT REVOLUTIONARY movements have taken years to work themselves out. Indeed, they cannot really be considered complete until a new political order blessed by constitutional rather than revolutionary legitimacy has been put firmly in place. As of early 2011 all that could be said with confidence is that the different revolutionary processes in the various Arab countries had a long, long way to go. And it remained just as likely that they would end with a new form of perhaps military-backed authoritarianism as with a fully functioning Western-style democracy with a set of well-developed rules and practices governing political accommodation between different competing parties and ideological movements. It could even be that, when the process is finally over, only Tunisia, with its substantial middle class and breadth of associational life, will have made the difficult transition from a system of presidents for life to one with the necessary balance between law, civil society, and government to prevent its return.

Writing early in 2011, I would pin my best hopes on one major set of factors: the end of the exceptionalism that produced so many similar presidential regimes up to 2010, coupled with the return of the Arab world to a place in the larger global historical processes that, on other continents, have allowed countries like South Korea and Brazil to make the necessary transition from a military or bureaucratic authoritarianism to a competitive party democracy.

Interaction with the larger world can be supportive of openness and democracy in many different ways. It provides useful information about different political practices. It allows for various processes of testing and experiment. It encourages an open-ended engagement with a country's own history and its own great men, something of particular importance to the Arab states where the previous authoritarian regimes insisted on placing everyone and everything in the straitjacket of a rigid version of the national narrative.

It is also important to note how different all this is from the previous practice of relying on foreign "democracy experts" sent from the United States and its war on terror allies, few of whom had any knowledge of Arabic and of the Arab world's previous political history. This is especially the case of Egypt, where the three decades of pluralist political practice before the Free Officers' revolution of 1952, with a quite regular alternation of governments and a parliamentary concern for ministerial accountability, had been dismissed by the Nasser regime as simply a process of social tyranny and needless division promoted by squabbling politicians.

So much for the early hopes rightly engendered by the Arab revolutions begun in 2011. Some no doubt will be quickly dashed. Others will be realized in complicated ways difficult to predict at this time.

But what is certain is that the era of multiple monarchical presidents for life had conclusively come to an end, with the president of Egypt and his sons in jail and the president of Tunisia in uncomfortable and precarious exile in Saudi Arabia. No more abuse of term limits; no more hereditary successions.

Conclusion

The era of Arab republican presidents for life was notable both for what it was and for how it ended. It began as a result of a necessary drive for sovereignty and independence that was marred from the start by its complicity with certain deeply unsatisfactory features of the postcolonial world that encouraged a particular form of authoritarian control, later institutionalized into something best described as a "mirror state" in which its presidents were encouraged not only to see what they wanted to see but also to imagine themselves as omnipotent, indispensable, and well loved by a grateful people in whose name they professed to govern. And it ended with an almost complete rejection of this form of semimonarchical government by many, or most, of their subject populations no longer able to stomach either the personal sense of humiliation this method of rule involved or the way in which it alienated them from their fellow citizens, whose humiliation they despised as much as their own.

Viewed chronologically, this is a story in three parts. First came the era of postindependence rootlessness leading to the creation of authoritarian political structures, flawed by their arbitrariness and bouts of gratuitous brutality and, increasingly, dominated by one man. Then, in the second part, the presidents who survived tended to become more monarchical in their ways, seeking to establish family dynasties with their associated inner circles of supporters, cronies, and lackeys. Finally, in the last part, the increasing political and economic contradictions that these structures necessarily engendered created enough popular resentment to lead either to their revolutionary overthrow—as in Egypt and Tunisia—or to a rumbling discontent that forced them to try to reform themselves from within, as in the remaining five presidential republics— Algeria, Libya, Syria, Sudan, and Yemen. I will isolate some of the main features of each of these parts in turn.

The Postcolonial Context

Few writers have attempted to depict the essential features of the postcolonial world in as dark a way as V. S. Naipaul. Nevertheless, there is a great deal in his stark depiction of it as a transitional and unstable stage in human history that seems to me to apply as much to the Arab region as to that of his chosen subject, sub-Saharan Africa. He writes:

> To be colonial was to know a kind of security, it was to inhabit a fixed world. . . . But in the new world I found the ground move below me. The new politics, the curious reliance of men on institutions they were yet working to undermine, the simplicity of belief and the hideous simplicity of actions, the corruption of causes, half-made societies that seemed doomed to remain half-made.[1]

Achille Mbembe made much the same point in 1992, when he described the "postcolony" as "characterized by a distinctive style of political improvisation, by a tendency to excess and lack of proportion. . . . It is a place where no divisions can be allowed to exist."[2]

Here, it seems to me, are the essential features of the dangerous and unstable context in which the early Arab presidents for life had to operate, and upon which they sought to impose their own type of order.

How they attempted to do this obviously depended on local circumstances. Nevertheless, one thing they had in common was a fixation on control. This can easily be seen at the political and ideological level by the way in which they sought to monopolize both the language and the practice of politics. It can also be seen as the begetter of a type of political arrangement in which the president, his family, and his cronies contrived to live in a closed world of mutual delusion in which everything was for the best and opposition was confined to a few, usually foreign-inspired, malcontents.

The Mirror State as a Form of Personal Government

The creation of systems that so closely mirrored presidential beliefs must have been a gradual process dependent on the institutionalized monopoly of all political activity in the hands of one long-serving president and his associated colleagues and cronies. At its center was the establishment of a coherent world of meaning in which the resources of an authoritarian state—its monopoly on political language, its control over the media, its management of the educational system, and so on—were put to the single use of presenting the image of an indispensable leader presiding over a grateful people.

Something of the way this took place in strong states with strong leaders like Egypt, Syria, and Tunisia has already been described in previous chapters. But the particular contribution of each president's own personality, and of the way this helped to shape the final outcome, can only be guessed at, given the almost complete lack of the necessary information on which such an exercise in biography must be based. We can surmise, for example, the importance of the corrosive effect of absolute power with its absence of checks and its nourishment of personal idiosyncrasies. We can also imagine the role of those who provide the ruler with support in the shape of information and advice, often, like Machiavellian courtiers, intent on flattering him and telling him only what they think he wants to hear.

Yet, in terms of hard facts, all that the outsider has to go on is a set of anecdotes and vignettes. We know, for example, some of the ways in which a president's independence of thought can be worn down by the sheer weight of flattery, further exacerbated at times of difficulty when extravagant professions of loyalty to the man at the helm seem especially de rigueur. There is a Mubarak who, despite the fact that he seems not to have wanted anything very much named after him, ended up, just before his fall, with hundreds, perhaps even thousands, of schools, streets, squares, and libraries that bore his and his wife's name, including a major subway station in central Cairo. There is a Bashar al-Asad appearing in public in Damascus at the start of the popular uprising against his rule in April 2011, surrounded by parliamentary supporters shouting his praise and members of an orchestrated crowd waving his picture. And there is a Qaddafi listening to crowds of supporters with their well-rehearsed chant of "Allah, Libya, Mu'ammar wa bas." We also have access to a particular form of presidential language, dutifully echoed by acolytes and officials throughout the land, replete with reminders of how the people love their leader and want what he wants.

Unfortunately, examples of this kind can only hint at the outlines of a larger system by which huge delusions about the true nature of government and of the actual relationship between government and people come to be intensified over time by an increasingly monarchical president supported by an inner circle of those who have a vested interest in his continued rule. Drawing on a few works by political psychologists like Jerrold M. Post, let my try to sketch out some of its most obvious components, bearing in mind that the construction and maintenance of the mirror state is always a work in progress, dependent on the ruler's age and length of time in office as well as his own personal and psychological characteristics.[3]

First and foremost is the significance that should be attached to the ruler's narcissism, seen most directly in his sense of the indispensability of his rule and his personal identification with the country and the people he rules, which he increasingly describes as "my" or "mine." This is usually accompanied by a sense of destiny, which may become particularly exaggerated in those rulers who have either survived attempts to kill them, such as Yasser Arafat or Muammar Qaddafi's, or whose country has been under direct attack, like Hafiz al-Asad or Gamal Abdel Nasser. Such narcissism, Post also argues, is likely to be accompanied by extreme self-confidence, the need for constant adulation, great sensitivity to criticism, difficulties in acknowledging ignorance, and a tendency to overestimate the probability of success. Just as significant is Post's observation that while narcissists can be assisted in achieving power by their appearance of great self-sufficiency, they may be consumed by self-doubt and feelings of inadequacy that drive them on in an endless search for attention and approval, making their abandonment of a heroic life unthinkable.[4] One thinks here of a Qaddafi continuing to imagine himself as the champion of the Arabs, or a Sadat proclaiming himself the "commander of the faithful" as a result of what seemed to him his God-given success in getting his troops across the Suez Canal in the 1973 war.

A second, and even more obvious, feature is the impact of a monarchical president's aging while in office. Some of this, for example, the narrowing of his inner circle of advisers, has already been mentioned in the case of Hafiz al-Asad and Hosni Mubarak. Just as important are Post's commonsense observations about a decline in judgment and intellectual ability, increased rigidity, a denial of physical disabilities, and a tendency toward marked fluctuations in personal behavior.[5] Often present too is a nostalgia for the past, and so a reliance on it for reassurance and to provide simple solutions to present difficulties.[6] Other factors may include an increased sense of urgency to accomplish long-stated goals, as well as, more worrying still, the way in which certain personality traits may become more exaggerated with old age, with distrust turning to paranoia, with an even greater dislike of critical advice, and, as observed in the case of Muammar Qaddafi, more and more "bad" days to balance the occasional "good" ones.[7]

Third, there is an aging president's response to any serious crisis that challenges his rule. On the one hand, loss of control, as Post observes, is "especially threatening to authoritarian personalities," impelling such persons to become particularly "repressive" at times of social unrest.[8] On the other, under pressure from the urgency, uncertainty, and surprise that necessarily accompany any major crisis, psychological traits, previously dormant or unnoticed, may now become decisive in directing a ruler's response, encouraging someone with paranoid tendencies to see his opponents as embodiments of evil, for example, while throwing others into a "panic-like state" marked by a "deterioration of judgment and an impairment of cognitive efficiency."[9] It is here that the observer, armed with enough information, may actually be able to discern some of the basic psychological features examined by Post, labeling some rulers—perhaps a Qaddafi or a Ben Ali—as paranoid, and so dysfunctional in a crisis, and others—perhaps an Omar al-Bashir or an Ali Abdullah Saleh—as compulsive, action-oriented personalities with a tendency toward instant response in situations where they might be better off looking before they leap.[10]

So much for the application of psychological theory. What we lack, or have lacked until recently, is the raw data required to use such insights to throw more light on the personalities of individual Arab republican presidents for life and on their influence on the way in which particular structures came to grow up around them, shaping them in important ways while at the same time being shaped by them. The narcissist, as we know, needs a mirror to reflect his own sense of worth. But it is a long way from this simple metaphor to understanding how a set of complex structures can be made to perform the same function. In my reading of Arab political systems, the only possible candidate for such an analysis is Qaddafi's Libya, and then only because so much can be learned from observing the leader and his inner circle on television and by reports of their attempts to steer outside perceptions of their rule during the crisis induced by the uprisings against them beginning in February 2011.

Whatever Qaddafi's mental state might have been when he first seized power in 1969, there is now some evidence to suggest that, over time, he developed the type of psychotic personality whose world must be rendered entirely predictable by becoming a closed entity in order to avoid psychic collapse.[11] This was certainly in evidence by the time of his interview with Italian journalist Oriana Fallaci in 1979, when he proclaimed to her that government no longer existed in Libya, that "the authority of the people is achieved, the dream is realized. The struggle is over." It was also on the same occasion, Fallaci reports, that he went on and on shouting that he was "the Gospel" for so long that "she had to quiet him down."[12]

We can imagine, too, that his associates, and then later his sons, sensing his condition and his needs, helped him to create a coherent system that protected his necessary sense of his own omnipotence, and then that they continued to pump up his personal image of himself as the beneficent guide of a loving people who only needed a bit of encouragement—or what Qaddafi himself has called "incitement"—to achieve great things. In functional terms, this would have had the double effect of calming him down, and so of preventing him from taking dangerous initiatives, while allowing his inner circle to get on with their own business of running the country—not always with his knowledge—and of feathering their own nests.

Support for such a hypothesis can be found in a number of recent episodes in Libya's history, without, of course, ever being able to pin it down for sure. There is Qaddafi's obvious need to seem to be in charge, to be in control. In day-to-day terms, this allowed him to operate without constraints, to treat the matter of government as something he could conduct without any consideration for the interests of others, for example, by keeping high officials waiting outside his tent for hours and hours while he entertained himself. Then there is the sense of omnipotence revealed in his interview with Oriana Fallaci when he told her that all the things she wished to discuss with him, apart from the teachings of his "Green Book," "bored" him profoundly.[13] Such, we may suppose, is the extreme narcissism of the man. Such is his deep underlying fragility.

Meanwhile, as far as Libya's relations with the rest of the world are concerned, Qaddafi has always tried to subvert organizations that he cannot control, like the Maghreb Union of North African States, while seeking fresh regions on which to try to impose his presence. Hence in 2010 he saw himself as the "King of Africa," bringing African heads of state to Libya and posturing before them in "African" costumes of his own design with absurd-looking little round caps. For him, it would seem, things can only be understood literally, at what seems to be their face value, the result, we might assume, of his limited ability to create metaphors and systems of meaning that others use to understand or to manage the world around him.

Clearly this is just a hypothesis. But it has the virtue of focusing on two, probably connected, central issues: each president's desire to control his own political environment combined with his own lack of personal boundaries. Some journalists have suggested much the same thing. Christopher Caldwell of the *Financial Times* imagines Hosni Mubarak during his very last days in office, a man he describes as a distant figure, stubborn, oblivious, late for a vital speech because there had never been anyone to insist that he be on time.[14] Other journalists have written of the way in which fallen dictators in exile never blame themselves for their overthrow, which they see as the result of a combination of some great world conspiracy and the terrible ingratitude of their own people.[15]

The System in Crisis
Opinions vary, and will obviously continue to vary, as to the weight of the specific causes that led most directly to the beginning of what soon

came to be called the "Arab Spring." Some, notably the advent of social networking by Twitter and other person-to-person communications and their ability to arouse and then focus dissent, are clearly of the greatest importance in bringing large crowds into the street. Nevertheless, it can certainly be argued that to find the basic causes of the wider popular discontent one should look rather at the changes in the political economy in the previous few years, as well as, more specifically, the growing impact of poverty, unemployment, and inequality, with their consequent deleterious effect on personal dignity and on hope.

True, this does not square with the widely held assumption that, prior to 2010, the two countries whose economies seemed to be performing the best in terms of annual growth—Egypt and Tunisia—were just the ones where the old political regimes fell the most quickly. Nor with the equally widely held belief that both economies had managed to weather the 2008 global downturn in international trade and tourism without too much difficulty. But, as the editors of the Winter 2010–2011 edition of *Maghreb/Machrek* argue, such conventional wisdom masked the basic failure of what they call the model of "authoritarian stability" and its inability to manage either the social question in the short run or the longer-term transition to a successful market economy open to global economic forces.[16] Based as it was on lack of transparency, institutionalized corruption, and the use of a tax system to reward and punish, its drive toward economic liberalization benefited only the middle class while leaving the bulk of the population unprotected.[17] If we add the impact of privatization and the removal of subsidies, as well as the effects of the rapidly rising prices that began to affect the Middle East in 2008, we see the makings of the perfect storm that undermined the old system of political management, leaving the republican presidents with no option but either to fight or to run.

Whatever new political orders emerge, they will have to deal with all the same problems and all the same challenges in the shape of youth unemployment, underfunded educational systems, and the other formidable obstacles in the way of creating a competitive knowledge-based economy. Clearly the impact of the long period of rule by presidents for life will continue for many decades after the presidents themselves are finally gone.

Afterword

Three years after the "fall" of several of the Arab presidents for life in the popular uprisings of early 2011 is a good time to look back at the reasons for their overthrow, as well as the various attempts that followed to create a new constitutional order. A good time, too, to examine the efforts of those, like the presidents of Sudan, Syria, and Yemen, who chose either to stand and fight or, in the case of the last, to make enough concessions to remain near the center of power. The well-entrenched Arab monarchies in Jordan and Morocco, though assailed by popular protest, have emerged more or less intact.

The first point to make is that though the uprisings of 2011 had much the same revolutionary character of mass protests against a corrupt and autocratic regime, the processes that followed, though superficially the same in terms of timetables, etc., followed paths largely determined by each nation's history, institutions, demography, and much more. This was particularly true of the two countries in the vanguard of change, Egypt and Tunisia, one of which ended up under military rule, and the other with a democratically elected parliament containing parties willing to make sufficient concessions to allow the government to begin to address many of the social and economic problems—such as high levels of youth unemployment—that had produced the revolutionary situation in the first place.

In what follows I will look first at the three North African states—Egypt, Libya, and Tunisia—in which the old order was overthrown in a matter of a few months, then Algeria and Sudan, where for reasons that need to be separately discussed, the management of the state remained more or less intact, although often beset by major difficulties. Lastly, I will turn to the countries of the eastern Arab world—Syria, Lebanon, Iraq, and Yemen—where existing systems of rule survived the uprisings yet often at very great cost to the social fabric, including the rise of more insidious types of political sectarianism dividing not just Sunni and Shi'i populations but also exacerbating dangerous divisions within each.

To begin with there was a considerable exchange of ideas and practices between Tunisia, where the uprisings started, and Egypt, where the vast crowds in Tahrir Square led by what is best described as "revolutionary youth" were soon instrumental in persuading the army that President Hosni Mubarak should step down in March 2011. These included above all the setting of a timetable leading, via elections, to the writing of a new and legitimate constitution laying the ground rules for a new constitutional order. Then, given the presence in each country of a well-organized and seemingly uncorrupt religious party, the Muslim Brothers in Egypt and the Nahda in Tunisia, it was more or less inevitable that members of these parties would not only win the first elections but also form the first post-revolutionary governments. It was equally inevitable that these same parties would soon run into a whole variety of difficulties stemming from a combination of their lack of administrative experience, the need to cater to the needs and expectations of their followers—including their demand for public sector jobs—and the huge economic challenges both countries faced.

Yet looked at with the perspective of time, the differences between the two experiences seem to have been at least as great, if not greater. In Tunisia, President Zein El Abidine Ben Ali fled the country in the first few days of the uprising, but in Egypt, Hosni Mubarak remained under house arrest, soon to become a rallying point for those anxious to preserve the economic and social status quo. The role of the army was also different: the Egyptian force was both much larger in size and much more dependent on US military assistance, a fact skillfully used by the Obama administration to persuade the commanders constituting the Supreme Council of the Armed Forces to force the president to step aside, a move taken all the more willingly because of the commanders' dislike of Mubarak's civilian son and proposed heir, Gamal.

From then on, and for better or worse, the Egyptian army became one of the essential arbiters of the revolution's fate, making a deal with the Muslim Brothers to allow one of its leaders, Mohamed Morsi, to become president in June 2012, and then removing him in a coup in July 2013 when he and his enthusiastic followers were adjudged to have become a threat to military interests. Once again, if looked at in terms of the revolutionary calendar established in the 1790s, this could be viewed as the moment when a military figure like Napoleon Bonaparte appears, clearing the streets of Paris with his famous "whiff of grapeshot" in October 1795 as a prelude to creating an autocratic Bonapartist state.

Tunisia, blessed as it were by Ben Ali's decision to allow only a relatively small army, was prevented from following the same path. Nor was it important enough to incur any particular American interest. What it also possessed was a relatively efficient police force far more adept at crowd control than the Egyptian one and useful at keeping order once the initial revolutionary commotion had died down. Thus it was that the Tunisian politicians obtained a little space in which to practice the arts of alliance building and conciliation, providing themselves with a weak presidency in the process as well as an institutionalized group of expert "wise" men to advise them on the vexing problems of the day, including what to do with the state properties forcibly annexed by some of Ben Ali's cronies, foremost among them his grasping wife, Leila Trebelsi. Lastly, Tunisia benefited from something else not to be found in Egypt: a vibrant civil society containing an influential group of young activists anxious to make absolutely sure both that the spirit of democracy continues to inform the political class between elections and that human rights for all are properly protected.

In Libya, the dramatic ousting of its flamboyant and vicious citizen leader, Muammar Qaddafi, as a result of a combination of internal uprisings and foreign intervention, was followed by an even more difficult process of transition than in its two North African neighbors. For one thing, Libya was hardly a unitary state to begin with, being cobbled together after the Second World War from three disparate provinces and then largely held together by a combination of fear and oil. For another, once its largely mercenary army crumbled, there was no single military force to take its place in a country awash with arms of every possible type. Then, too, the members of its small elite, though possessing many of the necessary administrative skills, were almost all tainted by their association with the old Qaddafi regime. The result was a situation much more like that of a failed state than of the long- and well-established polities of Egypt and Tunisia. Libya found itself with a weak central administration that experienced the greatest difficulty in either policing its borders or using its oil wealth to buy off a restive population, militant sections of which were just as likely to try to sell the oil themselves as to accept it as government largesse. From this, too, stemmed the worry that the draft constitution that finally emerged in late 2014 after months of fractious debate would remain like many other constitutions around the world a document honored more in the breech than by its observance.

Turn now to consider the case of the presidents who decided to fight back in Sudan, Syria, and Yemen. Sudan's Omar al-Bashir seems to have had the easiest task, given the fact that the popular challenges he faced were quite easily contained by a reasonably efficient army and police backed by the revenues he received from the country's oil wealth and the financial support he received from other Arab regimes to the east. True, he had to allow the secession of the provinces of the south. True, too, that he was named a war criminal for using one part of the population of the western province of Darfur to attack and control the other. Yet all this was offset by the support he seems to have received from his fellow generals, happy, it would appear, to let him take responsibility for Sudan's many woes in the confidence that, having no son, there was little chance he would try to create a family dynasty of his own.

Bashar al-Asad's struggle to keep power in Syria was much more violent once he had made the great initial mistake of shooting down the unarmed demonstrators in Damascus who were demanding reforms he largely agreed to but which he was only willing to enact from a position of strength. What saved him was the loyalty and brutal efficiency of his army, supported by weapons and other aid he received from Russia and Iran. But at what cost in terms of the staggering amount of destruction, displacement, and loss of life, which will not only take decades to recover from but leave the country's children—and future leaders—deeply scarred by patchy education they have received, not to speak of the deeper trauma inspired by fear, violence, and distrust. What also remains to be seen is whether Bashar will still try to ensure that his son succeeds him, as he succeeded his father, or whether that will be deemed impossible in the face of both popular and international outrage.

Lastly, the case of President Ali Abdullah Saleh of Yemen is unusual. He managed to preserve some of his authority in the face of demonstrations by student activists and others by agreeing to a plan for political transition put forward by his neighbors in the Gulf Cooperation Council, supported by Saudi Arabia. This called for him to hand over power to his vice president, Abd Al-Rabbih Mansur Hadi, who as head of a national unity government was charged with drafting a new constitution and holding new elections by the end of 2014. Yet such was his long-term experience of governing his fractious and divided country, Saleh continued to retain considerable power and influence, aided by his son, an army general. In this there are distinct echoes of the situation in Sudan, where the difficult skills required to manage a geographically large and tribally divided country are those more of the mediator and conciliator than of a military man able to impose his will by force. The need for these same skills is widely recognized in the east of the Arab world as well as by important members of the international community, notably the Americans, who fear that a weakened Sudan or Yemen could easily become a safe home and a training ground for jihadi militants.

The notion of the two other Arab presidents, in Lebanon and Iraq, amending their respective constitutions to obtain more than one (six year) or two (four year) terms respectively is impossible to entertain for many reasons. Both hold office as part of an arrangement designed to ensure harmony between their country's sections. Both have considerably less power than the prime minister, the chief of the army and, in Lebanon, the speaker of the Parliament. Not so in Algeria, though, where for historical reasons the risings of the Arab Spring were much more muted than elsewhere, with few among the popular forces wanting to return to the bloody situation that obtained during the violent civil war of the early 1990s.

Nevertheless, Algeria does have something to contribute to the story of the rise and fall of presidents for life. President Abdelaziz Bouteflika is not only the last of the Arab presidents to amend the constitution to remove the two-term limit in 2006 but also, at the time of this writing in 2014, is a woefully sick man of 76 seemingly determined to rise from his hospital bed in Paris to run for an unprecedented fourth term. And ludicrous though this might seem to many outsiders, there is good reason to suppose that he may easily succeed, given his and his local associates' obvious power to make it almost impossible for anyone else to get onto the ballot to oppose him. Bouteflika is regarded as safe by the generals who are the real power in the country. And it would seem that, in the usual way, his continuation in office is perceived by many powerful Algerian business leaders, inside and outside the gas and oil sector, as a reliable guarantee of continuity and a barrier to radical change. As so many times before in the Arab world and elsewhere, the known is perceived as safer than the unknown. And certainly much less costly in terms of remaking alliances with new political partners. Yet, as I hope readers of this book will recognize at once, the peace of mind that comes from association with a well-tried and tested leader can so easily be disturbed by worries about his health, his popularity, and, in the last resort, his disposability by a younger and much more energetic rival.

What are the general lessons to be derived from the impact of the revolutionary events of 2011 on the system of presidents for life? I will list five.

1. The republican form of government is a difficult one to establish in new states in which the notion of popular sovereignty can easily be overwhelmed by the perceived need for a powerful president to protect the national interest. Then, after the overthrow of a strong man by a large section of the people comes the problem of drawing up a new constitution to create a system of representative government via the formation of political parties, while limiting the powers of the president compared to those of the prime minister and other elected officials. And all this in an unruly climate of great excitement, enthusiasm, and agitation.

2. Although the revolutionary processes that took place in Egypt, Tunisia, Libya, and elsewhere had many things in common, the final outcome was the result of significant local differences in terms of institutional structures, traditions, and even simple size. It mattered greatly whether the president fled, was executed or, like Hosni Mubarak, stayed to be tried for various crimes. It mattered whether the army was large or small. And it mattered whether or not the nonreligious political forces were skilled and experienced enough to create mass parties able to challenge the scope and appeal of the religious ones.

3. The need to develop new systems of government encouraged constitution makers and then, sometimes, the new governments, to consider a wide range of possible forms from the parliamentary to the Bonapartist and the syndicalist, particularly in Egypt. Bonapartism of the kind developed by Emperor Napoleon III was bound to have some appeal to military rulers like General Abdel-Fatah Al-Sisi, consisting as it does of a powerful presidency legitimated by popular referendums and an emphasis on a strong army with a bellicose foreign policy. Syndicalism of the type developed in Mussolini's Italy provides a possible way of incorporating sections of the population into the political system on the basic of workplace identity rather than individual ideology or preference.

4. A major source of difference was the nature of civil society, its institutions and traditions, and the opportunities it provided for alternatives to state-sector employment in the new, post-2011 era, when budgets were tighter and international support dependent on lowering the public payroll. By and large it seems that it was easier for unemployed Tunisians to find work in such activities as cross-border smuggling than it was for their Egyptian and Libyan counterparts.

5. To step outside the world of republics, it should be noted that the two major Arab monarchies, though not exempt from waves of popular criticism, managed to survive by making only limited concessions to the demonstrators. In part this was due to their more tempered use of the same types of security systems as their republican neighbors, and in part to the mere fact of monarchy, which placed their dynastic form of succession beyond serious criticism while allowing some form of family selection to ensure that the crown prince was both experienced and tough enough to cope with all future possible eventualities. There was even space to use the new constitutions forced upon them by the Arab Spring to introduce much more humane and sophisticated forms of human rights regimes, as in Morocco, which became, for example, the first Arab state to recognize the particular category of "political refugee."

In conclusion, what pointers do the events of 2011–2014 give to the political future of the Arab presidential republics? What can be said for sure is that the process of political change has a long way to go before future stability can be assured. Even in Tunisia there is every sign that presidents, legislators, and others still want to tinker with different parts of the system, particularly the rules relating to parliamentary elections, whether they relate to the boundaries of constituencies, the numbers of members per constituency, or the use of proportional representation as opposed to the British method of one man/one vote. This is to be regretted, as historical evidence suggests that parliamentary systems would appear to work best when there is some stability, and so some predictability, concerning the methods used. Yet, after a period of such revolutionary intensity it would be utopian to expect everything to settle down that quickly.

What can also be expected with some degree of certitude is that the present use of highly charged and highly divisive political language will also continue, with political rivals routinely referring to their opponents as "evil" men, "terrorists," "fascists," or even worse. Just why this development occurred in countries with reasonable traditions of public civility is unclear. But it must have something to do with the invasion of language drawn both from a religious and a sectarian vocabulary, as well as, perhaps, with the fact that the political stakes relating to power and control over the post-despotic futures are now so high.

On the more positive side, it is to be hoped that, for the bulk of the political classes in the Arab republics the events of the last three years will be seen as a vital learning process in the arts of compromise, accommodation, and concession, the more so as examples of these virtues, as well as what can happen when they are set aside, abound. One such example would be the way in which the Tunisian religious leader Rachid Al-Ghannouchi is said to have moderated his pursuit of certain goals when he saw what had happened as a result of the intransigence of Mohamed Morsi and the Muslim Brotherhood elite in Egypt.

As this book seeks to demonstrate, the era of the Republican Presidents for Life lasted long enough to have an enormous effect on the conduct of Arab political life, just as it did in other parts of the former colonial world. And though it now seems destined to give way to a period of greater pluralism and accountability, encouraged by a spate of new constitutionally created structures, there is little reason to suppose that this will be a smooth and easy transformation, with publics divided between an enthusiasm for change and an equally strong desire for law, order, and stability.

February 2014

Notes

Introduction

1. For example, Jason Brownlee, "Hereditary succession in modern autocracies," *World Politics*, 59/4 (July 2007), 595–628; Kristina Kauch, "Presidents for life: Managed successions and stability in the Arab world," Fundación para las Relaciones Internacionales y el Diálogo Exterior Working Paper no. 104 (Madrid, November 2010); Larbi Sadiki, "Like father, like son: Dynastic republicanism in the Middle East," Policy Outlook no. 52 (Washington, DC: Carnegie Endowment for International Peace, 2009). See also the bibliography at the end of this book.

2. For example, Muhammad Abdul Aziz and Youssef Hussein, "The president, the son and military succession in Egypt," *Arab Studies Journal*, 9/11 (Fall 2001/Spring 2002), 73–100; Robert Springborg and John Sfakianakis, "The military's role in presidential succession," *Les notes de l'Ifri* (Institution Français de Relations Internationales), 31 (February 2001), 57–72.

3. Steffen Hertog, *Princes, Brokers and Bureaucrats: Oil and the State in Saudi Arabia* (Ithaca, NY: Cornell University Press, 2010), 3.

4. Holger Albrecht, "How do regimes work? Formal rules and informal mechanisms in Middle Eastern politics," in Eberhard Kienle, ed., *Democracy Building and Democracy Erosion* (London: al-Saqi Books, 2009), 235.

5. Mubarak, personal information. For Qaddafi see Dirk Vandewalle, *Libya in the Twenty-First Century* (Cambridge: Cambridge University Press, 2006), 177.

6. International Crisis Group, "Reshuffling the cards? Syria's evolving strategy," *Middle East Report* no. 92 (14 December 2009), 4.

1. The Search for Sovereignty in an Insecure World

1. Mohammed Ayoob, *The Third World Security Predicament: State Making, Regional Conflict and the International System* (Boulder, CO: Lynne Rienner, 1995), 4. Also Jean-François Bayart, *The State in Africa: The Politics of the Belly*, 2nd ed., trans. Stephen Ellis (Cambridge: Polity Press, 2009), 218–227.
2. Gamal Abdel Nasser, *Egypt's Liberation: The Philosophy of the Revolution*, intro. Dorothy Thompson (Washington, DC: Public Affairs Press, 1955), 43.
3. Eliezer Be'eri, "The waning of the military coup in Arab politics," *Middle Eastern Studies*, 18/1 (1982), 69–128, table 1.
4. Ibid., 75–76.
5. Kristina Kauch, "Presidents for life: Managed successions and stability in the Arab world," Fundación para las Relaciones Internacionales y el Diálogo Exterior Working Paper no. 104 (Madrid, November 2010), 10.
6. Ibid., 11.

2. The Origins of the Presidential Security State

1. Sami Zubaida, *Islam, the People and the State: Political Ideas and Movements in the Middle East*, 2nd ed. (London: I. B. Tauris, 1993), 122.
2. Gamal Abdel Nasser, speech delivered on the occasion of the eleventh anniversary of the revolution, July 22, 1963 (Cairo: Information Department, 1963).
3. Jean Lacouture, *The Demigods: Charismatic Leadership in the Third World*, trans. Patricia Wolf (New York: Knopf, 1970), 151.
4. Béchir Ben Yahmed, "Le pouvoir personnel," *Afrique-Action* no. 53, 7–13 October 1961, quoted in Lacouture, *The Demigods*, 172.
5. Quoted in Lacouture, *The Demigods*, 173.
6. *Le Quotidien d'Oran*, 16 March 2004, quoted in Isabelle Werenfels, *Managing Instability in Algeria: Elites and Political Change since 1995* (London: Routledge, 2007), 2.
7. Lacouture, *The Demigods*, 119ff.
8. Ibid., 123.
9. Jean-François Bayart, *The State in Africa: The Politics of the Belly*, 2nd ed., trans. Stephen Ellis (Cambridge: Polity Press, 2009), 207–227.

10. Michael Hudson, *Arab Politics: The Search for Legitimacy* (New Haven, CT: Yale University Press, 1977), appendix, 405–410.

11. James T. Quinlivan, "Coup-proofing: Its practical consequences in the Middle East," *International Security*, 24/2 (Fall 1999), 131–165.

12. Philippe Droz-Vincent, *Moyen-Orient: Pouvoirs authoritaires: Sociétés bloquées* (Paris: Presses Universitaires de France, 2004), 209.

13. Quoted by David Hirst, "The terror from Tikrit," *The Guardian*, 26 November 1971, 15.

14. Lacouture, *The Demigods*, 15.

15. Ibid., 108.

16. Ibid., 110.

17. Ibid., 113.

18. Ibid., 120.

19. Ibid., 122–122.

20. Dirk Vandewalle, *A History of Modern Libya* (Cambridge: Cambridge University Press, 2006), 127.

21. Lacouture, *The Demigods*, 124.

22. Ibid., 125.

23. Tawfiq al-Hakim, *The Return of Consciousness*, trans. Bayly Winder (New York: New York University Press, 1985), 24.

24. Lacouture, *The Demigods*, 135.

25. Ibid., 152.

26. Ibid., 176.

27. Ibid., 177.

28. Ibid., 191.

29. Lisa Wedeen, *Ambiguities of Domination: Politics, Rhetoric and Symbols in Contemporary Syria* (Chicago: University of Chicago Press, 1999), 6.

30. Ibid., 29.

31. Ibid., 34–35, 48, 149.

32. Ibid., 34.

33. Ibid., 55–60.

34. Ibid., 60.

35. Ibid., 27–28.

3. Basic Components of the Regimes

1. Nazih Ayubi, *Over-stating the Arab State: Politics and Society in the Middle East* (London: I. B. Tauris, 1995), 394.

2. *House of Saddam*, Episode 1, BBC2, 30 July 2008. The original quotation is from an exchange between Saddam and a citizen broadcast on Iraqi television (information from Sinan Antoon).

3. "US Embassy Cables: Gaddhafi's modest life style," Tripoli, 5 May 2006, in Guardian.co.uk, 18 December 2010. Later the complex was revealed to sit athwart an extensive set of underground bunkers.

4. Patrick Seale, *Asad of Syria: The Struggle for the Middle East* (London: I. B. Tauris, 1988), 340.

5. For example, ibid., 342.

6. Evidence from Egypt from Chibli Telhami.

7. Information from Joseph Sassoon.

8. Robert Baer (former CIA operative), "Assad's Alawite army still calls all the shots," *Financial Times*, 31 March 2011.

9. Robert Springborg, *Mubarak's Egypt: Fragmentation of the Political Order* (Boulder, CO: Westview Press, 1989), 15, 195.

10. Ibid., 15.

11. Samer Soliman, *The Autumn of Dictatorship: Fiscal Crisis and Political Change in Egypt under Mubarak* (Stanford, CA: Stanford University Press, 2011), 106.

12. Max Rodenbeck, "A special report on Egypt: The long wait," *The Economist*, 15 July 2010, 13; Springborg, *Mubarak's Egypt*, 15.

13. Reem Leila, "Ongoing emergency," *Al-Ahram Weekly*, 3–9 June 2010.

14. Soliman, *The Autumn of Dictatorship*, 299–300; Amnesty Report 2009, quoted in Rodenbeck, "Special report," 13.

15. Rodenbeck, "Special report," 13.

16. Robert Springborg, "Civilian control of Arab armed forces: Lessons from non-Arab experiences" (unpublished manuscript).

17. Dirk Vandewalle, *A History of Modern Libya* (Cambridge: Cambridge University Press, 2006), 150.

18. Yezid Sayigh, "'Fixing broken windows': Security reform in Palestine, Lebanon and Yemen," Carnegie Paper (Washington, DC: Carnegie Endowment for International Peace, 2009).

19. Riad Ziadeh, *Power and Policy in Syria: Intelligence Services, Foreign Relations and Democracy in the Modern Middle East* (London: I. B. Tauris, 2011), 21.

20. "US Embassy Cables: Gaddafi's modest life style."

21. Bassam Haddad, "Business as usual in Syria?," Middle East Report Press Information Note (U.S.), no. 66 (7 September 2001).

22. Lina Saigol, "Assad cousin accused of favouring the family," *Financial Times*, 21 April 2011.

23. Haddad, "Business as usual."

24. Daniel Brumberg, "Liberalisation versus democracy," in Thomas Carothers and Marina Ottaway, eds., *Uncharted Journey: Promoting Democracy in the Middle East* (Washington, DC: Carnegie Endowment for International Peace, 2005), 23.

25. Hugh Roberts, "Algeria: The subterranean logics of a non-election," Real Instituto Elcano, ARI 68/2009, 22 April 2009.

26. Lisa Blaydes, *Elections and Distributive Politics in Mubarak's Egypt* (Cambridge: Cambridge University Press, 2011), 2–3.

27. Mona El-Gorbashy, "The liquidation of Egypt's illiberal experiment," Middle East Research and Information Project, *MER Online*, 29 December 2010, http://www.merip.org/mero/mero122910.

28. See, e.g., Holger Albrecht, "How do regimes work? Formal rules and informal mechanisms in Middle Eastern politics," in Eberhard Kienle, ed., *Democracy Building and Democracy Erosion* (London: al-Saqi Books, 2009), 240.

29. Rodenbeck, "Special report."

30. Figures from the Tunisian Institut National de la Statistique, http://www.ins.nat.tn/indexen.php, accessed 2 March 2011.

31. Eva Bellin, "Coercive institutions and coercive leaders," in Marsha Pripstein Posusney and Michele Penner Angrist, eds., *Authoritarianism in the Middle East: Regimes and Resistance* (Boulder, CO: Lynne Rienner, 2005), 29.

4. Centralized State Systems in Egypt, Tunisia, Syria, and Algeria

1. Kirk J. Beattie, *Egypt during the Nasser Years: Ideology, Politics and Civil Society* (Boulder, CO: Westview Press, 1994), 120–121.

2. Ibid., 122.

3. Information from Tarek el-Bishri.

4. P. J. Vatikiotis, *Nasser and His Generation* (London: Croom Helm, 1978), 164.

5. Jean Lacouture, *The Demigods: Charismatic Leadership in the Third World*, trans. Patricia Wolf (New York: Knopf, 1970), 130.

6. Beattie, *Egypt during the Nasser Years*, 210, 215.

7. Anwar Sadat, *In Search of Identity*, quoted in David Hirst and Irene Beeson, *Sadat* (London: Faber and Faber, 1981), 100.

8. Hirst and Beeson, *Sadat*, 212–213.

9. Ibid.

10. John Waterbury, *The Egypt of Nasser and Sadat: The Political Economy of Two Regimes* (Princeton, NJ: Princeton University Press, 1983), 368.

11. Helen Chapin Metz, "The president and the power elite," in *Egypt: A Country Study* (Washington, DC: Federal Research Division, Library of Congress, 1990), chapter 4, 2.

12. Aamer S. Abu-Qarn, J. Paul Dunne, Yasmine M. Abdelfattah, and Shadwa Zaher, "The demand for military spending in Egypt," School of Economics, University of the West of England, Discussion Paper Series (March 2010), 5, http://carecon.org.uk/DPs/1001.pdf.

13. Eberhard Kienle, "More than a response to liberalism: The political de-liberalization of Egypt in the 1990s," *Middle East Journal*, 52/2 (Spring 1998), 219–235.

14. Ibid., 235.

15. Information from Shibli Telhami.

16. Bruce K. Rutherford, *Egypt after Mubarak: Liberalism, Islam, and Democracy in the Arab World* (Princeton, NJ: Princeton University Press, 2008), 211.

17. Larbi Sadiki, "Like father, like son: Dynastic republicanism in the Middle East," Policy Outlook no. 52 (Washington, DC: Carnegie Endowment for International Peace, 2009), 5.

18. Ibid.

19. Clement H. Moore, "The single party as a source of legitimacy," in Samuel P. Huntington and Clement H. Moore, eds., *Authoritarian Politics in Modern Society: The Dynamics of Established One-Party Systems* (New York: Basic Books, 1970), 327.

20. Ibid., 330.

21. Kenneth J. Perkins, *A History of Modern Tunisia* (Cambridge: Cambridge University Press, 2004), 181.

22. Ibid., 206.

23. Ibid., 203.

24. Nicolas Beau and Jean-Pierre Tuqoi, *Notre Ami Ben Ali: L'envers du "miracle tunisien"* (Paris: La Découverte, 1999), 28–29.

25. Ibid., 13.

26. Rachid Khechana, "Tunisia on the eve of presidential and parliamentary elections: Organising a pro-forma democracy," Arab Reform Initative, 13 October 2009, 1, http://www.arab-reform.net/spip.php?article2412.

27. Quoted in Heba Saleh, "Tunisia keeps 'single-party mentality,'" *Financial Times*, 23 October 2009.

28. Eric Grobe, "Deceptive liberal reforms: Institutional adjustments and the dynamics of authoritarianism in Tunisa (1997–2005)," in Eberhard Kienle, ed., *Democracy Building and Democracy Erosion* (London: al-Saqi Books, 2009), 101.

29. Beatrice Hibou, *La force de l'obéissance: Economie politique de la répression en Tunisie* (Paris: La Découverte, 2006), 95.

30. Beatrice Hibou, "Domination and control in Tunisia: Economic levers for the exercise of authoritarian power," *Review of African Political Economy*, 108 (2006), 185–206.

31. Perkins, *A History of Modern Tunisia*, 198.

32. Hibou, *La force de l'obéissance*, 44.

33. Grobe, "Deceptive liberal reforms," 94.

34. *New York Times*, World Briefing (AP), 27 November 2009.

35. Florence Beaugé, "Tunisia: Political vengeance," *Le Monde*, 30 January 2010.

36. Patrick Seale, *Asad of Syria: The Struggle for the Middle East* (London: I. B. Tauris, 1988), 318.

37. Raymond A. Hinnebusch, *Authoritarian Power and State Formation in Ba'thist Syria: Army, Party and Peasant* (Boulder, CO: Westview Press, 1990), 145–149.

38. Bassam Haddad, "Asad and after: Syria between continuity and change," paper presented at Georgetown University, 11 October 2003.

39. Seale, *Asad*, 334.

40. Ibid., 426.

41. Haddad, "Asad and after."

42. Ibid.

43. Radwan Ziadeh, *Power and Policy in Syria: Intelligence Services, Foreign Relations and Democracy in the Modern Middle East* (London: I. B. Tauris, 2011), 56; Bashar al-Asad, "President Bashar al-Assad: Inaugural address," Syrian Arab News Agency, 2000, http://www.al-bab.com/arab/countries/syria/basharooa.htm, accessed 2 March 2011.

44. Ziadeh, *Power and Policy in Syria*, 57–61.

45. Bassam Haddad, "Reshuffling the cards? (I): Syria's new hand," *Middle East Report*, no. 93 (16 December 2009), 7–8.

46. Ibid., 18–19.

47. Haddad, "Asad and after."

48. Jay Solomons, "Syria cracks open its frail economy," *Wall Street Journal*, 1 September 2009.

49. Hugh Roberts, "Demilitarizing Algeria," in Marina Ottaway and Julia Choucair-Vizoso, eds., *Beyond the Façade: Political Reform in the Arab World* (Washington, DC: Carnegie Endowment for International Peace, 2008), 9.

50. Ibid., 138.

51. E.g., Isabelle Werenfels, *Managing Instability in Algeria: Elites and Political Change since 1995* (London: Routledge, 2007), 59; Mohamed Benchicou, *Bouteflika: Une imposture algérienne* (Paris: J. Picollec, 2004), 37–39.

52. Werenfels, *Managing Instability*, 58.

53. Isabelle Werenfels, "Algeria: System continuity through elite change," in Volker Perthes, ed., *Arab Elites: Negotiating the Politics of Change* (Boulder, CO: Lynne Rienner, 2004), 189.

54. U.S. Department of State, Bureau of Near Eastern Affairs, "Background Note: Algeria," http://www.state.gov/r/pa/ei/bgn/8005.htm, accessed 24 February 2011.

55. Ahmed Aghrout and Yahia H. Zoubir, "Introducing Algeria's president-for-life," Middle East Research and Information Project, *MER Online*, 1 April 2009, http://www.merip.org/mero/mero040109.

56. Oxford Business Group, "The report: Algeria 2010," http://www.oxford businessgroup.com/country/Algeria/2010, 12.

57. Information from Hugh Roberts.

58. See, e.g., "Said Bouteflika obtient de nouvelles functions après la reelection de son frère," *El Khaber*, 17 June 2009.

5. Presidents as Managers in Libya, Sudan, and Yemen

1. Max Rodenbeck, review of Victoria Clark, *Yemen: Dancing on the Heads of Snakes, New York Review of Books*, 30 September 2010, 39.

2. Sheila Carapico, *Civil Society in Yemen: The Political Economy of Activism in Modern Arabia* (Cambridge: Cambridge University Press, 1998), 203.

3. Dirk Vandewalle, *A History of Modern Libya* (Cambridge: Cambridge University Press, 2006), 101.

4. Ibid., 85, 105, 130.

5. I am indebted to Dr. Judith Gurewich for this suggestion.

6. For example, Vandewalle, *A History of Modern Libya*, 99.

7. Dirk Vandewalle, *Libya since Independence: Oil and State Building* (Ithaca, NY: Cornell University Press, 1998), 158.

8. Ibid., 158.

9. Vandewalle, *A History of Modern Libya*, 185, 190.

10. Larbi Sadiki, "Like father, like son: Dynastic republicanism in the Middle East," Policy Outlook no. 52 (Washington, DC: Carnegie Endowment for International Peace, 2009), 8.

11. Ibid., 8.

12. Landon Thomas, "Reinventing Libya," *New York Times*, 1 March 2010.

13. Rachid Khechana, "Bedouinocratic Libya: Between hereditary succession and reform," Arab Reform Initiative, 29 January 2010, 2.

14. Ibid., 2–3.

15. Quoted in Landon Thomas Jr., "Memo from Tripoli: Unknotting father's reins in hope of 'reinventing' Libya," *New York Times*, 28 February 2010.

16. Ian Black, "Gaddfi's son retreats on human rights," *The Guardian*, 16 December 2010.

17. Alex de Waal, "Dolarised," *London Review of Books*, 24 June 2010, 38–41.

18. Ibid.

19. "President Bashir declared winner of Sudan poll," *BBC World News*, 26 April 2010.

20. Sadiki, "Like father, like son," 4.

21. Jillian Schwedler, *Faith in Moderation: Islamist Parties in Jordan and Yemen* (Cambridge: Cambridge University Press, 2006), 58.

22. "Yemen leader rules himself out of polls," Al-Jazeera (English), Archive, 17 July 2005.

23. "Yemen: In eleventh-hour reversal, President Saleh announces candidacy," IRIN Humanitarian News and Analysis, http://www.irinnews.org/report.aspx?reportid=27058, accessed 2 March 2011.

24. Paul Dresch, *A History of Modern Yemen* (Cambridge: Cambridge University Press, 2000), 151, 193–194, 201–202.

25. Sadiki, "Like father, like son," 12.

26. Barak A. Salmoni, *Regime and Periphery in Northern Yemen: The Huthi Phenomenon* (Santa Monica, CA: RAND, 2010), 8.

27. Robert F. Worth, "In Yemen, a war centers on authority not terrain," *New York Times*, 25 October 2009.

28. Susanne Dahlgren, "The snake with a thousand heads: The southern cause in Yemen," *MERIP Reports*, 40/3 (Fall 2010), 28–33.

29. Andrew England, "Yemen leader faces test of reputation as political survivor," *Financial Times*, 6 January 2010.

30. Almawludi Al Ahmar, "The labour pains of a new Libya," Arab Center for Research and Policy Studies, 7 July 2011, http://english.dohainstitute .org/file/pdfViewer/55e90f6e-e67e-4175-8108-57ff81837005.pdf, 3.

6. Constrained Presidencies in Lebanon and Iraq after Hussein

1. Lebanese jurist Antoyne Khayr, quoted in Fawwaz Traboulsi, *A History of Modern Lebanon* (London: Pluto Press, 2007), 109.

2. Sami Zubaida, "Religion, community, and class in Iraqi politics and society," The Peter Green Lectures on the Modern Middle East, Brown University, 1 April 2009.

3. Sami Zubaida, *Islam, the People and the State: Political Ideas and Movements in the Middle East*, 2nd ed. (London: I. B. Tauris, 1993), 152–154.

4. Traboulsi, *A History of Modern Lebanon*, 110–111.

5. Ibid., 115.

6. Oren Barak, *The Lebanese Army: A National Institution in a Divided Society* (Albany, NY: SUNY Press, 2009), 37–38.

7. Traboulsi, *A History of Modern Lebanon*, 245.

8. Quote from Hanna Batatu, *The Old Social Classes and the Revolutionary Movements of Iraq: A Study of Iraq's Old Landed and Commercial Classes and Its Communists, Ba'thists and Free Officers* (Princeton, NJ: Princeton University Press, 1978), 835–836; Charles Tripp, *A History of Iraq* (Cambridge: Cambridge University Press, 2000), 151.

9. Tripp, *A History of Iraq*, 151–152.

10. Zubaida, "Religion, community, and class in Iraqi politics and society."

11. Raad Alkadiri and Chris Toensing, "The Iraqi Governing Council's sectarian hue," Middle East Research and Information Project, *MER Online*, 20 August 2003, http://www.merip.org/mero/mero082003.

12. Ibid. Translation from *Washington Post*, 12 October 2005, credited to the Associated Press.

13. Najde al-Ali and Nicola Pratt, *What Kind of Liberation? Women and the Occupation of Iraq* (Berkeley: University of California Press, 2009), 115.

14. Kadhim Ajrash and Nayla Razzouk, "Iraq names officials, leaves security appointments unfilled," *Bloomberg News*, 13 February 2011, http://www .bloomberg.com/news/2011-02-13/iraq-names-officials-leaves-security -appointments-unfilled.html.

15. For example, Steven Lee Myers, "Iraqi prime minister is given 30 days to form new government," *New York Times,* 26 November 2010.

7. The Monarchical Security States of Jordan, Morocco, Bahrain, and Oman

1. Khair el-Din Haseeb et al., *The Future of the Arab Nation: Challenges and Options,* trans. R. M. Dennis (London: Routledge, 1991), 94.
2. Walid Hazbun, *Beaches, Ruins, Resorts: The Politics of Tourism in the Arab World* (Minneapolis: University of Minnesota Press, 2008), 169.
3. Sufian Obaidat, "Security reform in Jordan: Where to start?," Arab Reform Initiative, 18 December 2009.
4. Jillian Schwedler, "Jordan's risky business as usual," Middle East Research and Information Project, *MER Online,* 30 June 2010, http://www .merip.org/mero/mero082003, 1.
5. Ibid., 3–4.
6. Jamal Halaby, "King's allies win majority in Jordan," *Boston Globe,* 11 November 2010.
7. "Jordan protests: Thousands rally over economic policies," *BBC News Middle East,* 21 January 2011.
8. Bruno Callies de Salies, "Mohamed VI et la rénovation du champ politique," *Magheb/Machrek,* 197 (Autumn 2008), 103–104.
9. Pierre Vermeren, *Le maroc de Mohammed VI: La transition inachevée* (Paris: La Découverte, 2009), 72–90, 157–165.
10. David Mednicoff, "The wrong friends," *Boston Globe,* Ideas, 30 January 2011.

8. The Politics of Succession

1. Anthony Billingsley, *Political Succession in the Arab World: Constitutions, Family Loyalties and Islam* (London: Routledge, 2010), 4.
2. Riad Ziadeh, *Power and Policy in Syria: Intelligence Services, Foreign Relations and Democracy in the Modern Middle East* (London: I. B. Tauris, 2011), 41.
3. Ibid., 33–34.
4. See William Harris, "Bashar al-Assad's Lebanon gamble," *Middle East Quarterly,* Summer 2005, 33–44.
5. Ziadeh, *Power and Policy in Syria,* 28n.
6. Personal information.
7. Larbi Sadiki, "Like father, like son: Dynastic republicanism in the Middle East," Policy Outlook no. 52 (Washington, DC: Carnegie Endowment for International Peace, 2009), 5.

8. Landon Thomas Jr., "Unknotting father's reins in hope of 'reinventing' Libya," *New York Times*, 28 February 2010; and Landon Thomas Jr., "Son of Libyan leader says charity to quit politics," Reuters, 16 December 2010.

9. "Libya: A mixed story," Reuters Africa, 7 July 2010.

10. Sheila Carapico, "Successions, transitions, coups and revolutions," in Louis J. Cantori and Augustus Richard Norton, eds., "Political succession in the Middle East," *Middle East Policy*, 9/3 (September 2002), 110.

9. The Question of Arab Exceptionalism

1. Jason Brownlee, "Hereditary succession in modern autocracies," *World Politics*, 59/4 (July 2007), 595–628.

2. Ibid., 602 and 603, figures 1 and 2.

3. Jean-François Bayart, "Africa in the world: A history of extraversion," *African Affairs* 99 (2000), 217–267, 226.

4. Stephen Smith, "Nodding and winking," *London Review of Books*, 11 February 2010, 10–12.

5. Sally N. Cummings and Raymond Hinnesbush, eds., *Sovereignty after Empire: Comparing the Middle East and Central Asia* (Edinburgh: Edinburgh University Press, 2011), 15.

6. Kirk Beattie, *Egypt during the Nasser Years: Ideology, Politics and Civil Society* (Boulder, CO: Westview Press, 1994), 120.

7. Larry Diamond, "Why are there no Arab democracies?," *Journal of Democracy*, 21/1 (January 2010), 99.

8. "Disturbing moves to create a super-police for Arab satellite TV stations," Reporters without Borders, 23 January 2010, http://en.rsf.org/middle-east-north-africa-disturbing-moves-to-create-super-23-01-2010,36189.

9. "Libya's Gaddafi pained by Tunisian revolt, blames WikiLeaks," Monsters and Critics, Africa News, 16 January 2011, http://www.monstersand critics.com/news/africa/news/article_1612073.php/Libya-s-Gaddaffi-pained-by-Tunisian-revolt-blames-WikiLeaks.

10. Yezid Sayigh, *Armed Struggle and the Search for State: The Palestinian National Movement, 1949–1993* (Oxford: Oxford University Press, 1997), 20–23, 670–674, 679–682.

11. Moshem Mohammed Saleh, "The Palestinian Authority and the problem of reform under the occupation," Al-Zaytouna Centre for Studies and Consultations, Beirut, 18 December 2010, http://www.alzaytouna.net/arabic/?c=1522&a=132122.

12. Information from Aaron Shakow.

13. Steven Heydemann, "Authoritarian learning and current trends in Arab governance," in Shibley Telhami, ed., *Oil, Globalization, and Political Reform in the Middle East,* The Brookings Project on U.S. Relations with the Islamic World: Doha Discussion Papers (Washington, DC: Saban Center, Brookings Institution Press, 2009), 27–36.

10. The Sudden Fall

1. Eva Bellin, "Coercive institutions and coercive leaders," in Marsha Pripstein Posusney and Michele Penner Angrist, eds., *Authoritarianism in the Middle East: Regimes and Resistance* (Boulder, CO: Lynne Rienner, 2005), 21–41.

2. Timur Kuran, "Sparks and prairie fires: A theory of unanticipated political revolution," *Public Choice,* 61 (1989), 41–74.

3. Arne Klau, "Socio-economic ripple effects," *Al-Ahram Weekly,* 17–23 March 2011, 17.

4. Jonathan Steele, "Half a revolution," *London Review of Books,* 17 March 2011, 36–37.

5. Mohamed Abdel-Baky, "Cyber revolution," *Al-Ahram Weekly,* 10–16 February 2011, 2.

6. Azzadine Layachi, "Algeria's rebellion by installments," Middle East Research and Information Project, *MER Online,* 12 March 2011, http://www.merip.org/mero/mero031211.

7. Quoted by Anthony Shadid, "Syrian protests regain momentum, draw fire," *Boston Globe,* 22 May 2011.

8. Abigail Fielding-Smith and Lina Saigol, "Uprising exposes weakness of economy," *Financial Times,* 27 April 2011. See also David Gardner, "This can only end with the Assads' fall," *Financial Times,* 9 August 2011.

9. Neil MacFarquhar, "Mubarak faces more questions on gas deal with Israel," *New York Times,* 23 April 2011.

10. Shiela Carapico, "No exit: Yemen's existential crisis," Middle East Research and Information Project, *MER Online,* 3 May 2011, http://www.merip.org/mero/mero050311-1.

11. Dena Rashed, "New concerns for women?," *Al-Ahram Weekly,* 21–27 April 2011, 20.

12. Amy Knight, "The concealed battle to run Russia," *New York Review of Books,* 13 January 2011, 48–51.

Conclusion

1. V. S. Naipaul, "Conrad's darkness," in *The Return of Eva Perón* with *The Killings in Trinidad* (New York: Vintage Books, 1981), 233.

2. Achille Mbembe, "Provisional notes on the postcolony," *Journal of the International African Institute*, 62/1 (1992), 3–37.

3. Jerrold M. Post, *Leaders and Their Followers in a Dangerous World: The Psychology of Political Behavior* (Ithaca, NY: Cornell University Press, 2004), 27–28. Post was the founder of the Center for the Analysis of Personality and Political Behavior, which provided President Jimmy Carter with political profiles of the Israeli and Palestinian leaders with whom he was negotiating in 1979.

4. Ibid., 109–110.

5. Ibid., 94–95.

6. Ibid., 37–38.

7. Ibid., 36, 94–96.

8. Ibid., 21, 77–78.

9. Ibid., 101.

10. Ibid., 104–105.

11. I am indebted to Judith Gurewich for many of these ideas.

12. Margaret Talbot, "When Qaddafi met Fallaci," News Desk, *The New Yorker*, 12 February 2001.

13. Ibid.

14. Christopher Caldwell, "Egypt shakes a distant dictator from his dream," *Financial Times*, 12 December 2010.

15. Riccardo Orizio, *Talk of the Devil: Encounters with Seven Dictators*, trans. Avril Bardoni (New York: Walker and Co., 2003).

16. Mohamed Haddar and Jean-Yves Moisseron, "Editorial," *Maghreb/Machrek*, 206, Winter 2010/2011, 9–15.

17. Jean-Francois Daguzan, "De la crise économique à la revolution politique," *Maghreb/Machrek*, 206, Winter 2010/2011, 9–10.

Bibliography

Articles and Chapters

GENERAL

Albrecht, Holger. "How do regimes work? Formal rules and informal mechanisms in Middle Eastern politics." In Eberhard Kienle, ed., *Democracy Building and Democracy Erosion* (London: al-Saqi Books, 2009), 230–247.

Anderson, Lisa. "Absolutism and resilience of monarchy in the Middle East." *Political Science Quarterly*, 106/1 (1991), 1–15.

Bayart, Jean-François. "Africa in the world: A history of extraversion." *African Affairs*, 99 (2000), 217–267.

Be'eri, Eliezer. "The waning of the military coup in Arab politics." *Middle Eastern Studies*, 18/1 (1982), 69–128.

Bellin, Eva. "Coercive institutions and coercive leaders." In Marsha Pripstein Posusney and Michele Penner Angrist, eds., *Authoritarianism in the Middle East: Regimes and Resistance* (Boulder, CO: Lynne Rienner, 2005), 21–41.

Brownlee, Jason. "And yet they persist: Explaining survival and transition in neopatrimonial regimes." *Studies in Comparative International Development*, 37/2 (2002), 35–63.

Brownlee, Jason. "Hereditary succession in modern autocracies." *World Politics*, 59/4 (July 2007), 595–628.

Brumberg, Daniel. "Liberalisation versus democracy." In Thomas Carothers and Marina Ottaway, eds., *Uncharted Journey: Promoting Democracy in the Middle*

East (Washington, DC: Carnegie Endowment for International Peace, 2005), 15–25.

Cantori, Louis J., and Augustus Richard Norton, eds. "Political succession in the Middle East." *Middle East Policy*, 9/3 (September 2002), 105–123.

Daguzan, Jean-Francois. "De la crise économique à la revolution politique." *Maghreb/Machrek*, 206, Winter 2010/2011, 9–10.

Diamond, Larry. "Why are there no Arab democracies?" *Journal of Democracy*, 21/1 (January 2010), 93–104.

Droz-Vincent, Philippe. "From political to economic actors: The changing role of Middle Eastern armies." In Oliver Schlumberger, ed., *Debating Arab Authoritarianism: Dynamics and Durability in Nondemocratic Regimes* (Stanford, CA: Stanford University Press, 2007), 195–211.

Hale, Henry E. "Regime cycles: Democracy, autocracy and revolution in post-Soviet Eurasia." *World Politics*, 58 (October 2005), 133–165.

Heydemann, Steven. "Authoritarian learning and current trends in Arab governance." In Shibley Telhami, ed., *Oil, Globalization, and Political Reform in the Middle East.* The Brookings Project on U.S. Relations with the Islamic World: Doha Discussion Papers (Washington, DC: Saban Center, Brookings Institution Press, 2009), 27–36.

Heydemann, Steven. "Social pacts and the persistence of authoritarianism in the Middle East." In Oliver Schlumberger, ed., *Debating Arab Authoritarianism: Dynamics and Durability in Nondemocratic Regimes* (Stanford, CA: Stanford University Press, 2007), 21–38.

Kuran, Timur. "Sparks and prairie fires: A theory of unanticipated political revolution." *Public Choice*, 61 (1989), 41–74.

Mbembe, Achille. "Provisional notes on the postcolony." *Journal of the International African Institute*, 62/1 (1992), 3–37.

Naipaul, V. S. "Conrad's darkness." In *The Return of Eva Perón* with *The Killings in Trinidad* (New York: Vintage Books, 1981).

Quinlivan, James T. "Coup-proofing: Its practical consequences in the Middle East." *International Security*, 24/2 (Fall 1999), 131–165.

Sevier, Caroline. "The costs of relying on ageing dictators." *Middle East Quarterly*, Summer 2008, 13–22.

Smith, Stephen. "Nodding and winking." *London Review of Books*, 11 February 2010, 10–12.

COUNTRY SPECIFIC

Abdul Aziz, Muhammad, and Youssef Hussein. "The president, the son and military succession in Egypt." *Arab Studies Journal,* 9/11 (Fall 2001/Spring 2002), 73–100.

Alkadiri, Raad, and Chris Toensing. "The Iraqi Governing Council's sectarian hue." Middle East Research and Information Project, *MER Online,* 20 August 2003. http://www.merip.org/mero/mero082003.

Callies de Salies, Bruno. "Mohamed VI et la rénovation du champ politique." *Maghreb/Machrek,* 197 (Autumn 2008), 103–104.

Dahlgren, Susanne. "The snake with a thousand heads: The southern cause in Yemen." *MERIP Reports,* 40/3 (Fall 2010), 28–33.

Drysdale, Alasdair. "The succession question in Syria." *Middle East Journal,* 39/2 (Spring 1985), 247–250.

Erdle, Steffen. "Tunisia: Economic transformation and political restoration." In Volker Perthes, ed., *Arab Elites: Negotiating the Politics of Change* (Boulder, CO: Lynne Rienner, 2004), 207–236.

Gorbashy, Mona el-. "The liquidation of Egypt's illiberal experiment." Middle East Research and Information Project, *MER Online,* 29 December 2010. http://www.merip.org/mero/mero122910.

Haddad, Bassam. "The formation and development of economic networks in Syria: Implications for economic and fiscal reforms." In Steven Heydemann, ed., *Networks of Privilege in the Middle East* (New York: Palgrave Macmillan, 2004), 37–66.

Harris, William. "Bashar al-Assad's Lebanon gamble." *Middle East Quarterly,* Summer 2005, 33–44.

Hibou, Beatrice. "Domination and control in Tunisia: Economic levers for the exercise of authoritarian power." *Review of African Political Economy,* 108 (2006), 185–206.

Khechana, Rachid. "Bedouinocratic Libya: Between hereditary succession and reform." Arab Reform Initiative, 29 January 2010.

Khechana, Rachid. "Tunisia on the eve of presidential and parliamentary elections: Organising a pro-forma democracy." Arab Reform Initiative, 13 October 2009. http://www.arab-reform.net/spip.php?article2412.

Kienle, Eberhard. "More than a response to liberalism: The political deliberalization of Egypt in the 1990s." *Middle East Journal,* 52/2 (Spring 1998), 219–235.

Layachi, Azzadine. "Algeria's rebellion by installments." Middle East Research and Information Project, *MER Online*, 12 March 2011. http://www.merip.org/mero/mero031211.

Obaidat, Sufian. "Security reform in Jordan: Where to start?" Arab Reform Initiative, 18 December 2009.

Nasser, Gamal Abdel. Speech delivered on the occasion of the eleventh anniversary of the revolution, July 22, 1963 (Cairo: Information Department, 1963).

Perthes, Volker. "Syria's difficult inheritance." In Volker Perthes, ed., *Arab Elites: Negotiating the Politics of Change* (Boulder, CO: Lynne Rienner, 2004), 1–32.

Roberts, Hugh. "Algeria: The subterranean logics of a non-election." Real Instituto Elcano, ARI 68/2009, 22 April 2009.

Rodenbeck, Max. "A special report on Egypt: The long wait." *The Economist*, 15 July 2010.

Schwedler, Jillian. "Jordan's risky business as usual." Middle East Research and Information Project, *MER Online*, 30 June 2010. http://www.merip.org/mero/mero082003.

Sfakaniakis, John. "The whales of the Nile: Businessmen and bureaucrats during the era of privatization in Egypt." In Steven Heydemann, ed., *Networks of Privilege in the Middle East* (New York: Palgrave Macmillan, 2004), 67–99.

Shehata, Samer. "Political succession in Egypt." *Middle East Policy*, 9/3 (September 2002), 110–113.

Springborg, Robert, and John Sfakianakis. "The military's role in presidential succession." *Les notes de l'Ifri* (Institution Français de Relations Internationales), 31 (February 2001, 57–72.

Stacher, Joshua. "Reinterpreting authoritarian power: Syria's hereditary succession." *Middle East Journal* 65/2 (Spring 2011), 197–212.

Steele, Jonathan. "Half a revolution." *London Review of Books*, 17 March 2011, 36–37.

Waal, Alex de. "Dolarised." *London Review of Books*, 24 June 2010, 38–41.

Weaver, Mary Anne. "Pharoahs-in-waiting." *The Atlantic*, 292/3 (October 2003), 79–82.

Reports

Dunne, Michele, and Marina Ottaway. "Incumbent regimes and the 'King's Dilemma' in the Arab world" (Washington, DC: Carnegie Endowment for International Peace, 2007). Carnegie Paper, Middle East, 88, December 2007).

International Crisis Group. "Reshuffling the cards? Syria's evolving strategy." *Middle East Report* no. 92 (14 December 2009), 4.

Kauch, Kristina. "Presidents for life: Managed successions and stability in the Arab world." Fundación para las Relaciones Internacionales y el Diálogo Exterior Working Paper no. 104 (Madrid, November 2010).

Sadiki, Larbi. "Like father, like son: Dynastic republicanism in the Middle East." Policy Outlook no. 52 (Washington, DC: Carnegie Endowment for International Peace, 2009).

Sayigh, Yezid. "'Fixing broken windows': Security reform in Palestine, Lebanon and Yemen." Carnegie Paper (Washington, DC: Carnegie Endowment for International Peace, 2009).

Books

GENERAL

Albrecht, Holger, ed. *Contentious Politics in the Middle East: Political Opposition under Authoritarianism* (Gainesville: University Press of Florida, 2010).

Ayoob, Mohammed. *The Third World Security Predicament: State Making, Regional Conflict and the International System* (Boulder, CO: Lynne Rienner, 1995).

Ayubi, Nazih. *Over-stating the Arab State: Politics and Society in the Middle East* (London: I. B. Tauris, 1995).

Bayart, Jean-François. *The State in Africa: The Politics of the Belly*, 2nd ed., trans. Stephen Ellis (Cambridge: Polity Press, 2009).

Billingsley, Anthony. *Political Succession in the Arab World: Constitutions, Family Loyalties and Islam* (London: Routledge, 2010).

Blondel, Jean. *World Leaders: Heads of Government in the Post-war Period* (London: Sage Publications, 1980).

Brown, Nathan J. *Constitutions in a Nonconstitutional World: Arab Basic Laws and the Prospects for Accountable Government* (Albany, NY: SUNY Press, 2002).

Carothers, Thomas, and Marina Ottaway, eds. *Uncharted Journey: Promoting Democracy in the Middle East* (Washington, DC: Carnegie Endowment for International Peace, 2005).

Cook, Steven A. *Ruling but Not Governing: The Military and Political Development in Egypt, Algeria and Turkey* (Baltimore, MD: Johns Hopkins University Press, 2007).

Cummings, Sally N., and Raymond Hinnesbush, eds. *Sovereignty after Empire: Comparing the Middle East and Central Asia* (Edinburgh: Edinburgh University Press, 2011).

Droz-Vincent, Phillipe. *Moyen-Orient: Pouvoirs authoritaires: Société bloquées* (Paris: Presses Universitaires de France, 2004).

Gelvin, James A. *The Modern Middle East: A History* (New York: Oxford University Press, 2008).

Halliday, Fred. *Nation and Religion in the Middle East* (London: al-Saqi Books, 2000).

Haseeb, Khair el-Din, et al. *The Future of the Arab Nation: Challenges and Options*, trans. R. M. Dennis (London: Routledge, 1991).

Hazbun, Walid. *Beaches, Ruins, Resorts: The Politics of Tourism in the Arab World* (Minneapolis: University of Minnesota Press, 2008).

Heydemann, Steven, ed. *Networks of Privilege in the Middle East* (New York: Palgrave Macmillan, 2004).

Hudson, Michael. *Arab Politics: The Search for Legitimacy* (New Haven, CT: Yale University Press, 1977).

Huntington, Samuel P., and Clement H. Moore, eds. *Authoritarian Politics in Modern Society: The Dynamics of Established One-Party Systems* (New York: Basic Books, 1970).

Kamrava, Mehran. *The Modern Middle East: A Political History since the First World War*, 2nd ed. (Berkeley: University of California Press, 2011).

Khoury, Philip S., and Joseph Kostiner. *Tribes and State Formation in the Middle East* (Berkeley: University of California Press, 1990).

Kienle, Eberhard, ed. *Democracy Building and Democracy Erosion* (London: al-Saqi Books, 2009).

Lacouture, Jean. *The Demigods: Charismatic Leadership in the Third World*, trans. Patricia Wolf (New York: Knopf, 1970).

Mufti, Malik. *Sovereign Creations: Pan-Arabism and Political Order in Syria and Iraq* (Ithaca, NY: Cornell University Press, 1996).

Ottaway, Marina, and Julia Choucair-Vizos, eds. *Beyond the Façade: Political Reform in the Arab World* (Washington, DC: Carnegie Endowment for International Peace, 2008).

Owen, Roger. *State, Power and Politics in the Making of the Modern Middle East*, 3rd ed. (London: Routledge, 2004).

Perthes, Volker, ed. *Arab Elites: Negotiating the Politics of Change* (Boulder, CO: Lynne Rienner, 2004).

Post, Jerrold M. *Leaders and Their Followers in a Dangerous World: The Psychology of Political Behavior* (Ithaca, NY: Cornell University Press, 2004).

Posusney, Marsha Pripstein, and Michele Penner Angrist, eds. *Authoritarianism in the Middle East: Regimes and Resistance* (Boulder, CO: Lynne Rienner, 2005).

Roy, Olivier. *The Politics of Chaos in the Middle East* (New York: Columbia University Press, 2008).

Salamé, Ghassan, ed. *Democracy without Democrats: The Politics of Renewal in the Muslim World* (London: I. B. Tauris, 1994).

Schedler, Andrea, ed. *Electoral Authoritarianism: The Dynamics of Unfree Competition* (Boulder, CO: Lynne Rienner, 2006).

Schlumberger, Oliver, ed. *Debating Arab Authoritarianism: Dynamics and Durability in Nondemocratic Regimes* (Stanford, CA: Stanford University Press, 2007).

Sirrs, Owen S. *A History of the Egyptian Intelligence Service: A History of the Mukhabarat, 1910–2009* (Abingdon: Routledge, 2010).

COUNTRY SPECIFIC

Alexander, Christopher. *Tunisia: Stability and Reform in the Modern Meghreb* (Abingdon: Routledge, 2010).

Ali, Najde al-, and Nicola Pratt. *What Kind of Liberation? Women and the Occupation of Iraq* (Berkeley: University of California Press, 2009).

Allawi, Ali A. *The Occupation of Iraq: Winning the War, Losing the Peace* (New Haven, CT: Yale University Press, 2007).

Barak, Oren. *The Lebanese Army: A National Institution in a Divided Society* (Albany, NY: SUNY Press, 2009).

Batatu, Hanna. *The Old Social Classes and the Revolutionary Movements of Iraq: A Study of Iraq's Old Landed and Commercial Classes and Its Communists, Ba'thists and Free Officers* (Princeton, NJ: Princeton University Press, 1978).

Beattie, Kirk J. *Egypt during the Nasser Years: Ideology, Politics and Civil Society* (Boulder, CO: Westview Press, 1994).

Beau, Nicolas, and Catherine Graciet. *La régente de Carthage: Main basse sur la Tunisie* (Paris: La Découverte, 2009).

Beau, Nicolas, and Jean-Pierre Tuqoi. *Notre Ami Ben Ali: L'envers du "miracle tunisien"* (Paris: La Découverte, 1999).

Benchicou, Mohamed. *Bouteflika: Une imposture algérienne* (Paris: J. Picollec, 2004).

Benchicou, Mohamed. *Notre Ami Bouteflika: De l'État rêve à l'état scélérat* (Paris: Riveneuve, 2010).

Blaydes, Lisa. *Elections and Distributive Politics in Mubarak's Egypt* (Cambridge: Cambridge University Press, 2011).

Cailles de Salies, Bruno. *La grand Maghreb contemporain: Entre régimes authoritaires et islamistes combatants* (Paris: Jean Masonneuve successeur, 2010).

Carapico, Sheila. *Civil Society in Yemen: The Political Economy of Activism in Modern Arabia* (Cambridge: Cambridge University Press, 1998).

Crystal, Jill. *Oil and Politics in the Gulf: Rulers and Merchants in Kuwait and Qatar* (Cambridge: Cambridge University Press, 1990).

Davis, John J. *Libyan Politics: Tribe and Revolution: An Account of the Zuwaya and Their Government* (Berkeley: University of California Press, 1988).

Dresch, Paul. *A History of Modern Yemen* (Cambridge: Cambridge University Press, 2000).

Firro, Kais M. *Inventing Lebanon: Nationalism and the State under the Mandate* (London: I. B. Tauris, 2003).

Gause, F. Gregor, III. *Oil Monarchies: Domestic and Security Challenges in the Arab Gulf States* (New York: Council on Foreign Relations, 1940).

Gelvin, James L. *Divided Loyalties: Nationalism and Mass Politics in Syria and the Close of Empire* (Berkeley: University of California Press, 1998).

Hakim, Tawfiq al-. *The Return of Consciousness*, trans. Bayly Winder (New York: New York University Press, 1985).

Hertog, Steffen. *Princes, Brokers and Bureaucrats: Oil and the State in Saudi Arabia* (Ithaca, NY: Cornell University Press, 2010).

Hibou, Beatrice. *La force de l'obéissance: Économie politique de la répression en Tunisie* (Paris: La Découverte, 2006).

Hinnebusch, Raymond A. *Authoritarian Power and State Formation in Ba'thist Syria: Army, Party and Peasant* (Boulder, CO: Westview Press, 1990).

Hinnebusch, Raymond A. *Syria: Revolution from Above* (London: Routledge, 2001).

Hirst, David, and Irene Beeson. *Sadat* (London: Faber and Faber, 1981).

Khalil, Samir (Kanan Makiya). *Republic of Fear: The Politics of Modern Iraq* (Berkeley: University of California Press, 1990).

Kienle, Eberhard. *A Grand Delusion: Democracy and Economic Reform in Egypt* (London: I. B. Tauris, 2001).

Lacey, Robert. *Inside the Kingdom: Kings, Clerics, Modernists, Terrorists and the Struggle for Saudi Arabia* (New York: Viking, 2009).

Liverani, Andrea. *Civil Society in Algeria: The Political Functions of Associational Life* (London: Routledge, 2008).

Nasser, Gamal Abdel. *Egypt's Liberation: The Philosophy of the Revolution*, intro. Dorothy Thompson (Washington, DC: Public Affairs Press, 1955).

Orizio, Riccardo. *Talk of the Devil: Encounters with Seven Dictators*, trans. Avril Bardoni (New York: Walker and Co., 2003).

Perkins, Kenneth J. *A History of Modern Tunisia* (Cambridge: Cambridge University Press, 2004).

Perthes, Volker. *Syria under Bashar al-Asad: Modernization and the Limits of Change* (Oxford: Oxford University Press, 2004).

Robins, Philip. *A History of Jordan* (Cambridge: Cambridge University Press, 2004).

Rutherford, Bruce K. *Egypt after Mubarak: Liberalism, Islam, and Democracy in the Arab World* (Princeton, NJ: Princeton University Press, 2008).

Salibi, Kamal. *The Modern History of Lebanon* (New York: Caravan Books, 1977).

Salmoni, Barak A. *Regime and Periphery in Northern Yemen: The Huthi Phenomenon* (Santa Monica, CA: RAND, 2010).

Sayigh, Yezid. *Armed Struggle and the Search for State: The Palestinian National Movement, 1949–1993* (Oxford: Oxford University Press, 1997).

Schwedler, Jillian. *Faith in Moderation: Islamist Parties in Jordan and Yemen* (Cambridge: Cambridge University Press, 2006).

Seale, Patrick. *Asad of Syria: The Struggle for the Middle East* (London: I. B. Tauris, 1988).

Seale, Patrick. *The Struggle for Syria: A Study of Post-War Arab Politics, 1945–1958* (London: Oxford University Press, 1965).

Selvik, Kjetil, and Stig Stenslie. *Stability and Change in the Modern Middle East* (London: I. B. Tauris, 2011).

Soliman, Samer. *The Autumn of Dictatorship: Fiscal Crisis and Political Change in Egypt under Mubarak* (Stanford, CA: Stanford University Press, 2011).

Springborg, Robert. *Mubarak's Egypt: Fragmentation of the Political Order* (Boulder, CO: Westview Press, 1989).

Traboulsi, Fawwaz. *A History of Modern Lebanon* (London: Pluto Press, 2007).

Tripp, Charles. *A History of Iraq* (Cambridge: Cambridge University Press, 2000).

Vandewalle, Dirk. *A History of Modern Libya* (Cambridge: Cambridge University Press, 2006).

Vandewalle, Dirk. *Libya in the Twenty-First Century* (Cambridge: Cambridge University Press, 2006).

Vandewalle, Dirk. *Libya since Independence: Oil and State Building* (Ithaca, NY: Cornell University Press, 1998).

Vandewalle, Dirk, ed. *North Africa: Development and Reform in a Changing Global Economy* (Basingstoke: Macmillan, 1996).

Vatikiotis, P. J. *The Modern History of Egypt* (London: Weidenfeld and Nicolson, 1969).

Vatikiotis, P. J. *Nasser and His Generation* (London: Croom Helm, 1978).

Vermeren, Pierre. *Le maroc de Mohammed VI: La transition inachevée* (Paris: La Découverte, 2009).

Waterbury, John. *Commander of the Faithful: The Moroccan Political Elite* (London: Weidenfeld and Nicolson, 1970).

Waterbury, John. *The Egypt of Nasser and Sadat: The Political Economy of Two Regimes* (Princeton, NJ: Princeton University Press, 1983).

Wedeen, Lisa. *Ambiguities of Domination: Politics, Rhetoric and Symbols in Contemporary Syria* (Chicago: University of Chicago Press, 1999).

Werenfels, Isabelle. *Managing Instability in Algeria: Elites and Political Change since 1995* (London: Routledge, 2007).

Ziadeh, Riad. *Power and Policy in Syria: Intelligence Services, Foreign Relations and Democracy in the Modern Middle East* (London: I. B. Tauris, 2011).

Zubaida, Sami. *Islam, the People and the State: Political Ideas and Movements in the Middle East,* 2nd ed. (London: I. B. Tauris, 1993).

Acknowledgments

This book could not have been written without the advice and encouragement of many friends and colleagues as well as the works that they and others have written about the Middle East, its recent history, and its particular structures of government. Its origins lie in a set of discussions with Yezid Sayigh and Robert Springborg, later joined by Lisa Blaydes and Tarek Masoud. It was also given a great lift by Jim Robinson and the support he gave for a grant from the Mindich Fund for organizing a detailed chapter-by-chapter discussion of the first draft.

Others who I would like to acknowledge for their particular advice, insights, and general encouragement are Betty Anderson, Mona Anis, Mohammed Bamyeh, Oren Barak, Jason Brownlee, Melanie Cammett, Ruth Culleton, Beshara Doumani, Bassam Haddad, Terry Martin, Yoram Meital, Pascal Menoret, Mustapha Nabli, Hugh Roberts, Joseph Sassoon, Jillian Schwedler, Patrick Seale, Aaron Shakow, Shibley Telhami, Fawwaz Traboulsi, Dirk Vandewalle, Leonard Wood, Malika Zeghal, and Radwan Ziadeh.

Many thanks too to Joelle Abi-Richard for her help with finding appropriate illustrations; to Kathleen McDermott, the History Editor at Harvard University Press; and to the useful comments from the Press's two anonymous readers.

All mistakes, misunderstandings, and other mishaps are, of course, entirely my own.

Index

Abbas, Mahmoud, 167, 168
Abdullah I, King of Jordan, 126, 127
Abdullah II, King of Jordan, 126, 129, 130, 132, 133
Abu Dhabi, family coups, 17
Abu Ghazala, Abd-Halim, 67
Access, as political coin, 41, 42
Ackerman, Bruce, 184
Addis Ababa agreement (1972), 102
El-Adli, Habib, 177
Adulation, power and, 31
Advisers, presidential style and, 42
Africa, illegal migration from, 78
Afrique-Action, 25
Afro-Asian Solidarity Conference, 16
Agricultural sector, 51
Al Ahmar, Almawludi, 109
Al-Ahram Weekly, 177
Air transport, domestic (Syria), 52
Akayev, Askar, 156
Alawis, 36, 45, 80, 81, 140, 143, 176, 177
Albrecht, Holger, 7

ALESCO. *See* Educational, Social, and Cultural Affairs (ALESCO)
Algeria, 2, 6, 94, 106, 146; anticolonial struggle, 88; Houari Boumedienne, 26; coup, 1; coup (1965), 17; cronyism, 45, 49; demonstration effect, 10; division among the officer corps, 90; economic diversification debated, 58; election management, 55, 57, 76, 90; end of military rule, 62; French, 12, 19; influence of foreign settlement, 14; influence of Nasserite revolution, 159; international debt, 90; nationalists, 16, 73; National People's Assembly dissolved, 90; 1996 constitution, 91; non-Muslim and foreign populations, 17; oil resources and economic evolution of, 62; political conditions that supported president for life, 157; power of the military, 89;